HORRIBLE MOTHERS

Horrible Mothers

Representations
across Francophone
North America

Edited by Loïc Bourdeau

UNIVERSITY OF NEBRASKA PRESS   LINCOLN

Library of Congress Cataloging-in-Publication Data
Names: Bourdeau, Loïc, editor.
Title: Horrible mothers: representations across
francophone North America / edited by Loïc Bourdeau.
Description: Lincoln: University of Nebraska Press,
[2019] | Includes bibliographical references and index.
Identifiers: LCCN 2019003994
ISBN 9780803293984 (cloth: alk. paper)
ISBN 9781496218278 (ePub)
ISBN 9781496218285 (mobi)
ISBN 9781496218292 (PDF)
Subjects: LCSH: French-Canadian literature—History
and criticism. | French American literature—History and
criticism. | Mothers in literature. | Franco-Americans—In
literature. | Motion pictures—Québec (Province)—
History. | Mothers in motion pictures.
Classification: LCC PQ3902 .H67 2019
| DDC 840.9/352520971—dc23
LC record available at https://lccn.loc.gov/2019003994

Set in Garamond Premier by Mikala R. Kolander.
Designed by N. Putens.

To Marie-Thérèse, my mother

Aujourd'hui maman est morte.
Ou peut-être hier, je ne sais pas.

ALBERT CAMUS, *L'étranger*

CONTENTS

ACKNOWLEDGMENTS

Putting together this volume has been a wonderful reminder of the importance of collaboration in academia. As such, the first people I would like to thank are the generous and patient scholars who have joined me in this adventure (in order of appearance in the book): Pauline Henry-Tierney, Susan Pinette, Chelsea Ray, Alison Rice, Natalie Edwards, Lucie Hotte, Ariane Brun del Re, Susan Ireland, Patrice Proulx, and Amy Ransom. I am exceedingly grateful for your exciting contributions, your timeliness, and your overall flexibility.

I owe a significant debt to the late Prof. Lucille Cairns, who supervised my MA research at Durham University (UK) and introduced me to Jean-Marc Vallée's film *C.R.A.Z.Y.* The beauty of the maternal character and its reception sparked a lasting interest for questions of motherhood in literature and film. Lucille was a kind and supportive human being whose dedication to research has also been truly inspiring. During my doctoral studies at the University of California, Davis, I was fortunate to work under the supervision of equally outstanding and inspiring scholars. In particular, I would like to thank Dr. Jeff Fort for his constantly thorough feedback and encouragements, as well as his continued support after graduation. I thank the entire Department of French and Italian for its intellectual and financial support, as well as Dr. Elizabeth Constable (Women and Gender Studies) for making me a stronger feminist/queer scholar. I am also grateful to Dr. Jarrod Hayes, who codirected my dissertation and whose work in queer studies has influenced me greatly.

As a faculty member in the Department of Modern Languages at the University of Louisiana at Lafayette, I have received significant support from Dr. Caroline Huey (chair), who has helped me secure travel awards to present my work, along with an endowed professorship. Thank you to Ms. Regina LaBiche (operations manager) for chatting with me about "horrible mothers" and sharing her own maternal insights. I am grateful to all my colleagues in French and francophone studies, especially Prof. Fabrice Leroy and Prof. Monica Wright. They have become role models and generous friends. Monica, thank you for helping me proofread parts of this project and for your overall enthusiasm toward the project. Finally, I must express gratitude to Dean Jordan Kellman for his financial support (summer grants, travel expenses, etc.) and to my students for making teaching a joy.

This project would not have been possible and enjoyable without the unwavering support I received from Alicia Christensen, my editor at the University of Nebraska Press. Her professionalism, kindness, and overall understanding of the collaborative process lifted a weight off my shoulders. I thank her for choosing dedicated external readers whose comments have helped me (and the contributors) strengthen the final product. I am indebted to these readers, who spent a significant amount of time reading the entire book and provided detailed feedback.

I feel fortunate to have wonderful friends in my life who have listened to me when I needed to vent or discuss the project and distracted me when I needed a break. I thank my special someone for all the love and support I receive every day. Finally, I must thank my own mother, Marie-Thérèse, who showed me what a strong, independent woman looks like, made sacrifices for my education, and remains a constant source of awe and inspiration. Thank you all for making my world a better place.

HORRIBLE MOTHERS

Introduction

Failing Successfully

LOÏC BOURDEAU

> Le problème, peut-être, c'est que la maternité normale n'est plus seulement,
> justement, normale. On ne peut plus se "contenter" (je mets entre guillemets
> parce que c'est déjà énorme) de fournir nourriture, sécurité et chaleur à nos
> enfants. Il faut aussi être *créative*. Elle fait des biscuits! . . . La mère créative
> n'est qu'une autre variante de la mère parfaite . . . Mais elle colporte la même
> pression, la même étroitesse de modèles, le même impératif de juger sa valeur
> selon le nombre de "j'aime" qu'elle reçoit sur Facebook.
>
> FANNY BRITT, *Les tranchées*

There is nothing new about motherhood. There is still so much to say about it. A quick database search in one of Québec's leading newspapers, *Le Devoir*, using the keyword "maternité / motherhood" yields over eighty articles on the subject since 2007. A similar search on Huffingtonpost.fr yields close to 250 pieces over the past six years. Spanning just a single decade, these numerous contributions show how the topic of motherhood continues to make headlines. Single motherhood, work-life balance, postpartum depression, childfree women, good or bad parenting, and maternal struggles—these are some of the most recurring, trending themes. What further emerges from these

1

sources is an overall move toward empathy and visibility, shedding light on a variety of lived experiences in an attempt, on the one hand, to validate one's choices and, on the other, to broaden the spectrum of acceptability. Likewise, twenty-first-century literary and cinematographic works seek to "[r]endre présent et visible l'autre" ("[m]ake the other present and visible") (Gefen 150) not so much to "guérir la marginalité, mais [pour] l'exposer" ("heal marginality but to reveal it") (46). In this context of prolific media contributions on the subject of motherhood, this collaborative volume brings together a series of essays about literature, film, politics, and social issues relevant to francophone North America and constitutes a commitment to keeping the conversation going and to refuse silence. In this way, *Horrible Mothers* also owes a significant debt to post-2000 Québec cinema and to Michel Tremblay's timeless maternal characters—from *Les belles-soeurs* (1968) to *Encore une fois, si vous permettez* (1998)—who engage proudly and boisterously in the denunciation and deconstruction of restrictive norms for women.

The larger debt, however, is an academic one. Since the 1970s, the topic of motherhood has been central to numerous scholarly endeavors, in part because of the initial prominence and continued relevance of feminist studies. What follows is a nonexhaustive account of such endeavors, of critical and theoretical works on the question of motherhood. But before looking at the French and francophone North American landscape, I turn to Andrea O'Reilly's influential edited volume *Feminist Mothering* (2008) because it demonstrates similar scholarly objectives to those of *Horrible Mothers*. Featuring essays on women's emancipation and empowerment, O'Reilly's contributors examine women's struggles and challenges, rejecting the "patriarchal profile and script of 'good mothering' . . . [and highlighting] the various ways patriarchal motherhood becomes oppressive to women" (11). This work also adopts her eight-point categorization of the "perfect mother" under patriarchal ideology, which the contributors in this volume likewise challenge:

(1) children can only be properly cared for by the biological mother; (2) this mothering must be provided 24/7; (3) the mother must always put children's needs before her own; (4) mothers must turn to the experts for instruction; (5) the mother must be fully satisfied, fulfilled, completed, and composed in

motherhood; (6) mothers must lavish excessive amounts of time, energy, and money in the rearing of their children; (7) the mother has full responsibility, but no power from which to mother; (8) motherwork, and childrearing more specifically, are regarded as personal, private undertakings with no political import. (O'Reilly 10)

Unlike O'Reilly's work, however, this volume is not a work of social science; instead, it is an investigation of the literature and cinema that treat motherhood but also childlessness.[1] The francophone context of North America also comes with its own specificities and history. The influence of the language, the colonial past, and the relationship to France add singularity to a universal topic. Such considerations emerge in the scholarship that follows.

Of recent interest, Allison Connolly's 2016 *Spaces of Creation: Transculturality and Feminine Expression in Francophone Literature* investigates "the trying experiences of literary mothers and daughters" (122) across the French Caribbean, North Africa, and Canada. In a similar way, a broader reflection on the diversity of maternal models, as well as the question of agency, lies at the heart of this volume. Connolly's interest in "women's interpersonal exchanges and creative actions" also echoes earlier works by Lori Saint-Martin, whose article "Le corps et la fiction à réinventer: Métamorphoses de la maternité dans l'écriture des femmes au Québec" deals with similar topics, such as silent and absent mothers and female creativity, while highlighting a major representational change in fiction. Indeed, she argues: "[À] faire de la mère un sujet plutôt qu'un objet, on ouvre de nouveaux espaces romanesques qui pourront à leur tour transformer le réel" ("[B]y making the mother a subject rather than an object, one opens the way to new fictional avenues that can in turn transform the real") ("Le corps" 132). Gill Rye's *Narratives of Mothering: Women's Writing in Contemporary France* (2009) offers analogous reflections on and detailed analyses of the objectification of mothers and the ways in which, in French literary texts, "women themselves are expressing and defining mothering" in the period from the 1990s to the early 2000s (17), during which "mothers in reasonably large numbers have become narrative subjects and . . . motherhood has become the subject of their narratives" (33). As Rye initially points out, any "new work on mothers is situated . . . in relation to an enormous body of feminist work on mothers and motherhood, from North America, the United Kingdom, France, and beyond" (22).

In the case of the present volume, I likewise acknowledge this inheritance but focus more specifically on francophone North America and the concept of the bad mother, who goes against or fails to fit into O'Reilly's categorization.[2] This current enterprise seeks to make sense of and bring forth strategies of representation of failing motherhood in Québec, Ontario, New England, and California at the turn of the twenty-first century. While the selected texts and films range from the 1990s to 2015, their temporalities and engagement with the past provide historically informed representations of "horrible mothering." As the title of this project suggests, I address the significant impact of new technologies and social media vis-à-vis motherhood, but I must first clarify that the title *Horrible Mothers* is above all intended to be ironic, especially as every chapter aims to deconstruct such judgmental and limiting rhetoric and underscores the empowering potential behind each maternal experience.

Regarding the more specific trope of the overbearing or monstrous mother, this collection of essays owes a debt to previous academic works that have, in particular, shed light on the connections between motherhood, national identity, and oppressed womanhood. For instance, Mary Jean Green's *Women and Narrative Identity: Rewriting the Quebec National Text* (2001) situates women's writing in relation to "Quebec's identitary project" (3) and examines how the Quiet Revolution produced narratives of monstrous mothers "as a means of understanding and representing a radical process of social change" (75). With the same intent, *Horrible Mothers* considers the potential of these quintessential archetypes in more recent works while unearthing new ones (the working, multitasking mother, the absent mother, the liberated mother, the nonmother, etc.) along with new patterns that are informed by current social and theoretical developments in feminist and queer studies. Overall, the chapters focus on the predominant and symbolic theme of the mother in an attempt to reassess questions of identity, guilt, heteronormativity, culture, childlessness, and matricide, to name a few.[3] As such, a particular objective of this volume is first and foremost to reiterate that "[w]hereas the 'Mother' has often traditionally been represented as a quintessentially 'natural' figure (even as the very figure of 'Nature' itself, as in 'Mother Nature') and birth is often assumed to be an incontestably empirical and knowable event . . . 'the maternal function' is anything but natural" (Marder 2).

Not only do these chapters explore all of these concepts in relation to the historical contexts in which the works were produced, but they also provide a broader discourse on motherhood and womanhood in times of persisting anxieties and backlash in the Western world.[4] Ironically (or perhaps regrettably), Miléna Santoro makes similar remarks in the introduction to her 2003 monograph, *Mothers of Invention: Feminist Authors and Experimental Fiction in France and Quebec*, bewailing "the current period of considerable anti-feminist backlash and ebbing commitment to feminist activism" (3). Beyond these remarks, and as far as Québec is concerned, Santoro examines, among other themes, the mother figure in the works of Madeleine Gagnon and Nicole Brossard in order to show "how women were challenging the boundaries and possibilities of the [novel] genre as part of their efforts to rethink questions of gender" (8). Santoro's work serves also as a reminder of Brossard's major contribution to Québec feminism. Brossard's words echo earlier comments and concerns about women's subjectivity: "La conscience féministe permet de passer d'un monde où les femmes sont invisibles ou, quand elles sont visibles, uniquement charnelles et moralement coupables de tout, à un monde où les femmes deviennent sujets, centre d'intérêt, et sont valorisées comme individus et comme groupe" (Larose and Lessard 18).[5]

In addition to these texts, a number of other contributions have had an impact on this project and testify to the lasting consideration for women's writing and mother figures. As most of them focus either on the Québécois context or on the relationship between France and Québec, they are listed in the works cited section. Although Québec constitutes the largest French-speaking community in North America—and almost half of the following chapters discuss that—Québec should not be considered the sole focal point of our analysis. Experiences from the other geographical areas are equally relevant and are thus included here.

If visibility and making visible are at the heart of this undertaking, then the texts and films discussed in this study doubtlessly join in those efforts. Given the contemporary nature of these contributions, I wish to draw specific attention to the role that new technologies play in our lives and the ways in which they resonate for contemporary motherhood. This is not to say that the primary texts and films analyzed here deal explicitly with technology and its effects, because they do not; instead, our current era of heightened visibility and surveillance brought about by technology calls for new reflections on women's rights and emancipation. We must remember that "[d]isciplines will define not a code of conduct, but a code of normalization" (Foucault, *"Society"* 38) and thus call for an investigation of the modes of representation, as well as the excavation of nonnormative models of motherhood, kinship, and individuality. The proliferation of discourses around the maternal subject, the predominance of questions of self-representation in a "society [that] is finding new ways to regulate who will be heard and who will be taken seriously" (Walker Rettberg 19), requires, more than ever, examples of diversity and loud voices to reject alleged natural orders.

In titling this collection *Horrible Mothers*, I refer to all those instances in our lives when parents, especially women, are called "terrible," "horrible," or "unfit" by external observers. Not limited to pronouncement in our homes, streets, or public parks, these judgments permeate and inundate the media. The current propensity for taking selfies, posting pictures on social media, and documenting every detail of one's life intensifies the impact of such accusations on the alleged bad parent. "One of the most frequent reasons given for enjoying taking selfies is that it allows the subject full control over the photographic process" (Walker Rettberg 80); however, control over the reception of those images may quickly flounder—when it does not backfire. In her review of Elsa Godart's *Je selfie donc je suis*, journalist France Lebreton confirms the narcissistic dimension of selfies, which seek to "transformer son image en la faisant coïncider avec un idéal de soi et en la soumettant au regard de l'autre" ("transform one's image by making it coincide with an ideal of oneself and by submitting it to the other's gaze"). Yet reality catches up. Our filtered perfect selves vanish in the meanders of the Web as mental health disorders develop at worrying speed, including body dysmorphic disorder, obsessive compulsive disorder, and even suicide. In the case of motherhood, similar practices of online expression (blogs, Facebook pages, and articles in major news outlets) lead to similar obsessions with perfect parenting and being recognized and valued as such by virtual communities, as highlighted by Fanny Britt in the epigraph to this introduction. As lifestyle sections in newspapers and magazines and lifestyle blogs multiply and gain ever more appeal, so too do modes of surveillance multiply.[6] Indeed, Walker Rettberg confirms: "In the decades since Foucault wrote about the panopticon, the nature of surveillance has changed greatly. We are watched to a far greater degree than when Foucault was alive" (85). She continues:

> In many cases we know exactly how we are being watched. For instance, several companies are now offering discounts on health insurance to employees who agree to wear a Fitbit activity tracker. Progressive, a US car insurance company, offers its customers a device they call the Snapshot that will track their driving for 30 days, and promise a discount. . . . Wildflower Health is a company that offers a pregnancy tracker. . . . Maternity and newborn care are a major expense in health care, so if high-risk pregnancies can be caught early on, better care can be provided and a lot of money, and possibly lives, can be saved. . . . If my data shows me (and my insurer) that I am a safe driver, that I am doing a great job looking after my baby, or that I am walking 10,000 steps a day . . . I will feel good about myself. . . . Imagine if Wyoming Medicaid starts offering smart onesies to newborns that track breathing, sleep, heart rate, temperature, feeding and more. Imagine if you start getting visits from child services if your baby doesn't get enough sleep or there are other risk indicators. That might also save lives, but imagine parenting under constant government surveillance. (Walker Rettberg 86–87)

Not only are we aware of the variety of ways we are being watched, we are also complicit in monitoring our every move. Such an exacerbated "volonté de savoir," to use Foucault's expression, that is, the desire to know ourselves, comes at a high cost.[7] That our data have actually more value than our lives in this capitalistic market, which uses those data to sell us new products, seems to matter little. Likewise, the interference of technology only reinforces judgments: Who is good and who is bad?[8] Once again, perfectionism creeps into our lives in more ways than one, making failure something to be avoided.

This is where the notion of failure, in particular from a queer perspective, actually provides the potential to subvert and expand our conceptions of motherhood. In light of our capitalistic, neoliberal environment, the turn to queer studies is a logical one.[9] Indeed, as much as the field tackles questions of sex and sexuality—especially nonnormative sexualities—queer is also a tool to subvert hegemonic ideologies and actions. The potential of queer lies in its intersectional consideration of gender, race, sex, class, sexuality, identity, and nationhood, as well as the effects of dominant structures of power. In that sense, this volume aims to further bridge the gap between queer studies and feminism, as Mimi Marinucci did in *Feminism Is Queer: The Intimate Connection between Queer and Feminist Theory* (2016), because "[t]here is an unmistakable sense of solidarity linking concern about women's issues and concern about lesbian, gay, bisexual, and transgender issues" (140). Queer also offers a new direction within feminism, ensuring that mainstream, dominant structures are criticized rather than lauded for offering alleged freedom of choice.

As far as motherhood is concerned, queer studies also serve as a reminder that contemporary family models are constantly evolving and reshaping. Yet these new structures, Shelley M. Park argues, continue to function according to the notion that "children must have *one and only one mother*," thus highlighting the fact that "[h]eteronormative power cannot countenance polymaternal families and practices of childrearing" (3). Park's contribution is a necessary intervention in that it shows how queer broadens the spectrum of motherhood and offers a tool to resist "both the good mother / bad mother dichotomy as well as the good queer / bad queer dichotomy," all the while "contest[ing] hierarchies of worthiness that pit mothers against one another" (15). As I discussed above, failure offers one means of resistance to dichotomies and hierarchies, to which I now turn.

Drawing on Jack Halberstam's *The Queer Art of Failure* (2011), *Horrible Mothers* likewise seeks "to articulate an alternative vision of life, love, and labor and to put such a vision into practice" (2). Particularly, this volume reintroduces alternatives to normative motherhood, other "ways of being in the world" (2–3) as both a parent and a nonparent. I would further argue that if "[f]ailing is something queers do and have always done exceptionally well," mothers experience similar failures but have yet to voice them publicly, as well as to fully see that "maybe failure is easier in the long run and offers different rewards" (3). At times when perfect models of motherhood, tutorials to be a creative mother, or tips for successful parenting flood the internet, being a "bad mother" comes with the embarrassment of stigmatization and the fear of expressing one's reality. Even more so, when one considers that "[n]early everyone, it seems, wants to be normal. And who can blame them, if the alternative is being abnormal, or deviant" (Warner 53). Normalcy thus remains a powerful tool of erasure and silencing. However, the essays in this volume refuse or denounce silence and conformation, just as some mothers today are turning to the internet to express the flaws they embrace.[10] "I'm Not a Bad Mom" is one such example of a mother sharing her struggles while showing that not all mothers are perfect. Like her, "other mothers hide in the closet for just a moment's peace" or "are positive they're screwing up their children." Nevertheless, expressing one's flaws becomes a powerful reminder that "I'm not a bad parent. I'm just normal" (Hammer). In a similar fashion, countless examples seek to alleviate the guilt that some mothers feel whenever they start caring for themselves and not just for their children. It certainly takes courage to express one's failures, to stand out in a pool of publications on perfect parenting.

On a positive note, "failure allows us to escape the punishing norms that discipline behavior and manage human development. . . . Failure preserves some of the wondrous anarchy of childhood" (Halberstam 3). As far as feminism is concerned, Halberstam goes on to argue that

> failure has often been a better bet than success. Where feminine success is always measured by male standards, and gender failure often means being relieved of the pressure to measure up to patriarchal ideals, not succeeding at womanhood can offer unexpected pleasures. In many ways this has been the message of many renegade feminists in the past. Monique Wittig (1992) argued in the 1970s that if womanhood depends upon a heterosexual framework, then lesbians are not "women," and if lesbians are not "women," then they fall outside of patriarchal norms and can re-create some of the meaning of their genders. (4)

Following a comparable logic, if motherhood depends upon a patriarchal/heteronormative framework, then bad mothers are not "mothers," given that the only normative model is that of the perfect one. Historian Andrée Lévesque asserts that during the first half of the twentieth century, "the mother was primarily a figure of love and self-sacrifice" (23). Official discourses "constructed an ideal of femininity with which every woman laying claim to a place in the social order would have to align herself" (12) and that depended for the most part on her reproductive abilities. As such, a bad mother (one who does not demonstrate sufficient love and self-sacrifice), failing to secure "a place in the social order," would step out of the realm of oppression and enjoy "unexpected pleasures," as well as allow for the reassessment of the maternal role and its expectations. Instances of monstrous mothers in Québec are, as mentioned earlier, common representational schemes to advocate for emancipation, as evidenced by Anne Hébert's iconic novella, *Le torrent* (1948). Yet, whereas "Hébert summed up all the forces of social oppression in her maternal figure, Claudine Perrault, making her a fitting target for violent revolt and, ironically, turning the mother into a monster" (Green 75), Claudine's identity is so limited to the realm of motherhood that even her monstrous nature precludes any possibility of stepping out of the social order.

Granted, writers like Hébert broke "new ground by integrating women's quest for personal and sexual autonomy" (Green 76) in other narratives such as *Kamouraska*. Contrary to Claudine, in the selection of texts included in this volume, writers and filmmakers rely on monstrous or horrible mothers to showcase a diversity of nonhierarchical maternal practices, as well as a way to expand our understanding of womanhood. In that sense, through failure, women are to a certain extent extricated from a constraining social order in which reproduction or motherhood is the only way of being in the world and are able to express their pleasures, desires, and subjectivities as women.

Today's media interactions do tend to advocate for more progressive notions of family and relationships. They do so, however, by offering so many different models that parents/mothers become trapped in a schizophrenic world of unattainable ideals. Further, journalists often rely on social media comments (Twitter for the most part) to generate sensational or alleged controversial pieces, giving global attention to minor events without providing enough distance or critical reflection.[11] A consequence of such journalistic practices lies in the widening of ideological gaps between who is considered right and who is considered wrong. As a matter of fact, the usual response to shaming practices is a radical one that tends to chastise the detractors. Such a response is neither productive nor educational. "Preaching-to-the-choir" strategies have little to no transformative effect on nonbelievers. Perhaps this is where literature and films come to the rescue with contextualized, in-depth commentaries on social events and practices, allowing readers and viewers of all stripes to ponder and reevaluate their beliefs.

Horrible Mothers contains nine chapters and follows a chronological order. Chapter 1 opens the volume by showing how past models of motherhood, particularly oppressive ones, result in fear. Indeed, Pauline Henry-Tierney explores matrophobia and its roots in Nelly Arcan's *Putain* (2001), along with the trope of the whore. Dealing with corporeal degradation, desexualization, prostitution, and death, Henry-Tierney underscores the effects of past representations and sheds light on the subversive strategies at play in Arcan's work to disrupt the maternal cycle and offer new mother-daughter configurations, new female genealogies. In that sense, this chapter provides interesting echoes with the later chapter by Natalie Edwards.

The relationship between mother and child lies at the heart of Susan Pinette's analysis of works by Franco-American writers Paul Monette, David Plante, Allan Bérubé, and Steven Riel, ranging from the 1990s to 2006. In this second chapter, Pinette reminds us that Franco-Americans are tightly linked to motherhood (be it the motherland or the maternal body as a site of social reproduction) and investigates strategies by gay writers to explore their identities in the past heteronormative regimes of francophone New England. Relying on the myth of the Franco-American mother, these writers manage to articulate their queer identities. Further, they provide tools to apprehend the past without romanticizing it or playing into nationalist rhetoric.

Turning to the past and the predominance of the mother figure is Chelsea Ray's work on Franco-American playwright Grégoire Chabot, whose 2006 unpublished piece, "A Life Lost," discusses issues of class, gender, ethnicity, and social divides in the context of French-Canadian immigration to

Maine in the 1930s. Not only does Ray show how Chabot relies on the main character to denounce the burden of large families and clerical hypocrisy, she also posits the mother as a "feminist-in-the-making." Though focused on the past and Chabot's personal family stories, this contribution displays strong examples of feminine empowerment.

If these early chapters offer strict and oppressive models of motherhood, Alison Rice's reading of Nancy Huston's *Lignes de faille* (2006) in chapter 4 provides a counterexample whose consequences are not necessarily positive. Rice shows how permissive parenting, in particular, can prove damaging for children and often hides deeper, traumatic secrets. In the end, Huston's novel advocates for constant adjustments, not just good intentions, and demonstrates the effects of American mothering practices. While some women struggle to find the right balance or to conform to ideals of motherhood, others choose not to have any children.

In chapter 5, Natalie Edwards tackles the autobiographical expression of voluntary childlessness in twenty-first-century Québec literature, especially in the work of Lucie Joubert (2010). As scholarship on the matter is still developing, Edwards provides a necessary commentary on nonmothering or childlessness and the ways women voice such a rejection. Beyond literary expressions, this essay testifies to a contemporary interest and growing phenomenon.

Also dealing with autobiographical materials, Lucie Hotte and Ariane Brun del Re give a voice to Franco-Ontarian literature. Chapter 6 delves into Marguerite Andersen's 2013 *La mauvaise mère* in relation to her larger oeuvre. Looking at Andersen's narrative structures and choices of genre, Hotte and Brun del Re argue that the progression from fiction to confessions serves to express maternal failure. Through close readings of Andersen's latest text and cross-references with previous publications, the authors discuss the problematics of shame, guilt, and inadequacy and the potential of writing as means of doing penance.

Along similar lines and in the form of another collaboration, chapter 7, by Susan Ireland and Patrice Proulx, offers a complementing and contrasting piece to that of Rice (in chapter 4) and looks at Nancy Huston's *Bad Girl* (2014), a semi-autobiographical narrative, discussing the predominant theme of abandonment in relation to pregnancy, abortion, motherhood, and procreation. Highlighting the unconventional nature of Huston's narrative, the trauma of being an unwanted child, Ireland and Proulx reflect on the historical construction of good or bad mothering, as well as the act of writing as a means to produce and destabilize knowledge. The last two chapters in this volume look at cinematographic productions from Québec.

In chapter 8, Amy Ransom provides a survey of mother figures in Québec cinema from the first decade of the twenty-first century. These figures show a clear intention to move away from classic, negative representations of mothers to more understanding and forgiving portrayals. Engaging with Québec's sociohistorical changes, Ransom argues that more works showcase nuanced treatments of the mother and increasingly complex female characters, and these works broaden the spectrum of maternal practices.

With similar intentions, chapter 9 focuses more specifically on recent films by critically acclaimed filmmaker Xavier Dolan. Loïc Bourdeau's contribution draws a parallel between *J'ai tué ma mère* and *Mommy* to shed light on the progression in Dolan's representation of motherhood from one that relies on references to Québec's history to one that is a reflection on contemporary sociopolitical difficulties. While the first feature advocates for new models of motherhood, the second demands that we be aware of the effects of politics, as well as current processes of domination, even where we least expect them.

This collection is not intended to provide an exhaustive survey of all the horrible mother figures in francophone North America; instead, it is a contribution to ongoing developments in the field of feminist, queer, and francophone (literary and cinematographic) studies, providing an account of post-1990s and contemporary works on the subject. Louisiana has unfortunately been left out of this project insofar as its relevant works date back to the nineteenth century. Although analyses of these texts and the trope of the mother figures are important, the volume could not afford such a significant temporal gap. Further, as queer studies calls for intersectionality, one might also deplore the lack of diversity. For instance, studies of mothers in literary works by First Nations writers would have added to the spectrum of lived experiences and offered other forms of resistance. As these works gain more scholarly attention, we can expect essays on the topic to appear. Nevertheless, the diversity of geographies, histories, and portrayals in this collaborative project manages to show the difficulty in attaining or maintaining maternal perfection, sometimes with the accompanying trauma or fear of failure. *Horrible Mothers*, however, provides a space for failing more or less successfully, for voicing anxieties, rejections, regrets, and for offering alternatives. This volume rejects the belief that "success happens to good people and failure is just a consequence of a bad attitude" (Halberstam 3). In doing so, this project proves unapologetically committed to denouncing lasting clichés, forms of prejudice, and misrepresentations. *Horrible Mothers* is an *acte engagé* in line with Geoffroy de Lagasnerie's recent philosophical reflections on systemic violence and academia, and our duty is to reject complicity and to resist and oppose existing domination, exploitation, and oppression at large. In *Penser dans un monde mauvais* (2017), he argues:

> [S]itôt que l'on écrit, sitôt que l'on prend la décision de publier, de chercher, de créer, tout change. Se lancer dans de telles activités suppose d'avoir décidé, plus ou moins consciemment, à un moment ou à un autre, de faire partie des producteurs d'idées, de faire circuler des discours, et donc *de contribuer à façonner le cours du monde.* Par conséquent, à ce moment-là, *nous avons choisi de nous engager. Nous sommes engagés dans quelque chose.* Et là, nous ne pouvons plus reculer et nier la dimension politique de notre action. (12)[12]

Horrible Mothers engages in similar, perhaps grand, objectives to make the world better. Finally, it demands an understanding of deeply rooted past and present systems of marginalization and oppression. It demands acceptance of all mothering practices and of those who do not wish to be mothers; it rejects tolerance. I borrow from Nicholas Giguère's *Queues* (2017), a novel in verse on homosexuality and normativity whose words on tolerance strongly resonate with being a "horrible mother" and this volume's objectives:

> j'en ai rien à crisser d'une société qui m'endure
> comme on endure
> une otite
> une verrue plantaire
> un mal de gorge qu'on essaie de guérir avec des
> Vicks
>
> . . .

je veux rien savoir d'une société qui m'accepte comme une attraction touristique
une bête de foire des années 1930
une monstruosité pour les promeurs du
dimanche
qui me lanceraient des peanuts
tout en sifflant d'admiration et d'étonnement (64–65)[13]

The women and mothers portrayed in this collection call for our attention, for acceptance, for the ability to express all facets of their identities. They call for diversity. In the end, the francophone contexts under scrutiny reveal more universal concerns at a time of global exchanges and border and identity blurring. If mothering is a losing game, failing at it is a winning strategy.

NOTES

Epigraph: "The problem, perhaps, is that normal motherhood no longer is, in fact, normal. One can no longer 'satisfy oneself' (I use quotation marks because it is already a lot of work) with providing food, safety, and warmth to one's children. One must also be *creative*. She bakes cookies! . . . The creative mother is nothing but a derivative of the perfect mother. . . . Yet she spreads the same pressure, the same narrowness of models, the same imperative to appraise one's value based on the number of 'likes' she receives on Facebook."

1. As far as the potential of literature is concerned, see Pierre Jourde, whose thorough demonstration says it all and with whom I agree in his conclusion that "il me paraît clair qu'une société fondée sur le pur utilitarisme, l'intérêt à court terme, perd sa raison d'être" ("it seems clear to me that a society founded on mere utilitarianism, short-term interest, loses its *raison d'être*").

2. Chapter 2 of Rye's monograph provides an outstanding survey of the Western contributions on the topic. Drawing on Simone de Beauvoir, Adrienne Rich, Nancy Chodorow, Marianne Hirsch, Anne Oakley, Luce Irigaray, Julia Kristeva, and Hélène Cixous, among others, Rye showcases the variety and history of discourses on motherhood.

3. I turn to Eve Kosofsky Sedgwick for her distinction between shame and guilt: "The conventional way of distinguishing shame from guilt is that shame attaches to and sharpens the sense of what one is, whereas guilt attaches to what one does" (51)—an important distinction that in the case of mothers or nonmothers leads to the partial conflation of the two insofar as motherhood, although a performative act, is inextricable from womanhood as an identity. As such, what one is *is* what one does and vice versa. There is no escaping these feelings.

4. While Simone de Beauvoir and Luce Irigaray have had an undeniable impact on women's liberation and the field of feminist studies, reminding us that "on ne naît pas femme on le devient" ("one is not born woman: one becomes one") (Beauvoir 13) or that "we live in accordance with exclusively male genealogical systems" (Irigaray 8), decades later the same fights are being fought. Women face similar expectations and similar normative violence. French journalist Nadia Daam reports on one such instance of violence against women who do not wish to have children: "Les personnes qui ne veulent pas d'enfants, et en particulier les femmes, sont quotidiennement les réceptacles de remarques acides, voire franchement dégueulasses de la part de leur entourage, parfois même très proche. . . . Mais les professionnels de santé, pourtant avertis et censés s'interdire d'émettre une opinion sur les choix de vie de leur patients, participent aussi parfois à ce tribunal populaire" ("Individuals who do not want children, and in particular women, are constantly the targets of harsh comments, even some frankly disgusting ones, coming from their loved ones, sometimes even very close relations. . . . But health professionals, although informed and officially forbidden to share their opinion on their patients' choices, also take part in this popular trial"). In the Québécois context, journalist Isabelle Paré examines a documentary on "childfree" women and notes: "L'incompréhension autour du non-désir d'enfant aboutit inévitablement aux contingences du genre: 'Que vas-tu faire de ta vie? Fais-tu du bénévolat? Est-ce qu'on doit faire plus pour justifier notre choix?' Ça véhicule l'idée qu'une femme sans enfants est incomplète" ("The lack of understanding concerning voluntary childlessness leads inevitably to gender contingencies: 'What will you do with your life? Do you volunteer? Do we have to do more to make up for our choice?' It propagates the idea that a childless woman is incomplete"). With regard to the specific question of "childfree/childless" women, see Edwards, who studies the strategies of expressing one's decision to not be a mother along with the struggles and stereotypes these women face and deconstruct.

5. Feminist consciousness allows us to go from a world where women are invisible, or when they are visible they are only sexual or morally guilty of everything, to a world where women become subjects and a center of interest and are valorized as individuals and as a group.

6. Walker Rettberg also shows the potential of these new modes of expression and self-representation: "In a study of NSFW (not safe for work) blogs where women and men share erotic photos . . . this woman developed a 'new gaze' that 'taught' her to feel sexy in her body, but it also altered her material body-practices in terms of how she held herself, how she dressed, and accessorized, whether she used make-up" (84). Undeniably, self-representation can grant the subject more autonomy and agency.

7. I use Foucault's "volonté de savoir" to allow a comparison with his analysis of institutional and categorizing discourses on sexuality: "[M]ore importantly was the multiplication of discourses concerning sex in the field of exercise of power itself: an institutional incitement to speak about it, and to do so more and more" (*History* 18). Furthermore, "Doctors counseled the directors and professors of educational establishments, but they also gave their opinions to families; educators designed projects which they submitted to the authorities" (28). What emerges in our current era is a shift with regard to the sources of knowledge. While similar institutionalized and systemic processes of domination and normalization occur, individuals are now providing personal data willingly, in hopes of gratification. In turn, the multiplication of discourses pertaining to parenting—as it is the main focus of this project—generates horizontal regulating power structures (among the individuals, in opposition to vertical, that is, from the institutions to the people). The leveling between doctors, educators, and now individual opinions blurs the lines of influence yet contributes just as much to moralizing our actions. This diversity of opinions certainly gives way to more acceptance, but it often does so by reinforcing paralyzing identity categories and binaries.

8. In 1999 Michael Warner's *The Trouble with Normal* investigated the impact of monitoring technologies: "Now they [people] are surrounded by numbers that tell them what normal is: census figures, market demographics, opinion polls, social science studies, psychological surveys, clinical tests, sales figures, trends, the 'mainstream,' the current generation, the common man, the man on the street, the 'heartland of America,' etcetera. Under the conditions of mass culture, they are constantly bombarded by images of statistical populations and their norms, continually invited to make an implicit comparison between themselves and the mass of other bodies" (53–54). As is the case with Foucault, it is now striking and worrying to see individuals who take part in producing additional statistics and comparisons, individuals who are bombarded by and bombard others with images of normalcy and deviance.

9. For more information on the subject, see Sears.

10. In his analysis of *Little Miss Sunshine* (2006, directed by Jonathan Dayton and Valerie Faris) "a young girl [Olive] with her sights set on winning a Little Miss Sunshine beauty pageant . . . is destined to fail, and to fail spectacularly. But while her failure could be the source of misery and humiliation, and while it does indeed deliver precisely this, it also leads to a kind of ecstatic exposure of the contradictions of a society obsessed with meaningless competition" (Halberstam 5). I would argue that motherhood too has become its own competition. Yet, failing at it not only reveals its meaninglessness but also breaks apart oppressive expectations.

11. In "Hilary Duff Fires Back after Being Mom-Shamed for Kissing Her Son," Caroline Bologna briefly summarizes the events: "After receiving criticism for kissing her 4-year-old son on the lips, the actress and singer fired back with a strong message." Following this appeared the official Instagram post, a sample of negative Twitter comments, and Duff's response, asking those with "warped minds and judgment" to unfollow her. Bologna's one-hundred-word piece takes on an alleged impartial standpoint, simply reporting facts on the dispute. Yet, the concluding "Leave mamas alone!" testifies to her agreeing with Duff. While we would too join in rejecting any form of mom shaming, the method falls short. The decision to give such events greater visibility should require a true *acte engagé*, one that includes different perspectives and seeks to educate without using the critics' tools.

12. "[A]s soon as one writes, as soon as one makes the decision to publish, to research, to create, everything changes. To engage in such activities implies to have decided, more or less consciously, at one moment or another, to be part of an idea-producing group, to circulate discourses, and as such to *contribute to the shaping of our world*. Consequently, at that moment, *we have chosen to be engaged. We are engaged in something*. And here, we can no longer back down and deny the political dimension of our action."

13. "i couldn't care less for a society that endures me
    like one endures
    an ear infection
    a foot wart
    a sore throat that one tries to heal with
    Vicks
    . . .
    I don't care to hear about a society
    that accepts me only as an attraction for tourists
    a fair's freak from the 1930s
    a monstrosity for those taking a stroll on
    Sundays
    who would throw peanuts at me
    while whistling with admiration and astonishment" (my translation).

WORKS CITED

Beauvoir, Simone de. *Le deuxième sexe*. Gallimard, 1949.

Bologna, Caroline. "Hilary Duff Fires Back after Being Mom-Shamed for Kissing Her Son." *Huffington Post*, 13 Dec. 2013, https://www.huffingtonpost.com/entry/hilary-duff-fires-back-after-being-mom-shamed-for-kissing-her-son_us_58503a14e4b0bd9c3dff1998.

Britt, Fanny. *Les tranchées: Maternité, ambiguité et féminisme, en fragments.* Atelier 10 (2013).

Chodorow, Nancy. *The Reproduction of Mothering: Psychoanalysis and the Sociology of Gender.* University of California Press, 1999.

Connolly, Allison. *Spaces of Creation: Transculturality and Feminine Expression in Francophone Literature.* Lexington Books, 2016.

Daam, Nadia. "La violence verbal inouïe envers les femmes qui ne veulent pas d'enfant." *Slate,* 21 Apr. 2016, http://www.slate.fr/story/117329/violence-verbale-inouie -femmes-qui-ne-veulent-pas-denfant.

Damlé, Amaleena, and Gill Rye, eds. *Women's Writing in Twenty-First-Century France: Life as Literature.* University of Wales Press, 2013.

Daoust-Boisvert, Amélie. "Fanny Britt et ses mères (indignes, parfaites, superwomen . . .)." *Le Devoir,* 16 Nov. 2013, https://www.ledevoir.com/lire/392715/fanny-britt-et -ses-meres-indignes-parfaites-superwomen.

Dufault, Roseanna Lewis. *Metaphors or Identity: The Treatment of Childhood in Selected Quebecois Novels.* Fairleigh Dickinson University Press, 1991.

———, ed. *Women by Women: The Treatment of Female Characters by Women Writers of Fiction in Quebec since 1980.* Fairleigh Dickinson University Press, 1997.

Edwards, Natalie. *Voicing Voluntary Childlessness: Narratives of Non-mothering in French.* Peter Lang, 2016.

Foucault, Michel. *The History of Sexuality.* Vol. 1. Vintage, 1990.

———. *"Society Must Be Defended": Lectures at the Collège de France, 1975–1976.* Trans. David Macey. Picador, 2003.

Gay, Roxane. *Bad Feminist: Essays.* Harper Collins, 2014.

Gefen, Alexandre. *Réparer le monde: La littérature française au XXIᵉ siècle.* Corti, 2017.

Giguère, Nicholas. *Queues.* Hamac, 2017.

Gilbert, Paula Ruth, and Miléna Santoro, eds. *Transatlantic Passages: Literary and Cultural Relations between Quebec and Francophone Europe.* McGill-Queen's University Press, 2010.

Gould, Karen. *Writing in the Feminine: Feminism and Experimental Writing in Quebec.* Southern Illinois University Press, 1990.

Green, Mary Jean. *Women and Narrative Identity: Rewriting the Quebec National Text.* McGill-Queen's University Press, 2001.

Halberstam, Jack. *The Queer Art of Failure.* Duke University Press, 2011.

Hammer, Toni. "I'm Not a Bad Mom." *Scary Mommy,* http://www.scarymommy.com /not-a-bad-mom/.

Hébert, Anne. *Le torrent.* 1948. Bibliothèque Québécoise, 1990.

Hirsch, Marianne. *The Mother/Daughter Plot: Narrative, Psychoanalysis, Feminism.* Indiana University Press, 1989.

Hotte, Lucie, and François Ouellet. *La littérature franco-ontarienne depuis 1996: Nouveaux enjeux esthétiques*. Prise de parole, 2016.

Irigaray, Luce. *Je, tu, nous: Toward a Culture of Difference*. Routledge, 1992.

Jones, Katie. *Representing Repulsion: The Aesthetic Disgust in Contemporary Women's Writing in French and German*. Peter Lang, 2013.

Joubert, Lucie, ed. *Trajectoires au féminin dans la littérature québécoise (1960–1990)*. Nota Bene, 2000.

Jourde, Pierre. "A quoi sert la littérature." *L'Obs*, 3 Mar. 2009, http://pierre-jourde.blogs .nouvelobs.com/archive/2009/03/03/a-quoi-sert-la-litterature-1.html.

Jurney, Ramond, and Florence McPherson, eds. *Women's Lives in Contemporary French and Francophone Literature*. Palgrave Macmillan, 2016.

Lagasnerie, Geoffroy de. *Penser dans un monde mauvais*. PUF, 2017.

Larose, Karim, and Rosalie Lessard. "Entretien avec Nicole Brossard." *Voix et Images*, vol. 37, no. 3, 2012, pp. 13–29.

Lebreton, France. "Génération Selfie." *La Croix*, 31 May 2016, https://www.la-croix .com/Famille/Generation-selfie-2016-05-31-1200764179.

Lévesque, Andrée. *Making and Breaking the Rules: Women in Quebec, 1919–1939*. Trans. Yvonne M. Klein. University of Toronto Press, 2010.

Marder, Elissa. *The Mother in the Age of Mechanical Reproduction: Psychoanalysis, Photography, Deconstruction*. Fordham University Press, 2012.

Marinucci, Mimi. *Feminism Is Queer: The Intimate Connection between Queer and Feminist Theory*. Zed Books, 2016.

Marshall, Bill. *Quebec National Cinema*. McGill-Queen's University Press, 2000.

Milot, Louise, and Jaap Lintvelt, eds. *Le roman québécois depuis 1960*. University Laval Press, 1992.

O'Reilly, Andrea, ed. *Feminist Mothering*. SUNY Press, 2008.

Paré, Isabelle. "En avoir ou pas?" *Le Devoir*, 12 Nov. 2015, https://www.ledevoir.com /societe/454994/en-avoir-ou-pas.

Park, Shelley M. *Mothering Queerly, Queering Motherhood: Resisting Monomaternalism in Adoptive, Lesbian, Blended, and Polygamous Families*. SUNY Press, 2013.

Rich, Adrienne. *Of Woman Born: Motherhood as Experience and Institution*. Norton, 1977.

Ruth, Gilbert, and Roseanna Lewis Dufault. *Doing Gender: Franco-Canadian Women Writers of the 1990s*. Fairleigh Dickinson University Press, 2001.

Rye, Gill. *Narratives of Mothering: Women's Writing in Contemporary France*. University of Delaware Press, 2009.

Saint-Martin, Lori. "Le corps et la fiction à réinventer: Metamorphoses de la maternité dans l'écriture des femmes au Québec." *Recherches Féministes*, vol. 7, no. 2, 1994, pp. 115–34.

———. *Le nom de la mère: Mères, filles et écriture dans la littérature québécoise au féminin*. Nota Bene, 1999.

Santoro, Miléna. *Mothers of Invention: Feminist Authors and Experimental Fiction in France and Quebec.* McGill-Queen's University Press, 2003.

Sears, Alan. "Queer Anti-capitalism: What's Left of Lesbian and Gay Liberation?" *Science & Society*, vol. 69, no. 1, 2005, pp. 92–112.

Sedgwick, Eve Kosofsky. "Shame, Theatricality, and Queer Performativity." *Gay Shame*, edited by David Halperin and Valerie Traub, University of Chicago Press, 2009, pp. 49–62.

Seghal, Parul. "In a Raft of New Books, Motherhood from (Almost) Every Angle." *New York Times*, 24 Apr. 2018, https://www.nytimes.com/2018/04/24/books/review-mothers-jacqueline-rose.html.

Stanley, Eric A., and Nat Smith, eds. *Captive Genders: Trans Embodiment and the Prison Industrial Complex.* AK Press, 2011.

Tremblay, Michel. *Encore une fois, si vous permettez.* Leméac, 1998.

———. *Les belles-soeurs.* Ed. Rachel Killick. Bristol Classical Press, 2000.

Walker Rettberg, Jill. *Seeing Ourselves through Technology: How We Use Selfies, Blogs and Wearable to Shape Ourselves.* Palgrave Pivot, 2014.

Warner, Michael. *The Trouble with Normal.* Harvard University Press, 1999.

1

The Whore and Her Mother

Exploring Matrophobia in Nelly Arcan's *Putain*

PAULINE HENRY-TIERNEY

J'ai eu trop de mères, trop de ces modèles de dévotes réduites à un nom de remplacement. . . . [J]'ai eu trop de ces mères-là et pas assez de la mienne, ma mère qui ne m'appelait pas car elle avait trop à dormir.

NELLY ARCAN, *Putain*

In the opening pages of Québécoise writer Nelly Arcan's autofictional debut novel, *Putain* (2001), the narrator proclaims that she has had too many mothers—an overabundance of the sister-mothers from her fervent Roman Catholic education, yet not enough of her own mother, a woman described by the narrator as "une larve" (18), a worm-like creature who exists only in a vegetative, mute state throughout the text.[1] The maternal dynamic dominates the text with the mother's shadowy absent-presence weighing down oppressively on the narrator as an ominous forewarning of what she considers to be her own impending destiny. For Arcan's protagonist, the fear of her own "destin de larve" (53) is all-consuming. In this study, I will explore the intense feelings of matrophobia experienced by the narrator. I will begin by examining how the narrator perceives her mother in terms of the images she employs to describe her and the feelings evinced from such portrayals. I will then look at the roots of the narrator's matrophobic angst, such as her phobias of corporeal degradation, desexualization, and social alienation. Finally, I will explore how prostitution and death are seen as subversive strategies to disrupt and ultimately reject the maternal cycle. Drawing upon maternal feminist theorist Adrienne Rich's elaboration of matrophobia and Simone de Beauvoir's critique of the phenomenological socialization of maternity, I will explore the specific interactions Arcan textually maps out between matrophobia, sexuality, and corporeality and their resultant implications for our understanding of maternal relations.

While the dynamics of mother-daughter relations have universal resonance, the specificity of the Québec context in which Arcan is writing is essential to our understanding of female genealogies in this sociocultural moment. Writing on the cusp of the third millennium, Arcan's voice joins with other contemporary Québécoise writers such as Marie-Sissi Labrèche, whose transgressive narratives explore maternal relationships through topoi such as sexuality and corporeality. While Gill Rye observes a trend in contemporary French literature in which "mothers are becoming narrative subjects in their own right" (15), the mothers in these texts remain silent, reflective, perhaps, of the persisting traditional values assigned to women in Québécois culture. As Andrée Lévesque explains, in efforts to populate and affirm the economic stability of the province, official discourses from the state and the Catholic Church sought to define women solely in relation to motherhood.[2] Over the years, many Québécoise writers have explored the persistence of this legacy and its repercussions for female genealogies,[3] and Arcan's text constitutes an important perspective on the mother-daughter issue in a postmillennial context. Despite the increasing audibility of Arcan's posthumous voice, scant critical attention has focused on her exploration of maternal relations and none on the question of matrophobia.

First appearing in Lynn Sukenick's 1973 essay on her study of Doris Lessing's female characters, the term "matrophobia" relates not simply to a fear of one's mother or maternity but rather to a fear of becoming one's mother. Sukenick explores the matrophobia experienced by Lessing's protagonist Martha Quest in *Children of Violence* (1952), describing the fear of becoming her mother as a catalyst for the development of the protagonist's own diametrically opposed subjectivity: "It is against her mother's vapidity that Martha Quest forms her character; her self-respect is fashioned out of her sense of difference from the woman who hovers uselessly in the margins of her life" (518). The term has been elaborated further by Adrienne Rich, who understands matrophobia as being manifested in a daughter's refusal to perpetuate subjugated patterns of female impotency inculcated through patriarchal order: "Thousands of daughters see their mothers as having taught a compromise and self-hatred they are struggling to win free of, the one through whom the restrictions and degradations of a female existence were perforce transmitted. Easier by far to hate and reject a mother outright than to see beyond her to the forces acting upon her" (235).

As my analysis of *Putain* will illuminate shortly, while the narrator does harbor feelings that vacillate from pity to sheer disgust for her mother, unlike Rich's definition, the narrator is acutely aware of the external forces acting upon her mother. Her castigation still remains sharp, since she is also admonishing her mother's complicity in those forces. Rich further delineates matrophobia as a self-splitting, an inward-looking form of self-annihilation in order to purge the latent maternal threat: "Matrophobia can be seen as a womanly splitting of the self, in the desire to become purged once and for all of our mothers' bondage, to become individuated and free. The mother stands for the victim in ourselves, the unfree woman, the martyr" (236).

As I shall discuss, this form of self-dissociation does take place in *Putain*, but in order to abate her matrophobia, the narrator subversively promotes extreme forms of splitting, ultimately seeing death (both real and symbolic) as a possible solution to the maternal dynamic. For now, let us consider who exactly the narrator fears becoming by analyzing the images the narrator employs to characterize her mother.

Maternal Imagery: Princesses, Cadavers, and Worms

From an early age the narrator is conscious of the maternal absence in her life, observing and framing her mother as an untenable figure and categorizing her progressive social withdrawal into different stages. For the narrator, the first stage, which lasted nearly four years, was "[la] période de cheveux" (9) ("the time of the hair" [3]), where only her mother's hair was discernible from the immobile mass under the bedsheets. Striking a parallel with the mother known as "la grande Claudine" in Anne Hébert's *Le torrent* (1989), whose hands were the only body parts perceptible to her son, such fragmented images are reminiscent of a queered version of Jacques Lacan's Mirror Stage, in which the infant's ego identity is formed through a process of identification with its mirror image by providing an illusory sense of mastery over the fragmented bodily experience that the mirrored alter ego provides. The persistence of the fragmented mother's body echoes Lacan's evocation of Renaissance painter Hieronymus Bosch's work, containing "images of castration, mutilation, dismemberment, dislocation, evisceration, devouring, bursting open of the body" (11), which he uses to illustrate the ever-present threat of the return of identity fragmentation. In this way, it seems that the narrator's subjectivity is precariously contingent upon the relationship to the mother. The mother's fragmented body incarnates Bosch's monstrous images, underlining the threat for the narrator of returning to a similar state of fractured identity. This state of staticity slowly gives way to "la période de la Belle au Bois dormant" (10) ("the time of Sleeping Beauty" [3]). The narrator's characterization of her mother in terms of a fairy tale heroine befits the narrator's childhood perspective. As Elizabeth Wanning Harries discusses in her study of women's autobiography and fairy tales, the use of this genre functions as an analogical, interpretative device, "a way of reading and even predicting the world" (103). According to Bruno Bettelheim, the fairy tale of *Sleeping Beauty* is symbolic of the adolescent's journey into sexual and corporeal maturity, with the period of sleep paradigmatic of the "long, quiet concentration on oneself" necessary for personal growth during puberty (225). In *Sleeping Beauty* the heroine's slumber ensues after she pricks her finger on a distaff (the blood symbolizes the bleeding in menstruation and first intercourse). The long sleep is a protective countermeasure against premature sexual encounters, and the wall of thorns enclosing the heroine only gives way "when Sleeping Beauty has gained both physical and emotional maturity and is ready for love, and with it for sex and marriage" (233). However, in *Putain*, the narrator's characterization of her mother as Sleeping Beauty offers a queering of the tale. In lieu of a period of quietude allowing for sexual maturation, the mother's sleeping represents her social regression and, conversely, her sexual degradation. As Wanning Harries explains, "[F]airy tales provide scripts for living, but they can also inspire resistance to those scripts and, in turn, to other apparently predetermined patterns" (103). Arcan's narrative disrupts the traditional script, with the Sleeping Beauty mother eventually dying from sleeping too much, having waited interminably for the kiss of a Prince Charming who, according to the narrator, "ne viendra jamais car il n'existe pas ou n'a pas voulu d'elle" (58) ("will never come, since he doesn't exist or didn't want her" [51]). By subverting the ending of the popular Brothers Grimm tale, we can read Arcan's dystopian version as a rejection of this idea of the heroine's fate being contingent upon masculine agency. In her study of female subjectivity in popular fairy tales, Marcia Lieberman observes that most heroines are characterized as "passive, submissive, and helpless" (190) and embedded in narratives that only serve "to acculturate women to traditional social roles" (185). Arcan's queering of *Sleeping Beauty* reflects her critique of the social structures it reifies, and her alternative ending serves as a way to stop the mother from further internalizing these subservient values. Nevertheless, the narrator's alternative of death for her mother remains equally bleak, since this solution does not empower the mother either.

Continuing with the fairy tale imagery, the narrator also describes her mother as a witch: "[Q]ue dire sinon cette fente de sorcière qui ne peut tenir lieu de bouche, non, ce n'est qu'un trait qui donne au visage un caractère mortuaire, et ses doigts rendus croches d'être si fort rongés, ses doigts tordus de ne servir à rien" (33) ("[W]hat is there except that witch's slit that can't substitute for a mouth, no, it's just a line that gives her face a funereal look, and her fingers gnawed into eighth notes, crooked from uselessness" [27]).[4] The description of the mother's mouth being no more than a slit presents her as an inaudible figure, thus emphasizing her lack of agency, as Andrea King underlines: "Cette sorcière nous fait penser à celle qui revient à travers la littérature, la femme-sorcière qui voudrait parler, mais qui est réduite au silence par l'ordre masculin et brûlée vive" (42) ("This witch reminds us of the recurring literary figure of the witch-woman who wishes to speak but who is silenced by the masculine order and burned alive").[5] Throughout the text, Arcan doubles the word *fente* to create an alignment between the mouth slit and the genital slit to underline the connection between women's capacity to speak and their sexuality, invoking Luce Irigaray's own doubling of the lips/labia sewn together by patriarchy ("Their words, the gag upon our lips" [212]), yet with women's sexuality promising the chance to reaffirm subjective agency ("Our lips are growing red again. They're stirring, moving, they want to speak" [212]). Furthermore, the funereal look of this slit links with the idea of the mortal decomposition of the mother's body, explicitly portrayed in the narrator's descriptions of her mother as a cadaver, "un cadavre qui sort de son lit pour pisser" (38) ("a corpse who leaves her bed to pee" [31]), "de mourir sous les couvertures d'être si peu vue, si peu touché" (49) ("dying under the covers from being so rarely seen or touched" [42]). This gnarled, macabre caricature of the mother as a witch runs through the text, with the threat of ensnarement looming over the narrator in a fairy tale–esque manner: "[C]e n'est pas eux mais moi qui suis du mauvais côté de la vie, celui du lit de ma mère, de sa cave humide de sorcière" (100) ("[T]he one who's on the wrong side of life is me, not them, I'm on the side of my mother's bed, in her damp witch's cellar" [91]). For the narrator, the comparison of her mother's bed to a witch's cellar highlights how she sees her as a force to be feared, and she is careful not to get too close to the mother for fear of entrapment in her own possible prostrate future.

Above all other characterizations, the narrator most frequently describes her mother as a worm.[6] It is both what she does ("j'ai la nausée de répéter ma mère qui larve" [186] / "I'm queasy from repeating my mother who worms" [171]) and who she is ("sa vie de larve, sa vie de gigoter à la même place se retournant sur son impuissance" [36] / "her worm of a life, a life spent wriggling in the same place, tossing and turning on her helplessness" [30]). A worm is a common literary trope often used as a symbol of putre-faction and death, yet although the English translation of the French word *larve* is most commonly "worm" (as it appears most often in the English translation, *Whore*), it is not a worm in the sense of an earthworm (*ver*). Instead, *larve* is more accurately "larva," namely, the juvenile form many creatures inhabit before their metamorphosis into adulthood. The narrator describes how her mother is suspended in this sleep-induced coma, "une larve entre le sommeil et l'attente de prendre forme" (55) ("a worm hovering between sleeping and waiting to take form" [48]), yet she sees the bleak reality of her mother's inability to metamorphose and stake claim to her own subjectivity: "son agonie de larve qui se tord de ne pas ouvrir les ailes, et puis de toute façon elle n'a pas d'ailes et n'en a jamais eu, elle s'est effondrée bien avant d'avoir pu voler" (103) ("her agony about being a larva writhing from its inability to open its wings, but actually she has no wings and never did, she collapsed long before she could fly" [93]). The narrator then changes the image, instead likening her mother to a baby bird who is left crushed in the nest, trampled on by her brothers. As a woman, her mother is unable to fly from the nest or transform from the larva stage and ascend to a state of empowered subjecthood. Arcan's critique here echoes Rich's earlier sentiment about the way in which the construction of motherhood continues to connect women with bondage to men and patriarchy. Furthermore, the details of the mother collapsing, being crushed and trampled, also underscore her vulnerability. While a sense of pathos is evinced over the mother's unfulfilled potential, the narrator's contempt is equally present, characteristic of what Fran Scoble describes as the daughter's anger at the mother who concedes to her powerlessness (130). Having established a sense of who the narrator is scared of becoming, let us turn now to look at which aspects of the mother's life the narrator fears reproducing.

Corporeal Matrophobia and Dialectics of Sexuality

The narrator's "manie d'être ma mère" (95) ("mania for being my mother" [86]) assumes myriad forms linked with issues of sexuality and corporeality. First and foremost, the narrator fears literally becoming her mother's body: "[C]e corps . . . n'étant jamais la même chose d'une fois à l'autre, un corps qui me rappelle trop celui de ma larve de mère" (46) ("[T]his body . . . is always changing, one thing today and another tomorrow, a body that reminds me too much of my worm of a mother's" [39]). The narrator fears corporeal degradation and the threat posed by the ageing body. Acutely aware yet simultaneously complicit in the reproduction of patriarchal constructions of femininity and beauty, the narrator evinces disgust at her mother's deteriorating body: "[C]hez les femmes c'est impardonnable, le flasque et les rides, c'est proprement indécent, il ne faut pas oublier que c'est le corps qui fait la femme" (48) ("[W]ith women, flab and wrinkles are unforgiveable, totally indecent, remember, it's the body that makes the woman" [41]). The narrator is conscious of what Naomi Wolf identifies as "the beauty myth," namely, a phenomenon imposed by patriarchal culture, which she delineates as the "last, best belief system that keeps male dominance intact" (12), since it invariably instigates a hierarchizing of women. A further consequence of the mother's ageing body that fills the narrator with angst for her own "destin de larve" has to do with the way in which the ageing body becomes socially ghettoized. Referring to her dystopian Sleeping Beauty mother, the narrator comments, "Mais j'allais oublier qu'elle est vieille et laide maintenant, personne ne voudra l'embrasser" (104) ("But I almost forgot that she's old and ugly now, no one will want to kiss her" [94]). As Beauvoir explores in *La vieillesse*, old people occupy the position of society's "Others," particularly in capitalist countries, where they are seen as economically inactive and, therefore, a social burden. In *Le deuxième sexe*, Beauvoir also attributes old people's marginalization to the materiality of the ageing body, which serves as an unwelcome reminder for active society of their own impending reality of ageing, illness, and death. Such marginalization, according to Beauvoir, is even more acute for women, whose physiological destiny carries greater signification than men's, since society continues to reify links between women and their biological functions: "Whereas the male grows older continuously, the woman is brusquely stripped of her femininity; still young, she loses sexual attraction and fertility from which, in society's and her eyes, she derives the justification of her existence and her chances of happiness" (633). Beauvoir's explanation substantiates the narrator's aversion to the mother's ageing body: the deteriorating, desexualized body functions as a mirror image for the narrator, reflecting her own eventual social decline and alienation.

For the narrator, there is also a fear of physical maternal embodiment: "Et je dois me tenir droite pour retarder le moment où elle me rattrapera, sa scoliose qui prendra le dessus, me pliant en deux, sa bosse qui ira me penchant toujours plus sur le repassage à faire" (35) ("I've got to stand up straight to keep back the moment when she catches up with me and I'm folded in two by her scoliosis, bent more and more towards the ironing board by her hump" [28]). This fear of corporeal colonization is elucidated by Rich, who writes, "[W]here a mother is hated to the point of matrophobia there may also be a deeper underlying pull towards her, a dread that if one relaxes one's guard one will identify with her completely" (235). The mother's body becomes a monstrosity, with its degenerative illnesses threatening to subsume the narrator's body. Embedded within this image of corporeal territorialization is also the threat of domesticity. The narrator fears the inheritance of a body that is ravaged by the constraints of female domestication. While universal, this fear of domestic inheritance is also specific to Québec. Louise Forsyth underlines that the province's survival as a French-speaking community in an Anglophone continent depended upon the perpetuation of very traditional values: "The mother was allowed no individual identity in this value system; she was seen solely in terms of her maternal function within the family unit, recognized and appreciated for her domestic virtues alone. The daughter was usually a mother's projection or else her replacement" (44). The narrator's reference here to "le repassage" takes on a double meaning: it is her refusal both to become domestically imprisoned and to perpetuate this cycle (literally, her refusal to *repasser* [to go back] in her mother's footsteps).

The narrator's other matrophobic preoccupation is with the postmaternal desexualized body of her mother. She blames herself for her mother's physical degradation: "[C]omment pourrais-je me faire pardonner de lui avoir creusé un ventre qui ne l'a plus quittée depuis et de lui avoir pris l'attention des hommes" (177) ("[H]ow could I have been forgiven for hollowing out her womb, which has never gone away since, and for having stolen the attentions of a man" [162–63]). The negative image the narrator paints of maternal relations clearly echoes Beauvoir's arguments on maternity as a source of both psychological and corporeal destruction: "Pregnancy is above all a drama playing itself out in the woman between her and herself. She experiences it both as an enrichment and a mutilation; the fetus is part of her body and it is a parasite exploiting her; she possesses it and she is possessed by it; it encapsulates the whole future and in carrying it she feels as vast as the world; but this very richness annihilates her, she has the impression of not being anything else" (551–52).

In line with Beauvoir's critique of maternity, the narrator feels culpable for having annihilated her mother both physically, in the sense that her postmaternal body is no longer desirable through the optic of the male gaze, and psychologically in Freudian terms, in the sense that she is responsible for averting her father's sexual attentions—an instrumental factor in precipitating the mother's emotional and social withdrawal. According to the narrator, this corporeal annihilation has an exclusively matrilineal heritage, since it is the daughter who gains the nubile, unblemished body that her own birth has stolen from the mother, and it is toward this coveted body that the paternal gaze is redirected. This accounts for the incestuous motif that punctuates *Putain*, as the narrator fears that one day it will be her own father who knocks upon the door of the room where she works as a prostitute. To abate her corporeal matrophobia, the narrator realizes that she must not become pregnant so as to break this cycle: "[M]oi je suis coupable de la laideur de ma mère et de la mienne aussi, je ne dois plus en contaminer le monde ni la transmettre à une autre qui devra en mourir à son tour" (80) ("I'm guilty of my mother's ugliness and mine as well, I should stop contaminating the world with it and not transmit it to another who will have to die of it in turn" [72]).[7] This perpetual perforced transmission echoes Beauvoir's sentiment about the cyclical nature of mother-daughter relations: "Becoming a mother in turn, woman somehow takes the place of the one who gave birth to her" (548). This act of replacing one's own mother then becomes an ultimate form of threat for the narrator, since this forewarns of her own impending purged maternal body and the consequent decline of her sexual desirability, which, for the narrator, is the most valuable form of currency in a porn-driven patriarchal culture, particularly given her role as a prostitute, which necessitates that she capitalize on such cultural values.

Performing Radical Surgery through Sex and Death

Returning to Rich's conceptualization of matrophobia as a form of self-splitting, she argues that the way women expulse maternal self-identification is via a process of severing: "Our personalities seem dangerously to blur with our mothers'; and, in a desperate attempt to know where mother ends and daughter begins, we perform radical surgery" (236). While Rich is not explicit as to what such "radical surgery" entails, for the narrator, the extrication from the shadow of the mother's life can only be achieved through prostitution and death. First, in response to the aesthetics of disgust displayed in relation to the mother's ageing, undesirable body, prostitution provides the narrator with the financial recompense to detach herself from her mother's body: "[L]'argent sert à ça, à se détacher de ma mère, à se redonner un visage à soi, à rompre avec cette malédiction de laideur qui se transmet salement" (35) ("That's what the money's for, to cut myself away from my mother, give myself a face that belongs to me, to break away from that curse of ugliness that's so messily passed on" [28–29]). The narrator spends her earnings on cosmetic surgery, beauty treatments, and cosmetic products in order to assuage the onslaught of old age with the purpose of keeping herself visible in an image-oriented society, which she criticizes yet with which she complies. Such patterns of behavior reflect Beauvoir's existentialist concept of "bad faith," whereby women's self-deception (through the internalization of patriarchal norms) denies the possibility for their radical freedom.

Second, there is a symbiosis between the mother and daughter in terms of sexuality, since the narrator sees marriage as a form of prostitution for women: "Ma mère n'aurait jamais fait ça, elle ne s'est prostituée qu'avec un seul homme, mon père" (33) ("My mother would never do that, she prostituted herself to only one man, my father" [26]). In this sense, the mother's prostitution takes the form of her subservience to her husband, specifically, the way in which her own happiness is directly contingent upon his affection for her. However, the mother's form of prostitution, which can be understood in terms of her relinquishment of self-determinacy, is differentiated from the narrator's prostitution. For the narrator, her life as a prostitute stands in sharp relief against the menial existence of her parents: "mon opposition radicale au couple vieillissant mal et s'ennuyant, l'un baisant les autres et l'autre mourant de ne pas être baisée" (46–47) ("my radical opposition to a bored, badly aging couple, one fucking others and the other dying from not being fucked" [40]). In this way, the narrator's prostitution can be understood as a symbolic rejection of heteronormative coupledom. Through her role as a prostitute the narrator subverts patriarchal constructions of both marriage and motherhood. The narrator's indiscriminate couplings with countless clients (whom, she attests, are all fathers themselves) threatens the sanctity (and therein the confines) of marriage by transgressing the boundaries of the sexual and moral parameters it institutionally delineates. Furthermore, prostitution, whose ends lie in sexual gratification as opposed to procreation, stands in diametrical opposition to maternity. It can be seen as a liberating force in the sense that it dissociates women's sexuality from childbirth and motherhood. As Ann Dally argues, "There have always been mothers, but motherhood was invented" (17). Dally is referring to the way in which motherhood has been packaged as a profession for women in replacement of their previous employment at various sociohistorical moments in Western culture (such as the transition from a society based on agriculture to an industrialized one and the return of men after World War II). The transgenerational transmission of motherhood perpetuates itself, according to Nancy Chodorow, "through social-structurally induced psychological mechanisms. It is not the unmediated product of physiology" (211). The narrator's prostitution, therefore, serves to disrupt such constructed maternal genealogies. In fact, the narrator states that her "putasserie" (27) ("whoredom" [21]) is performed expressly for her mother: "[S]i moi je baise c'est pour elle aussi" (33) ("[E]ven my own fucking is for her, too" [26]). Her prostitution functions as a form of mimetic maternal salvation, since the narrator sees her prostitution as a force to disrupt the socially constructed institutions of marriage and motherhood, which have instigated the mother's demise. Arcan's promotion of prostitution can be understood as a subversion of matrophobia in the sense that prostitution offers a symbolic rejection of the reified aspects of patriarchal society, which threaten to reinsert the narrator into her own worm-like existence.

The other resolution to matrophobia that Arcan proposes is death. The theme of death is intricately laced through the tapestry of Arcan's oeuvre, thus emphasizing the autofictional dimension of Arcan's work, the author having taken her own life in 2009.[8] In *Putain* the narrator fantasizes about getting rid of her mother: "[J]e devrais l'enterrer une fois pour toutes, la recouvrir des métaux les plus durs pour qu'elle ne puisse plus refaire surface et me pourchasser de son étreinte de pieuvre" (81) ("I should bury her once and for all, cover her with the strongest metals so she can't come to the surface again and hunt me down with her octopus's grip" [73]). The image of the octopus underlines the mother's monstrosity and suffocating presence for the narrator. Here the mother is likened to a poisonous weed that risks coming back to the surface to ensnare the narrator. Covering the ground with a sheet of metal is a common practice in agriculture to stop weeds resurfacing, yet this image also connotes the idea of interment. This recourse to death is consistent with the matricidal dimension of Western culture. According to Irigaray, this is evidence of the mechanics of patriarchy, and the act of (figuratively) killing the mother both substantiates and perpetuates phallic order. Irigaray cites the murder of Clytemnestra as the source of women's exclusion from Western culture and the attendant denigration of maternal genealogical relations: "One thing is plain, not only in everyday events but in the whole social scene: our society and our culture operate on the basis of an original matricide" (11). Prefiguring the Oedipal paradigm, this original matricide paves the way for the subsequent psychical matricide we undergo in pursuit of individuation and entry into Symbolic Order, namely, the disidentification from the mother as the primary object of desire. Yet in *Putain* death implicates not only the mother but also the daughter, as the narrator states: "Il faudrait que je ne sois pas si moi-même, tellement ma mère, il faudrait que ma mère se tue . . . et nous entre-tuer ainsi jusqu'à ne plus avoir aucune raison de s'en vouloir ou de s'aimer, jusqu'à ce que nous soyons devenues étrangères, défigurées" (53) ("I'd have to be myself less, my mother less, my mother would have to kill herself . . . and then have us kill each other to the point of no longer having any reason to bear a grudge or love each other, to the point of becoming mutilated strangers" [46]).

In this way, I would argue that Arcan proposes a radical reformulation of the paradigm. The death of both the mother and daughter is symbolic of the rejection of the way in which maternal relations have been fashioned and fixed according to phallic order. Arcan is calling for a dramatic overhaul of the patriarchal-driven social constructs and frameworks of reference, which position women in such a way that matrophobic angst becomes part of the fabric engrained in maternal relations. In opposition to established phallic order, Irigaray underlines the importance of a genealogy of women and "situat[ing] ourselves within that female genealogy so that we can win and hold on to our identity" (19). Echoing Irigaray, this reciprocal killing can be understood as the only way of obliterating this eternal cycle so that the mother and daughter can become strangers to one another, establish a tabula rasa, particularly at the level of the imaginary, in order to reinscribe new patterns of mother-daughter relations that assert women's subjective agency.

In conclusion, as Arcan's elaboration of matrophobia in *Putain* shows, not only is the phobia indicative of the complex dynamics at stake in mother-daughter relations, but more widely, the roots of matrophobia are revelatory of the specific positions women occupy within society. As Arcan's narrator enumerates, matrophobia exists because of the reification of specific images of women through narratives such as fairy tales that circulate within Western culture. From the impassive Sleeping Beauty to the grotesque witch, matrophobia germinates in response to the tropes that have been configured to depict women. Furthermore, the narrator's matrophobic angst surrounding her own "destin de larve," with its implications of a decline in sexual desirability and the incumbent social alienation, points to probing questions Arcan is implicitly posing regarding the place and status we assign ageing women within society. Similarly, her evocation of the corporeal matrophobia raises pertinent issues concerning the ways in which the female body is qualified in contemporary society. The narrator's fear of her mother's ageing, postmaternal body calls for us to face up to the realities of the value we continue to place on youth, the way in which corporeal hierarchies subsist, and the ever-present influence of the male gaze, particularly in our current image-driven technological culture. Finally, Arcan's resolution to matrophobia resides in the tenets of sex and death. Although such measures may seem drastic, Arcan considers these two practices as the sole precepts to challenge phallic order. Prostitution, despite its ambiguous status, represents, for Arcan, a symbolic subversion of the heteronormativity embedded in the patriarchal institutions of marriage and motherhood. Death, for Arcan, symbolizes the eradication of ancillary configurations of the mother constructed according to phallic order. For Arcan, the mutual death of mother and daughter represents the possibility of moving beyond such configurations, instead proposing new female genealogies with a mater-narrative that affords women the possibility of a radical and newly empowered sense of subjectivity.

Epigraph: "I had too many mothers, too many sanctimonious models reduced to a reinvented name. . . . I had too many of that kind of mothers and not enough of my mother, a mother who didn't say my name because she needed to sleep too much" (3).

1. Coined by Serge Doubrovsky in relation to his novel *Fils* (1978), autofiction represents a type of writing that elides fiction with reality, involving the speaking subject being coextensive with the authorial *je*. It can be understood as a narrative mode that flags itself as fictional yet features a narrator whose autobiographical details mirror those of its author. In an interview with Pascale Navarro, Arcan described her text as follows: "Elle est autobiographique, c'est vrai; mais en même temps, je l'ai écrite 'à côté de la réalité'" ("It is autobiographical, it's true; but at the same time, I wrote it 'alongside reality'").

2. See chapter 2, "La maternité," in Lévesque.

3. See Forsyth for a survey of the different ways in which the mother-daughter relationship has been interpreted by Québec women writers.

4. This is a possible mistranslation, since in Québec French, *croche* as an adjective means "hooked" or "deformed"; however, the translator's choice of the noun "eighth notes" could be due to the corresponding visual imagery suggested by this musical sign, which is made up of an oval dot and a hooked stem.

5. In her seminal text, *The Mother/Daughter Plot: Narrative, Psychoanalysis, Feminism* (1989), Marianne Hirsch traces the historical silencing of the mother in literary narratives.

6. In her study of recent Québécois transgressive mother-daughter narratives, Lori Saint-Martin highlights how animalistic vocabulary is often employed to qualify (and disqualify) mothers. Described as insects, cows, and spiders, these mothers embody degradation and revulsion, inspiring excessive acts such as cannibalism and even matricide. As in *Putain*, this animality is corporeally bequeathed to the child, symptomatic, as Saint-Martin argues, of the way in which society blurs the human-animal divide, likening women to reproducing farmyard mammals.

7. Arcan's insistence here on the matrilineal specificity of maternal degradation is not equivalently connoted in the English translation by the choice of the gender-neutral word "another." For a study of translation issues related to gender, sexuality, and corporeality in Arcan's texts, see Henry-Tierney.

8. The subject of death and suicide is most explicitly articulated in her posthumous novel *Paradis, clef en main* (2009), finished two days before Arcan committed suicide.

Arcan, Nelly. *Paradis, clef en main*. Coups de Tête, 2009.

——. *Putain*. Éditions du Seuil, 2001.

——. *Whore*. Trans. Bruce Benderson. Black Cat, 2005.

Beauvoir, Simone de. *Le deuxième sexe, vol. II: L'expérience vécue*. Gallimard, 1949.

——. *The Second Sex*. Trans. Constance Borde and Sheila Malovany-Chevallier. Jonathan Cape, 2009.

Bettelheim, Bruno. *The Uses of Enchantment: The Meaning and Importance of Fairy Tales*. Knopf, 1976.

Chodorow, Nancy. *The Reproduction of Mothering*. 1978. University of California Press, 1999.

Dally, Ann. *Inventing Motherhood: The Consequences of an Ideal*. Schocken, 1983.

Forsyth, Louise. "The Radical Transformation of the Mother-Daughter Relationship in Some Women Writers of Québec." *Frontiers: A Journal of Women Studies*, vol. 6, no. 1–2, 1981, pp. 44–49.

Hébert, Anne. *Le torrent*. Bibliothèque Québécoise, 1989.

Henry-Tierney, Pauline. "Transgressive Textualities: Translating References to Gender, Sexuality and Corporeality in Nelly Arcan's *Putain* and *Paradis, clef en main*." *Canada and Beyond: A Journal of Canadian Literary and Cultural Studies*, vol. 3, no. 1–2, 2013, pp. 161–79.

Hirsch, Marianne. *The Mother/Daughter Plot: Narrative, Psychoanalysis, Feminism*. Indiana University Press, 1989.

Irigaray, Luce. *Sexes and Genealogies*. Trans. Gillian C. Gill. Columbia University Press, 1993.

——. *This Sex Which Is Not One*. Trans. Catherine Porter. Cornell University Press, 1985.

King, Andrea. "Nommer Son Mal: *Putain* de Nelly Arcan." *Atlantis: A Women's Studies Journal*, vol. 31, no. 1, 2006, pp. 37–44.

Lacan, Jacques. *Écrits: A Selection*. Trans. Alan Sheridan. W. W. Norton, 1977.

Lévesque, Andrée. *La norme et les déviantes: Des femmes au Québec pendant l'entre-deux-guerres*. Editions du Remue-Ménage, 2009.

Lieberman, Marcia K. "Some Day My Prince Will Come: Female Acculturation through the Fairy Tale." *Don't Bet on the Prince*, edited by Jack Zipes, 1972, Methuen, 1986, pp. 185–200.

Navarro, Pascale. "Nelly Arcan: Journal intime." *Voir*, 6 Sept. 2001, http://voir.ca/livres/2001/09/05/nelly-arcan-journal-intime/.

Rich, Adrienne. *Of Woman Born: Motherhood as Experience and Institution*. Norton, 1986.

Rye, Gill. *Narratives of Mothering: Women's Writing in Contemporary France*. University of Delaware Press, 2009.

Saint-Martin, Lori. "Araignées, vers et vaches: Mères et filles excessives en littérature québécoise contemporaine." *Québec Studies*, vol. 63, 2017, pp. 31–55.

Scoble, Fran Norris. "Mothers and Daughters: Giving the Lie." *Denver Quarterly*, vol. 18, 1984, pp. 126–33.

Sukenick, Lynn. "Feeling and Reason in Doris Lessing's Fiction." *Contemporary Literature*, vol. 14, no. 4, 1973, pp. 515–35.

Wanning Harries, Elizabeth. "The Mirror Broken: Women's Autobiography and Fairy Tales." *Fairy Tales and Feminism: New Approaches*, edited by Donald Haase, Wayne State University Press, 2004, pp. 99–112.

Wolf, Naomi. *The Beauty Myth*. Random House, 1990.

2

Horrible Mothers in *Mémère*'s Kitchen

Queer Identity in New England Franco-America

SUSAN PINETTE

Franco-American identity has always had lots to do with mothers.[1] Whether negotiating allegiance to the Québec motherland, remaining faithful to the French mother tongue, or seeing the maternal body as the site of social reproduction, Franco-Americans are intricately linked to mothers. While this is true for other cultural identities as well, this is particularly the case for New England Franco-Americans, who came from a French-speaking Canada where, as Lori Saint-Martin notes, "le mythe de la mère y a atteint des proportions inégalées" ("the myth of the mother reached unparalleled heights") (48). It comes perhaps as no surprise, therefore, that Franco-American writers draw from this deeply rooted myth of the mother to create a highly charged representative symbol. Herbert Gans affirms that for ethnic identity, especially in the third generation, "[e]xpressive behavior can take many forms, but it often involves the use of symbols. . . . Ethnic symbols are frequently individual cultural practices which are taken from the older ethnic culture; they are 'abstracted' from that culture and pulled out of its original moorings, so to speak, to become stand-ins for it" (9). Franco-American literature is replete with mothers who symbolize both the ancestral homeland and Franco-American identity: Eglantine and Rose-Aimée in

Norman Beaupré's *Deux femmes, deux rêves*, Cecile in Gerard Robichaud's *Papa Martel*, the women who inhabit many of Grégoire Chabot's writings. In Kristin Langellier's argument it is through family stories centered on *mémère* that Franco-Americans "become linked with the motherland and mother tongue in [their] imagination of Franco American identity" (56). In Franco-American communities, "[t]he Franco American *mémère* is the most French of the French, a privileged icon and a locus of performative power" (61–62).

Integrally linked to all these mothers, Franco-American ethnic identity as it is articulated and performed in the Franco-American community is deeply heteronormative. French Canadian nationalism was grounded in high fertility rates and large families because "both the Catholic Church and the nationalists believed they could count on the proverbial high francophone fertility rate . . . to maintain the proportion and standing of French Canadians within the Canadian political landscape" (Baillargeon 236), and while the imagined "Revenge of the Cradle" was perhaps never as much in play in Franco-America as it was in French Canada, the importance of extended family and kinship ties is, as seen, for example, in Bruno Ramirez's and Yukari Takai's work on the prominence of extended family ties in French Canadian chain migration, in Tamara Hareven's documentation of French Canadian kinship networks in the Manchester mills, in Kristin Langellier's emphasis on the ongoing importance of extended family gatherings, or in the centrality of genealogical work to current Franco-American ethnic identity.[2] Franco-American ethnic identity is not unique in its reliance upon heteronormativity. As Anne McClintock has argued, the nation—which I would extend here to include ethnic identity—is often construed in terms of familial and domestic metaphors (62).

This chapter investigates how Franco-American authors, given this heteronormative discursive regime, write their queer identities, and it argues that it is the figure of the mother that enables the signification of Franco-American ethnic identity and, in particular, a Franco-American queer identity. What interests me in particular is how mothers—as a key site and symbol of Franco-American ethnic identity—are deployed in queer ethnic narratives. Gay identities often figure self-realization and self-knowledge in opposition to heterosexuality and the heterosexual family; they are based upon "a performative act, [that] constitut[es] identity by naming itself in public discourse" (Grindstaff 58), a naming that often figures self-realization and self-knowledge in opposition to the heterosexual family. As Anne-Marie Fortier notes, "A recurring theme in [coming-out] stories is the association of migration with the fulfillment of the 'true' homosexual self outside of the family home of one's childhood" (1). It is also a highly individual act, one that marks its speaker as individual and highlights his or her difference from the world he or she comes from. Given these discursive qualities, Franco-American queer identities in many ways seem to comprise what Eithne Luibhéid calls "'impossible subject[s]' with unrepresentable histories that exceed existing categories" (171). In struggling with this unrepresentability, Franco-American gay writers universally turn to one trope in particular to write their queer identity: the deeply rooted myth of the Franco-American mother. This chapter looks at the representation of mothers, grandmothers, and aunts in texts by Paul Monette, David Plante, Allan Bérubé, and Steven Riel; it argues that horrible mothers determine the possible signification of queer ethnic identities.

Paul Monette's memoir *Becoming a Man* won the 1992 National Book Award for Nonfiction and the Lambda Literary Award for Gay Men's Non-fiction, and it was nominated for the Stonewall Book Awards. Apart from his prominence and recognition as a gay writer, he is rarely recognized as Franco-American (e.g., Monette is not listed on the Wikipedia page of "American people of French Canadian descent," though he is included on the page "American people of French descent"). Yet to those of us studying Franco-America, just a short citation from his literary biography signals his ethnic background: "Paul Landry Monette was born on October 16, 1945, in Lawrence, Massachusetts, an industrial town on the Merrimack River known for textile mills" (Knox 149), and he himself clearly articulates this ethnic family in *Becoming a Man*:

> Sunday afternoons we'd go over to Lawrence in the '51 Buick, to visit the other
> side. The Monette grandparents were as stubbornly French as my mother's

people were English. They lived in a great peeling pile of a gingerbread Victorian, where Grandpa Joe still had his shingle out, though he was well into his eighties when I knew him. . . . Joe was a totem figure in Lawrence, lawyer and general sage to masses of immigrants from Quebec, the broken-French mill-workers who kept the hum going in the vast brick textile engines along the Merrimack. . . . Decidedly anticlerical, but that was nothing compared to his animus toward the Irish. Hardly alone in that: where I come from, Micks and Canucks are the Hatfields and the McCoys, with so much hate to spew about one another that they hardly had any left over for blacks and other exotic types. The only son among four sisters, Joe had taken his entrance exams to Harvard Law in classical Greek, because his English was still shaky. And told us once . . . that he'd added the last two letters to the family name because he got so tired of his Harvard profs mispronouncing Monet with a hard T. . . . Twenty years later I'd still run into the occasional elderly frog whose eyes would mist and voice choke when he heard I was Joe Monette's grandson. (14–15)

Monette's narrative of his grandparents is striking for its resonance with Franco-American ethnic signifiers: Sunday afternoons with extended family, textile mills, the animosity toward the Irish, the inability to speak English, and the pressure to change one's last name because of the inability of Anglophones to pronounce it. Yet despite these clear markers, it could be argued that Monette should not be included in this exploration of mothers and queer Franco-America. Not only does his text define this Little Canada as a world gone by ("That Sunday world of the ancients was my only regular foray into the urban stew of Lawrence, already half-dead in the 50's as the textile baronies fled to the South in droves. It always had the feel of a ghost city, mined out and long passed by" [Monette 16]), but his mother is not even Franco-American! Yet it is his mother—both as the key figure in the creation of Monette's closet and as a non-Franco-American—that makes this text a key if not exemplary candidate for this cursory survey of queer Franco-America. It is the protagonist's "horrible" mother who bears the full responsibility of putting the protagonist in the closet, and it is her explicit "non-Franconess" that provides the narrative structure of the way out.

Monette's narrative pinpoints his mother as the principal creator of his closet. His father remains silent throughout the text, speaking to Paul only once about the impropriety of his queer desire and only at the insistence of Paul's mother.[3] Instead, it is his mother who creates the shame that requires the closet and polices Paul's enclosure in it. She stumbles upon young Paul in his homosexual play with his friend Kite, and she is singled out as the one who stigmatizes that key awakening as something to be ashamed of: "No moment of my first twenty years is more indelible than the kitchen inquisition of my mother. All the ambiguity of sex reduced to a single question, the implication crystal clear that something very bad had happened—unnatural, even. The flinching of my heart from that point on would ensure our brief exchange a central place in therapy, fifteen years later" (Monette 29).

Throughout the text it is again and again his mother who is the key enforcer of his closet. When Paul's brother gets bullied because the neighborhood kids suspect Paul of being gay, their mother asks his brother to keep it quiet: "Secrets upon secrets. Thus by inexorable degrees does the love that dares not speak its name build walls instead, till a house is nothing but closets" (Monette 54). She stands guard over his place in the closet throughout his college years as she peppers him with questions about the girls he was dating: "My mother's subtext had to do with shaming back into the straight and narrow by letting me know she had my number. Her dread at having produced a homo son was shaped by her own wounded narcissism" (183). She remains there to the end of the novel, when the protagonist enters therapy: "Cantwell cut to the chase: my approval mechanism sprang from my desire to recover the relationship I'd lost with my mother the day she found me with Kite" (249). It is precisely this closeted, claustrophobic world created by his mother that the protagonist must leave behind in order to find "freedom" and a "real life": "The very act of remembering begins to resemble a phobic state—feeding on every missed chance, stuck forever in the place without doors. What's crazy about it is, I forget that I ever got out. For an hour or a day the pain wins. It throws a veil of amnesia over my real life, almost twenty years now since I took my first breath of freedom" (172).

Sociologists and literary scholars have repeatedly pointed to the importance of this "coming-out" story to gay identity. Matthew Rowe calls it a "formula story that maps gay men's and lesbians' experiences onto institutionalized understandings of collective identity" (3), and Monette's text is often cited as the paradigmatic example of the "closet," a space that Eve Kosofsky Sedgwick calls "the defining structure for gay oppression in this century" (71). Rowe's piece notes that recent explorations of this "formula story" have focused on how "social context affects identity-related understandings and practices"; Rowe in particular is interested in how the particularly American notion of voluntarism as a "broad cultural trope" is activated, "showing how a constituent feature of American culture figures in the concrete meaning-making practices of one social group today" (4). In a similar way, I argue that Paul Monette's "formula story" is anchored not only in this very American notion of voluntarism but also in another broad cultural trope that Rowe does not signal out and recognize: ethnic assimilation.

The mother in *Becoming a Man* creates and polices the protagonist's closet; she also—and perhaps more importantly—provides Monette's memoir with the rhetorical architecture that narratively structures his escape into his "real life." Paul's mother is not Franco-American but "English," and she is actively upwardly mobile: "Yet there was something more subtle at work in my family than money; call it an instinct for gentility that was equal parts Episcopal and English. . . . For my mother's people the move from Lawrence to Andover was a move up. . . . They were definitely out to better themselves. . . . [M]y parents clearly believed they'd cast their lot with a better class" (Monette 23).

Bruce Robbins highlights that upward mobility: "[W]hatever it may be to the sociologists, upward mobility is also a story" (xi), a powerful story, he argues, because it focuses "on the passage between identities and how one gets from here to there[.] [The stories] reveal something important about power, which can never be located within one identity alone" (xii). In Monette's text, his coming out into his "real life" is structured on this paradigm of upward mobility. Franco-Americans are represented only as working class and only seen in his father's working-class workplace. They are mentioned twice after the description of his grandfather's world, first, when Paul visited his dad's workplace when he was a child ("Maybe once a month my father would take me over to Cross Coal with him on a Saturday morning. . . . I was thrilled to the rough and tumble of the men, the purple streams of profanity, the cowboy moves as they loaded and weighed the trucks. Mostly Canuck, with names like Gus and Fat" [Monette 16]), and second, when he works for extra money to fund his studies ("Over Christmas I worked sidekick on one of Dad's coal delivery trucks. . . . I needed the money to keep up with the social life of the school. . . . So Proulx, the Canuck driver, and I battered our way through weeks of blizzards, chuting coal to snowbound customers like Saint Bernards" [109]). As he grows older, he shifts from accompanying his father to the workplace peopled with "Canucks" to mornings with his maternal grandmother and her escape from that world: "I'd outgrown going to the office with my father on Saturday mornings . . . but I'd still spend Friday nights at Nana Lamb's whenever I was on vacation. . . . She set great store by education, having been forced out of school and into the mills at ten. . . . Now in her eighth decade she wasn't about to deny herself. . . . Out on the town with Nana, I was worldly, and didn't have to watch my every gesture to see if I was man enough" (72–73).

It is his mother's and maternal grandmother's active identification away from his father's ethnic world that provides the narrative structure that creates Monette's queer identity. Monette's text harnesses a specifically American story, one of leaving behind one's ethnic origins in order to come into an individualized self not impinged on by the ethnic traditions of the past. This specifically American assimilationist story requires the absence of the symbolic Franco-American mother. And in Monette's mother's turn away from the ethnic toward an Americanized self free of communal demands and traditional ways, she provides a narrative structure that dominates the landscape of gay Franco-American fiction.

David Plante, a retired creative writing professor from Columbia University, is the author of more than twenty published volumes and numerous short stories. While Monette disavowed his Franco-American heritage, Plante is perhaps one of this ethnic community's most well known representatives. Many of his novels feature Franco-American characters set in New England Franco-American communities, and his autobiographical text, *American Ghosts*, explicitly engages with the ethnic milieu of his youth. Yet despite the differences in each author's identification, Plante's ethnic narrative resembles

Monette's both in the representation of his mother and in the way he harnesses his coming-out story to an assimilationist narrative structure.

Werner Sollors theorized that American ethnic literature exists in the crux between two opposing forces, "descent" and "consent": "Descent language emphasizes our positions as heirs, our hereditary qualities, liabilities, and entitlements; consent language stresses our abilities as mature free agents and 'architects of our fates' to choose our spouses, our destinies, and our political systems" (6). The figure of young David's mother, like Monette's, embodies Sollors's idea of consent. In *American Ghosts*, while the protagonist's father is repeatedly classified as a "Canuck," his mother "was, above all, American" (Plante 63). Her American identity is embodied first and foremost by her rejection of the Franco-American community: "My mother's mother had been against her marrying my father. '*Tu verras*,' she said, '*il est un vrai Canuck. Je les connais, les Canucks.*' My mother, who in marrying my father had married a real Canuck as if she herself, being French, were not, retained the feelings her mother had about the breed" (50). That identity is accompanied by a similar portrayal of the claustrophobic, dying ethnic community: "I found a strange freedom, confined as I was by the darkness of my parish. More and more, I saw emerge from the darkness mostly images of abandonment, as if abandonment were, finally, the fulfillment of the history of the parish" (60). It is in the abandonment of this ethnic community that the protagonist, like Monette, finds the freedom deemed necessary to express and fulfill his homosexual desires: "I wanted to get out of America" (76); "In Europe, I was free" (89).

Both Monette's *Becoming a Man* and Plante's *American Ghosts* rely upon similar tropes and mechanisms to write a "formula story," a story that is anchored in the figure of the upwardly mobile, nonethnic mother and harnessed to a narrative of "consent." That Plante, even though he actively identifies as Franco-American, continues to employ these specific literary devices shows the ways in which these tropes and narrative structures found and anchor American gay identity, even for those who actively identify with their ethnic heritage. Despite these discursive regimes, however, there are many gay writers who are not content to embrace this assimilationist story line, David Plante included. In the remaining pages, I will explore three different reinscriptions of an ethnic identity through the figure of the ethnic mother. In particular, I will explore how Plante in the remaining pages of *American Ghosts*, Bérubé in his essay "Intellectual Desire," and Riel in his poem "In My Grandmother's Kitchen" introduce and deploy a maternal figure. While the nonethnic mother is the figure of assimilation, the ethnic mother appears in all three attempts to write Franco-American queerness.

Plante, to use Sollors's vocabulary, spends the rest of *American Ghosts* reinscribing the language of descent into his narrative. Whereas Monette's story ends happily, like a fairy tale, in the loving embrace of his partner, Plante's doesn't. Like Monette, he finds the love of his life, Nikos, and with him he lives "a life . . . that was secure in his love for me" (Plante 176). But while Monette's narrative ends on this particularly American note of voluntary identity and fulfilling love (Monette meets his soul partner, Roger, in the last pages of the book), Plante's doesn't (Nikos and David become life partners on page 161 of 288). Instead, *American Ghosts* documents the insufficiency of this narrative plot. The protagonist, even though he has left behind his dying parish and found freedom in true love, is not happy: "I began to weep, and, unable to control myself, I went to a wall and stood facing it and sobbed, tears and saliva running down my face. When he asked, 'Why can't my love for you be enough?' I turned around to him and held him to me" (190). Finding a life-long soulmate is not the end of Plante's autobiographical narrative.

María del Pilar Blanco and Esther Peeren argue in their introduction to *The Spectralities Reader* that "ghosts and haunting can do more than obsessively recall a fixed past: in an active, dynamic engagement, they may reveal the insufficiency of the present moment" (16). The ghosts in Plante's narrative—the *American Ghosts* of the title—perform such a function. The ghosts in his text allow him to reinscribe the language of descent. It is their haunting that pushes him to visit his parish, to return to the birthplace of his parents in Canada, and to trace his genealogy all the way back to France. Blanco and Peeren also note that "ghosts are not interchangeable and it matters greatly . . . in what guise they appear and to whom" (309). The ghosts that come to haunt Plante, despite the fact that the text locates ethnic culture with his "Canuck" father in the beginning, are overwhelmingly Franco-American women: "As much as I told myself that with Nikos I was free of my parish, that with him I was free of my Canuck God, it would, however, happen, with or without Nikos, that I would suddenly become aware of my grandmother sitting next to me on the top of a bus going along Oxford Street, of my aunt Cora, in her nun's habit, at a table next to Nikos and me in a restaurant" (284). These specters, haunting Plante's text, figure both the ethnic culture that Plante's queer identity left behind and the ways in which that ethnic culture continues to haunt his "free" existence outside of the parish.

Bérubé and Riel take a different approach. Neither of them relies upon the "formula story," and in fact Bérubé expressly rejects it. An American historian and gay activist, Bérubé was best known for his work *Coming Out under Fire*. His keynote address given at the First Quebec Lesbian and Gay Studies Conference in Montreal in November 1992 was revised and published as an essay, "Intellectual Desire." In this keynote address, he explicitly rejects a traditional coming-out narrative: "How did I—a Franco American kid raised rural and working class in New England, whose earlier family history included no self-identified intellectuals or homosexuals—learn to become this new thing: a gay community–based historian who lives in a gay ghetto in San Francisco? I'm not going to answer this question with the happy-ending narrative of a coming out story" (Bérubé 44).

Bérubé's alternative is to reimagine and refigure the narration of his homosexuality as a migration narrative. Instead of harnessing his coming-out story onto a story line of assimilation and upward mobility, he uses one more aligned with the language of descent. For Bérubé, his identity is established not through his journey from an oppressed space to one of freedom but as a journey of migration, from one country to the next:

The history of working class Francos trying to survive in a fiercely Anglo North America in so many ways resonates with the emotional history of homos having to survive in a fiercely hetero world. . . . My own life's itineraries—coming out across sexualities, becoming a working-class intellectual in middle-class worlds, moving to California—all distanced me from my Franco-American family of origin. Yet it is our common history of migration that I and my Franco ancestors share most profoundly—crossing borders generation after generation for more than three centuries on this continent as we searched for ways to survive, creating new selves in the process. (47)

In his use of this narrative structure, Bérubé deploys different tropes, tropes that maintain a connection to the home he left behind and provide a space to articulate the pain and sense of loss that departure causes—a pain that the traditional coming-out story precludes, as it conceptualizes the home as a space of oppression. By harnessing this specifically ethnic trope to queer ends, Bérubé rearticulates his identity on different grounds, ones that maintain ethnic identity and that align him closely with *mémère* in her longing to "bridge the distances": "My interest in the queer, multiracial, working-class history of this union is part of the magnetic pull back to the past that haunts me as it has haunted at least four generations of my family.... From that farm, my *mémère* longed for her French community in Aldenville. There, her parents looked back toward their homes in Québec" (61).

While Bérubé uses the idea of his grandmother's migration and subsequent longing to rethink the coming-out narrative, Riel engages directly with the descent discourse centered on the all-powerful grandmother. A prolific contemporary poet living and writing in Massachusetts, Riel published "In My Grandmother's Kitchen" in Denis Ledoux's anthology *Lives in Translation*. The epigraph to Riel's poem cites the title of a cookbook, *Rien n'était gaspillé dans la cuisine de ma grand-mère / Nothing Went to Waste in My Grandmother's Kitchen*, a classic collection of recipes and folk remedies from the Lausier family of Grand Isle, Maine, originally published by the National Materials Development Center for French and Creole in 1981 as part of a Title VII grant for bilingual education.

Through the epigraph and his use of his grandmother's eponym, *mémère*, in the poem, Riel's text signals its engagement with the folkloric grandmother of Franco-American families. Yet the poem evokes this trope only to mark its inability to make space for him as a gay man: "'You'll never be rich,' you once barked at me, / snapping up the ends of celery stalk / I'd chopped off—'They'd make good stock'" (Riel 65). Like the grandmother in the title of his epigraph, nothing was wasted in his grandmother's kitchen either. Yet whereas the idealized *mémère* is the place for the articulation of an ethnic identity in the cookbook, Riel's poem uses this mythic figure to mark the space of his failure:

> You shoo me out of your pantry in disgust
> whenever I try to help with the dishes.
> I knew better than to ask for an unwritten recipe:
> "Bachelors shouldn't set up house.
> They should live at home until they marry.
> Next time, bring home a girl with you.
> There must be a girl somewhere!
> *You* made this bread? You'd make someone a good wife."
> . . . .
> . . . a good wife . . . a good wife . . .
> In a kinder mood, you advise, "Pray St. Jude,"
> but this lost cause will never be
> the kind of man your *shoulds* require. (66)

The narrator will never be the man his grandmother wants him to be, and she cuts off access to his ethnic identity.

It is in the space of the failure of the nationalist trope that the narrator articulates an alternative. He, despite his grandmother's inability to acknowledge him, has the recipe: "You see, I've weaseled the recipe out of you: my mother asked for it" and he makes the soup, "achiev[ing] that intricate, simple miracle of feeling a little closer to you" (Riel 66). Though the narrator has failed his grandmother's gender expectations, he nevertheless cooks. "[B]ut now I have the recipe," the narrator states, "and I can alter it." But lest we think that the narrator's win is a triumphant one, the poem also reminds us of the pain of that failure:

> *Mémère*, you fed a family on water and bones.
> For me, you've nothing but candy or stones?
> I warm my hands over the generous pot,
> watch the steam rise.

So much goes to waste
in my grandmother's kitchen. (Riel 67)

One might conceive of the protagonist's inability to meet his grand-mother's demands under Judith Halberstam's recent theorization of the importance of failure to queer identity: "Under certain circumstances failing, losing, forgetting, unmaking, undoing, unbecoming, not knowing may in fact offer more creative, more cooperative, more surprising ways of being in the world. Failing is something queers do and have always done exception-ally well" (1). It is through his failure that Riel articulates the liminal space of queer Franco-American identity. Yet Riel's poem also reminds us that Halberstam's attempt to recode abjection into resistance too easily ignores the pain that Riel, at least, does not want to simply chalk up and recuperate.

When Franco-American authors write about their ethnic identities, like other ethnic writers, they engage a whole range of preestablished tropes already recognized as the signifiers of American ethnicity: the narration of immigration, either one's own or that of past generations; the exclusion from the national community based upon cultural difference; the response to assimilatory forces; or the narration of past suffering and hardship. Most of these tropes are deeply embedded in a discourse regime that is over-whelmingly heteronormative, undermining from the very beginning the possibility of a queer ethnic identity. Franco-American gay writers turn to one trope in particular to write their queer identity: the deeply rooted myth of the Franco-American mother. The danger with these tropes of ethnicity, especially the Franco-American *mémère*, however, is the facility with which they can reduce the author's story into a romanticized past, stripping the narration of its particular content. Gay writers show us that queering those tropes paves the way for the rest of us as we aim to write stories that don't romanticize the past or rehearse the tropes of nationalist belonging but instead articulate the sometimes painful space of Franco-American identity.

NOTES

1. The term *Franco-American* typically designates descendants of Québécois and Acadian migrants from the late nineteenth and early twentieth centuries who settled in the northeastern United States, particularly in New England and New

York. Depending upon the state, Franco-Americans constitute from 10 to 25 percent of New England populations. In two New England states (Maine and Vermont), French is the leading non-English language, and Franco-Americans are the largest ethnic group. These Franco-American communities constitute one of the largest concentrations of French speakers in the United States.

2. It is just such centrality that makes Greg Chabot quip, "Les gens qui se tracassent au sujet de la perte des forêts au Brésil devraient parler aux Francos" ("People who are worried about the loss of the forests in Brazil should speak to Francos") (11).

3. "I got in the car, Dad and I exchanging the usual laconic pleasantries. Then he said, 'There's something we have to talk about. Your mother was cleaning your room this morning...' Hunkered against the car door in the dark, I could see her methodically tearing my room apart, going through everything till she found the evidence. I reeled from the violation as Dad went haltingly on. 'There's nothing wrong with those girlie magazines,' he declared. 'That's perfectly natural, you're almost a man. But the homosexual ones... that's not good.' I don't think it went any further than that, no hellfire and damnation. It seems almost decent in retrospect, compared to the ugliness and disownings that have rung down on my brothers and sisters, killing off parent and child for good" (Monette 96).

WORKS CITED

Baillargeon, Denyse. "Quebec Women of the Twentieth Century: Milestones in an Unfinished Journey." *Quebec Questions: Quebec Studies for the Twenty-First Century*, edited by Christopher John Kirkey, Stéphan Gervais, and Robert Jarrett Rudy, Oxford University Press Canada, 2010, pp. 231–48.

Beaupré, Normand R. *Deux femmes, deux rêves: Roman*. Llumina Press, 2005.

Bérubé, Allan. "Intellectual Desire." *Queerly Classed*, edited by Susan Raffo, South End Press, 1997, pp. 43–66.

Blanco, Maria del Pilar, and Esther Peeren. *The Spectralities Reader: Ghosts and Haunting in Contemporary Cultural Theory*. Bloomsbury Publishing USA, 2013.

Chabot, Grégoire. "Entre la manie et la phobie." 2000. Unpublished manuscript shared with the author.

Fortier, Anne-Marie. "'Coming Home': Queer Migrations and Multiple Evocations of Home." *European Journal of Cultural Studies*, vol. 4, no. 4, 2001, pp. 405–24.

Gans, Herbert J. "The Coming Darkness of Late-Generation European American Ethnicity." *Ethnic and Racial Studies*, 2013, pp. 1–9.

Grindstaff, Davin Allen. *Rhetorical Secrets: Mapping Gay Identity and Queer Resistance in Contemporary America*. University of Alabama Press, 2006.

Halberstam, Judith. *The Queer Art of Failure*. Duke University Press, 2011.

Hareven, Tamara K. *Family Time and Industrial Time: The Relationship between the Family and Work in a New England Industrial Community*. Cambridge University Press, 1982.

Knox, Melissa. "Monette, Paul 1945–1995." *American Writers: A Collection of Literary Biographies, Supplement 10*, edited by Jay Parini, Charles Scribner's Sons, 2002, pp. 145–61.

Langellier, Kristin M. "Performing Family Stories, Forming Cultural Identity: Franco American Mémère Stories." *Communication Studies*, vol. 53, no. 1, 2002, pp. 56–73.

Lindsay, Betty A. Lausier. *Nothing Went to Waste in My Grandmother's Kitchen / Rien n'était gaspillé dans la cuisine de ma grandmère*. National Materials Development Center for French and Creole, 1981.

Luibhéid, Eithne. "Queer/Migration: An Unruly Body of Scholarship." *GLQ: A Journal of Lesbian and Gay Studies*, vol. 14, no. 2, 2008, pp. 169–90.

McClintock, Anne. "Family Feuds: Gender, Nationalism and the Family." *Feminist Review*, vol. 44, 1993, pp. 61–80.

Monette, Paul. *Becoming a Man: Half a Life Story*. Harper Perennial Modern Classics, 2004.

Plante, David. *American Ghosts*. 1st ed. Beacon Press, 2005.

Ramirez, Bruno, and Yves Otis. *Crossing the 49th Parallel: Migration from Canada to the United States, 1900–1930*. Cornell University Press, 2001.

Riel, Steven. "In My Grandmother's Kitchen." *Lives in Translation: An Anthology of Contemporary Franco American Writers*, edited by Denis Ledoux, Soleil Press, 1990, pp. 65–67.

Robbins, Bruce. *Upward Mobility and the Common Good: Toward a Literary History of the Welfare State*. Princeton University Press, 2007.

Robichaud, Gérard. *Papa Martel: A Novel in Ten Parts*. 1st ed. University of Maine Press, 2003.

Rowe, Matthew. "Becoming and Belonging in Gay Men's Life Stories: A Case Study of a Voluntaristic Model of Identity." *Sociological Perspectives*, vol. 57, no. 4, 2014, pp. 434–49.

Saint-Martin, Lori. *Le nom de la mère: Mères, filles et écriture dans la littérature québécoise au féminin*. Éditions Nota Bene, 1999.

Sedgwick, Eve Kosofsky. *Epistemology of the Closet*. University of California Press, 1990.

Sollors, Werner. *Beyond Ethnicity: Consent and Descent in American Culture*. Oxford University Press, 1986.

Takai, Yukari. *Gendered Passages: French-Canadian Migration to Lowell, Massachusetts, 1900–1920*. Peter Lang, 2008.

3

"I'm Not the Virgin Mary"

Rebellious Motherhood in Grégoire Chabot's "A Life Lost"

CHELSEA RAY

Franco-American playwright Grégoire Chabot's poignant stories of Franco-American lives—often both miraculous and tragic—bring to the forefront issues of class, gender, ethnicity, and the social divide that was so common to the immigrant experience of French Canadians in Maine. A number of his published plays treat the issue of motherhood, especially *Chère Maman* and *No Trump*.[1] In the unpublished play "A Life Lost," set in Maine in the 1930s, Chabot moves beyond the stereotypes about large Franco-American families of the period, instead focusing on the very personal story of Zithée, a mother fearing that she is pregnant with her seventeenth child.[2] In her monologue, Zithée shares her most intimate feelings and worries, bringing the audience into a world fraught with physical dangers associated with childbirth, as well as economic uncertainty. Survival was paramount in this world. In showcasing Zithée's story, Chabot "re-present[s] [the] cultural mythology" of the fertile, nurturing, Franco-American or French Canadian mother, instead depicting the pain, fear of death, and deep frustrations that were also part of women's lives (Gilbert and Dufault 20). Not only does Chabot highlight the human cost of putting mothers on a pedestal in this way, but he also fashions Zithée as a kind of feminist in the making who criticizes the local priest and, by extension, the Catholic ideology of family and motherhood. In line with this volume's topic of "horrible" or rebellious mothers, she, too, does not wish to conform to society's mandate for endless birth and mothering, exhibiting what Barbara Almond terms "maternal ambivalence" and the "dark side of motherhood" (108). Though Zithée initially judges herself through her society's lens, deeming herself inadequate in many ways, she begins to see herself in a new light, apart from society's view of women and mothers in particular. She comes to see that she, indeed, is not a "horrible mother" for having lived her very real experience of mothering.

In bringing to life the singular voice of Zithée, Chabot's play helps the reader better understand the complexity of Franco-American women's lives, whose history remains in large part unwritten.[3] Born in 1944 and raised in a French-speaking household, Chabot drew on his own life in writing the monologue: the protagonist, Zithée, is based on an autobiographical composite of both Chabot's grandmother and his mother.[4] Like Zithée's mother, who died in childbirth, Chabot's grandmother died soon after giving birth to his mother. Although he never met his grandmother, he learned much about her through his mother's stories. One of his goals in writing this piece was to showcase the lack of options these women had. As Chabot puts it, "You don't want to have 17 or 20 kids, but you have never been to school, and you don't speak English—what do you do?" (personal communication, Mar. 2016).

Chabot's play highlights the stark contrast between the idealization of mothers—and the myths surrounding them—and the sobering reality of their lives. Zithée's portrayal as a mother stands in opposition to the image of French Canadian women promoted by the religious elite as "guardians of all that made for French-Canadian cultural superiority in North America[, holding] the key to the survival of religion, morality, education, and the family" (Mello, citing Bouliane 10). Instead, Zithée feels inferior and trapped in her situation. While it may appear anachronistic that Chabot's characters engage with concepts that later feminists would take up more formally, I would argue that he points to these women as precursors who struggled to articulate their own beliefs—kept to themselves or whispered to others—that subsequent feminists would theorize on a national and then a global scale.

While this chapter will primarily focus on "A Life Lost," I will also touch upon a second play, which Chabot cowrote with Jean-Claude Redonnet in 2013: "Jeanne et Osithée / Parallèles croisées." This work has also not been published and, unlike "A Life Lost," remains untranslated. The title could be translated as "Jeanne and Osithée: Parallel Lives Intertwined."[5] Although the title names the character Osithée, she is called Zithée in the actual play, just like her previous incarnation in "A Life Lost." Chabot confirms that the characters represented in the two plays are essentially the same, and both plays are set around the 1930s (personal communication, Mar. 2016). This time, Zithée no longer speaks in a despairing monologue—utterly alone—but rather reappears in the context of a (albeit halting) dialogue of sorts with Jeanne, a character based on Redonnet's great-grandmother, Jeanne Amiel.[6] Their dialogue spans geographical distance and time, as Zithée is from Madawaska in Maine and Jeanne is from Val d'Arn in Spain.[7] Despite this distance, they appear in the same physical space in the play; they strike up a friendship in what appears to be a kitchen in Madawaska where both women's chairs appear—a small chair in which Jeanne sits while she is cooking and warming herself by the fire and Zithée's rocking chair.[8]

Both women speak a nonstandard French that marks them as outsiders. Just as Chabot attempts to record the spoken language of Franco-Americans in New England, Redonnet captures the language of his great-grandmother, a rural French with Aranese words interspersed.[9] Jeanne learned to read and write in French in elementary school, whereas Zithée did not, thus making her dependent on the priests and nuns, who had access to education (Redonnet, personal communication, June 2016).[10] Both women were restricted at school in their choice of language: Jeanne was forbidden from speaking Aranese, and Zithée was forbidden from speaking French. So for Jeanne, French is the language of upward mobility, whereas for Zithée, it guarantees exclusion from the dominant Anglophone society. To their surprise, the women can understand each other, even though their French incorporates many local elements. This ability to communicate with each other validates their French and their place in the broader international francophone community, bringing to the fore the creativity and dignity inherent in asserting oneself through language.

Jeanne's and Zithée's lives run on parallel tracks, yet their encounter reveals how their lives intersect in meaningful and intimate ways. As I do not have space here to do justice to the complexities of this cowritten play, I will mainly discuss act 1 in terms of Zithée's character development. Zithée takes heart in hearing Jeanne's encouragement. Both women find ways to assert their independence against hypocritical Catholic imperatives for women and, especially, mothers. Because the cowritten play allows us to witness Zithée in the context of a budding friendship, it showcases the power of women to support each other; only with Jeanne's support is Zithée able to name her own reality and validate her experience as a mother. Their dialogue opens up the possibility of a kind of transnational solidarity among women that would challenge reigning notions of womanhood and motherhood.

For both Redonnet and Chabot, these works are deeply personal and based on family history and storytelling. In her article "The Problem with Speaking for Others," Linda Alcoff discusses in depth the challenges of speaking for/about marginalized groups and the limitations of this kind of binary thinking (e.g., you are either in the group or not). Redonnet and Chabot walk this line carefully as they attempt to embody these women's voices as accurately as possible. Since they are insiders of the cultures they portray, they use family stories to create as authentic voices as possible for their characters, no easy feat. They wish to leave a family legacy that showcases these women's lives, their struggles, and their accomplishments.

"A Life Lost"

In my discussion of "A Life Lost," I draw material from historical and critical scholarly works to give a sense of the context of Zithée's world and her French Canadian heritage. For the purposes of this chapter, I use sources that deal with Québécois and Franco-American history and culture, as the two were intimately interconnected due to travel, cultural exchange, and common French texts. For example, priests were routinely invited from Québec to visit New England to bolster the Catholic religion in the budding communities, and they eventually established new religious communities there. Key to understanding both traditional French Canadian and Franco-American culture is the concept of *survivance*, which tied the survival of the culture to language, religion, and procreation. In fact, scholar Susan Kevra points out, "Up until the Quiet Revolution, Quebec had one of the highest birthrates in the industrialized world" (3). She traces this phenomenon from the colonial period and beyond, when Native women were bearing children with French men. She also discusses the young women who were sent to New France expressly with the purpose of bearing children and populating the area, called "King's Daughters" because Louis XIV himself provided them with a dowry. As she puts it, "Cultural survival was predicated on population growth," and women often gave birth every two years during the colonial period (3).

This "maternal call to arms" was called *la revanche des berceaux* (revenge of the cradle) (Kevra 3).[11] Women's procreative function in society was emphasized and encouraged: "As policy, *la survivance* prescribed two roles for women: nuns, perceived to be asexual, to teach in schools; and fecund mothers to people the province. As the primordial role for women, motherhood and large families—more than ten children was not unusual—were exalted and eulogized. The myth of motherhood was enforced through Catholic Church hegemony and a variety of prenatal policies" (Langellier and Peterson 3). Chabot's play provides an implicit critique of these "pronatalist policies" by emphasizing the very real and human cost of this social imperative (Robbins, "Franco-American" 2).[12]

The concept of *survivance* connects the Québécois culture with the newly forming Franco-American identity in New England. By the start of the Great Depression, nearly one million French Canadians had migrated to the United States.[13] It was alarming for the Catholic elites to witness this exodus to the United States; the Catholic hierarchy was soon implanted in New England, becoming part and parcel of the fabric of budding *petits Canadas*. These "little Canadas" were enclaves of French-speaking immigrants, which became financial, linguistic, and social support networks. These communities revolved around the church, parochial schools, and local businesses that offered services entirely in French.[14] The *petits Canadas* remained relatively intact until after World War II, when the population began to intermarry.

While tracing the complexities of French Canadian history in New England is not feasible here, it is important to acknowledge the historic reasons why the concept of *survivance* became so important: "*Survivance* is important because it was a philosophy that was carried from Québec in response to English rule and later used in New England in response to the issue of Americanization" (Cleary). The theme of childbearing in Chabot's "A Life Lost" underscores the devastating effects of this philosophy, but in an individual, personal context. Mourning the loss of her own mother, who died in childbirth with her seventeenth child, Zithée fears the same fate, nearly certain that she, too, is pregnant with her seventeenth child. In one scene, Zithée describes her husband, Pierre's sexual advances after an evening out, which must have resulted in this pregnancy. Though she voices her fears to him about becoming pregnant again, he is inebriated and pays no attention to her misgivings or protests. In fact, it is not clear whether he even hears her at all. It is moving that she references the death of three of her children when trying to rebuff Pierre:

> This will be the fourteenth. The seventeenth if you count the three we lost. I told Pierre that I didn't want to. That it wasn't a good time. But you know how men are . . . once they get it in their heads, there's not much that can stop them. That night, we went to a party at his brother Leo's. He had a couple of drinks. Not enough to get him drunk but more than enough to give him "ideas." We got back here and he was on me in no time at all, calling me every sweet name he could think of. It was "chérie" this and "belle noune" that. That's when I told him I was afraid to get pregnant. But he didn't hear a thing, I don't think. *(Pause)* It was over in no time. (Chabot, "A Life Lost" 5)[15]

Zithée assumes that sex and pleasure are inextricably linked in Pierre's mind, whereas she associates sex with grief and the loss of three children. Zithée's lack of agency here is apparent, as she does not believe that she has the power to stop Pierre: "[T]here's not much that can stop them." The idea of her own pleasure and her own agency are noticeably absent from this scene, even though it appears that she submits to him willingly, if reluctantly. Thus, it is not so much that she does not want to engage in sexual intercourse (or perhaps please her husband); instead, it is that sex is inextricably intertwined with fear of loss. This heavy burden to bear is uniquely placed on the woman in this scene, as Pierre does not so much as hesitate and undoubtedly has acted similarly in the past. This privileging of the husband's sexual needs over those of the wife would have been undoubtedly part of the dominant discourse in Zithée's community. As scholars Andrée Lévesque and Yvonne Klein put it, "[F]rom the earliest centuries of the Christian era, the purpose of marriage was first and foremost to have children and then, in second place, to relieve the sexual needs of the husband" (27). Indeed, women were not considered to have sexual needs of their own: "It was, moreover, assumed that women, endowed by nature with less energy than men, found it easier to remain chaste" (54).

It appears that Zithée has internalized this hierarchy between men's and women's needs by discounting her own reality and experience. This time, however, she begins to feel angry, perhaps with a growing awareness of male (sexual) privilege. She doesn't have the word for it yet, but she appears to be growing more aware that she lacks a voice in her own life. She suggests that this feeling of anger has been brewing for a while, but perhaps she is more aware of it this time. In any case, she finds herself unable to let go of it:

> But this time, the whole thing got me mad, too. And that hasn't stopped either. Enough is enough. There's got to be more to life than cleaning, cooking, and washing, and making babies. If that's all there is . . . if that's all we're good for, then we're no better than Mickey Michaud's [a neighbor/farmer character who has a small role in the place] big fat sow. Sitting in our sties. Watching the world go by through the slats in the fence. Laying [*sic*] in the swill, rolling in the mud and manure and waiting for someone to come along someday and put us out of our misery. And always trying to recover from the last litter before the next one comes along. (Chabot, "A Life Lost" 5)[16]

Zithée concludes that this endless cycle of birthing, mothering, and domestic service is no better than a sow's life. Again, we note the helplessness and lack of agency in the image: "Watching the world go by through the slats in the fence." Zithée references the idea of death again, this time not in the form of losing a child or suicide (as we will see in the quotation below). Instead, she hints at the image of the farmer coming to kill the sow:

"put us out of our misery." In this cyclical hell, she has trouble imagining any exit other than death in her moments of greatest despair.

Zithée recounts the period of her life after her youngest child was born when she fell into what the audience might consider to be a (possibly post-partum) depression. She no longer feels like herself:

> But something happened after my youngest was born. It wasn't just here *(she indicates her stomach)*. Things started going wrong up here *(she indicates her head)*. And it changed me a lot. For weeks after he was born, I didn't want to do anything. Not even take care of him. And every once in a while, I'd get these really bad ideas. *(Pause)* When I think back on it now, it scares the daylights out of me. I didn't get out of bed for a couple of weeks at least. Pierre had the doctor come over and take a look, but he said that I wasn't really sick . . . that it was all in my head. So when Pierre saw that I wasn't getting any better, he called the priest. (Chabot, "A Life Lost" 5)

Zithée lacks the basic language and specific terminology to discuss mental illness, instead gesturing toward her belly and then her head. She feels very changed as a person and may have started thinking about suicide or perhaps even infanticide, which "scares the daylights" out of her. When she does have contact with a male doctor, he clearly does not understand her distress and dismisses her experience entirely, simply stating "that [she] wasn't really sick." Her husband, Pierre, is at a loss of what to do, so he calls on the support network that is in place in this small, rural, Franco-American community: he solicits the help of the priest. Scholar Yves Roby explains how the priest played a vital role in these *petits Canadas*: "The faithful expected all things, or just about, from their pastor. It was true that he enjoyed considerable power and authority; he instructed and led them as well as attending to the saving of their souls. . . . [H]e was pastor, teacher, social worker, doctor, architect, entrepreneur, even banker" (74–75). Pierre's reliance on the priest makes sense when we more fully understand the expansive role that the priest played in the social fabric of the community.[17]

Indeed, the conversation with the priest only serves to confirm Zithée's worst fears about the church's expectations of mothers, and this fuels her rage against the priest. Interestingly, even though it was Zithée who introduced the image of the fat sow into the narrative, she attributes this language to the priest: "Well, the priest comes over and talks to me for I don't know how long. And his point was that it was a really good thing to be a big fat sow and roll around in swill and manure all day long. That's not really what he said. Priests have a way with words. But that's what he really meant" (Chabot, "A Life Lost" 6).

Zithée struggles to name her own reality and experience. She insinuates that the priest somehow compares her to a sow (even though this is *her* term), concluding that the local priest propagates the submission of women through motherhood. She can thus be seen as a feminist in the making, revolting against the brutality of multiple pregnancies. She appears furious, too, with the fact that the priest can somehow label and name in ways that she cannot (perhaps because of her lack of education): "Priests have a way with words." At the same time, she claims the power to interpret as her own, stating that she knew what he "really meant." In this way, she supersedes the priest, parsing out the meaning of his words, at least for herself. As the priest's authoritative role entailed meaning making for the parishioners, telling them how and what to think, Zithée's questioning is a radical step in exploring her own independence.

As Zithée becomes more aware of her own voice as distinct from the voices of those in positions of authority (husband, doctor, priest), she gives herself permission to question the priest's vision of life and, indeed, the very foundation of Catholicism's devotion to the Virgin Mary. The priest alludes to the Virgin Mary and her sacrifice, but all Zithée hears is her own reality being discounted:

> He starts telling me that I'm like the Blessed Virgin Mary. She had to sacrifice and suffer and go through pain and misery . . . just like me. Just like all mothers do. As if that's all we were made for or good for. As if we didn't deserve to be happy. . . . Well, I've always liked the Blessed Virgin Mary, but with just one little one, there's no way she can know what it's like to have a dozen or more. And her little boy was the son of God. Come on, he couldn't have given her that much trouble, now could he. (Chabot, "A Life Lost" 6)

In this humorous scene, the ideology of *survivance* is satirized and debunked. Chabot echoes the modern-day feminist critique of the church, highlighting the way these traditional Catholic values must have rung false for many women like Zithée who were asked to obey social and religious imperatives that very often put their mental and physical health at great risk. Zithée inwardly refuses to accept the social and religious values that she perceives as serving to maintain a devastating status quo for mothers, but she does not voice her concerns lest she be labeled a "horrible mother." As someone who has lost a child to tragedy, she makes it clear that she wants her experience as a mother validated: "And that tractor made so much damned noise that he didn't hear anything either. Pierre ended up running over his own little boy. *(Pause)* Our little boy. So I think that maybe I could give the Virgin Mary a few pointers about what it means to have your heart broken . . . not the other way around" (Chabot, "A Life Lost" 6). Zithée's critique of the church's idealized image of the Virgin Mary suggests her defiance of religious values to a certain point. She knows that she is not a "horrible mother" but struggles to articulate more fully her rejection of these cultural and religious norms. As Chabot puts it, "Your entire survival strategy is to remain as invisible as possible. You don't have the words, because you never use them. Or you only use them to talk to yourself. You don't want anyone in the power structure—Anglo or Franco—to hear you, because that can only lead to one thing: trouble" (personal communication, June 2016).

Zithée laments the fact that, as the eldest child, she acted as surrogate mother to her siblings and never got a chance to attend school; she thus remains illiterate, feeling trapped and exhausted in this never-ending cycle of pregnancies and child rearing, as well as work in the house and on the farm. She begins to question her own values when comparing her situation to that of her younger sister, who clearly rejected outright the Catholic mandate for large families: "She's been married fifteen years, my little sister Yvette. And she has two kids . . . a boy and a girl. That's it. And it's not because she's been luckier than me. There's a lot more than luck involved, that's for sure. *(Pause)* And you know, she looked pretty happy for someone who was committing one mortal sin after another and who was going straight to hell for all eternity at the end of her days. Didn't seem to bother her at all" (Chabot, "A Life Lost" 7). She perceives her sister as happier than she is, even though Zithée is the one who follows the Catholic teachings against contraception.[18] Chabot's ironic tone here makes her statement about her sister's "mortal sin" humorous and bittersweet at the same time. The reader understands her wistfulness and struggle for a different life, a life that would emulate her sister's and involve more control over her body.

In struggling to find her voice and raise questions, Zithée becomes an example of a mother who could serve as a potential counterculture force against Catholic prescriptives for women. This runs in direct contrast with many traditional literary depictions of Franco-American women. For example, in her study of *mémère* stories, scholar Kristin Langellier notes that "[g]ood *mémères* are devoted to Catholicism; and if challenges to religion were made, they are muted or not narrated" (20). What is so compelling, then, about Zithée's voice is her struggle to express herself, both privately (to herself and her husband) and more publicly (to the priest and the doctor). She has had little formal schooling and cannot write, yet her sentiments come across in a powerful, raw way. Her story appears simple, yet her metaphor of the "fat sow" has the potential to disrupt the status quo for herself and other women. This image repudiates the tendency for "nostalgia for a more traditional past: more family-centered, more clearly demarked gender roles, more religious and less materialistic, and less assimilated," and calls into question the blind "celebrations of the heroic mother [that] serve a conservative political idealization of the traditional ethnic woman: pregnant, suffering, sacrificing, saintly, and serving, in the name of the family, faith, and French identity" (Langellier 22). Indeed, Chabot undermines society's idealization of Franco-American motherhood: Zithée is heroic to the reader not because she epitomizes society's expectations of a "good" Franco-American mother but because she dares to question these expectations. She points to the possibility of weaving a different narrative of motherhood, one that is more realistic and healthier for women. In this sense, then, Chabot's play can be seen as an example of women's desire to participate in cultural myth making.

Jeanne and Osithée: Parallel Lives Intertwined

Zithée keeps her objections to herself in "A Life Lost"; that is why meeting the rebellious Jeanne in the cowritten play "Jeanne and Osithée: Parallel Lives Intertwined" is so life-changing for her. Her encounter with Jeanne serves to embolden her feelings of rebellion and reaffirms her desire for a different life. Indeed, her exchange with Jeanne is a potentially healing experience, showcasing the kind of support that women can offer each other. Like Zithée, Jeanne has lived through great hardships: she is poor and earthy, living and working in harsh rural conditions in the mountains in southern France (the Central Pyrenees), where farming is extremely difficult due to the rough terrain. As the play progresses, the women come to see that they have more in common than meets the eye.

In act 1 both women give monologues on their lives. Zithée's monologue is nearly identical to her monologue from "A Life Lost," but this time, she has an interlocutor: Jeanne is listening to her describe her plight and appears to be preparing to talk with her. It is only at the end of this act that Jeanne tells Zithée that she can "see" her when the two women take their places at the front of the stage in their respective chairs and begin to interact. This acquaintanceship quickly becomes a friendship, as both women reveal deeply held secret thoughts to one other, including admonitions about priests. In acts 2 and 3 the women share from their own cultural traditions. In act 2 the women's children come onstage to perform traditional music for the other woman. In act 3 the women prepare food for their families, and they compare notes on differences between their traditional dishes. Both learn that the other has lost a son in World War I. The play ends on a poignant note when Zithée asks Jeanne to search for her lost son, who died in battle in France.

Jeanne's overt rebelliousness stands in contrast with Zithée's more subdued, private questioning. Jeanne introduces herself (to the audience) by claiming the title of "rebel" with pride: "I am Jeanne Amiel! I say it loud and clear! People don't like me very much in the village. They even call me 'Jeanne the rebel.' I am one of those women who want things to change, for tomorrow and forever. We aren't here to pull the wool over each other's eyes! We are here to ignite the truth!" (Chabot and Redonnet 1).[19] Jeanne is a self-proclaimed truth teller who wishes to "péter la vérité" ("ignite the truth"). Ultimately, she tries to teach Zithée about independence, validating her questioning of authority, especially the church's. Jeanne is more comfortable than Zithée with the idea of rebellion and names it as such: it is part of her core identity.

Both women feel judged by their society or confined in some way. In Zithée's case, she does not know how to read or write, so she describes herself as trapped, in contrast to the young people who are more educated: "Those young people, *they* had the chance to leave and make something of themselves. I don't even know how to read and write, so I am stuck here" (Chabot and Redonnet 1).[20]

Zithée describes the social imperative to move from her parents' house to live with her new husband: "I married Pierre when I was 17. That's how things were done. If you didn't have a man when you reached that age, you were going to be an Old Maid for the rest of your life and be alone . . . or else become a nun and live in a convent. . . . So to me, it feels like the only thing I did was switch houses. One day, I was working day and night for my mama and papa. The next day, I was working day and night in my own house" (Chabot, "A Life Lost" 3).[21] In her situation, Jeanne feels ostracized by her small community for "moral" reasons when she makes the choice not to disclose the names of the fathers of her first two children, born out of wedlock. She tires of the insults, however, and mocks those who criticize her: "Tcch, tchh, gnagnani, gnagnania!" ("blah blah blah") (Chabot and Redonnet 3). As the play progresses, the two women relate more directly with each other, and their common experience as mothers begins to surface more explicitly.

In act 1 Jeanne listens to Zithée's monologue from a distance and interprets it as a cry for help. Jeanne reacts and responds to Zithée's despair and tries to protect her from what Jeanne interprets as suicidal thoughts:

Come on, *Madame*, I see you. Come on, you are not going to throw yourself in the lake and come back to us drowned, are you? Stop listening to them. Remember, here or where you live there, these clergymen with their holy water are not all saints! They would very well let you jump in the lake, just because you can't go on making babies one after another in this hellish factory! That's right! These well-groomed *Messieurs* always have manicured hands, without any dirt under the nails. Believe me, they won't dirty their frocks! They know what to say; they sweet talk you just to take advantage of you. (Chabot and Redonnet 7)[22]

This is a powerful moment in the play, as Jeanne understands Zithée in a way that others (in particular, male authority figures) do not: "I see you." Jeanne uses the metaphor of the factory to underscore the "mechanization of motherhood" and consecutive pregnancies, and, by extension, she indirectly criticizes the entire philosophy of *survivance*, which keeps women in such a perilous position.[23] As a day laborer (*journalière*), Jeanne knows what it is like to work with her hands, and she mocks the priests who don't know anything about hard labor: "manicured hands, without any dirt under the nails."

Most importantly, perhaps, Jeanne reaffirms Zithée's critique of the church and its hypocrisy toward mothers. She condemns the church's posture toward women and calls into question the idea that the priests are "clean" and women "dirty," echoing Zithée's image of the "fat sow." She asserts that the priests try to trick or take advantage of women (*embobiner*) and control their access to information. Jeanne addresses a woman's decision to terminate a pregnancy: "It's like it's his job to make us keep them, and not go and make angels of them. They don't like that kind of angel, these men of the cloth! But the one who spoke to that lady over there—that priest is a hypocrite, a nefarious sort would let you have so many children that you keel over in the end" (Chabot and Redonnet 7).[24] She labels the priest a hypocrite for fighting against abortion (i.e., "mak[ing] angels"), yet she states that he does not worry about the death of the mother from childbirth or extreme exhaustion. In the middle of act 1 the two women sit down on chairs next to each other, and Zithée turns to address Jeanne for the first time. She wants to reassure her that she does not believe the priests: "Well, *Madame*, I haven't listened to a word they say for a long time. These people haven't worked a day in their life and they have never felt hardship. . . . They should come pick potatoes and eat watery soup with us" (8).[25] Jeanne's critique of the church opens up the possibility for Zithée to openly do so as well, something she likely would avoid in her day-to-day life.

Jeanne surprises Zithée by telling her a bit of history about the church during the French Revolution: "Well, our priests, we thought we had thrown them out during the Revolution. We even put some of them under the guillotine. We smashed their churches and drank the sacramental wine. *Bah, res a fa*, we push them out the door and they sneak back in through the window!" (Chabot and Redonnet 8).[26] Learning this confounds Zithée's stereotypes about the French, as she had regarded them as the "true Catholics." She responds to Jeanne: "But I must say that it surprises me to hear you speak like that about priests. You are French . . . and the French are supposed to be real Catholics. Not like us. The priest even told us that France is the eldest daughter of the Church" (8).[27]

This underscores a kind of Franco-American nostalgia for France and an oversimplification of the role of the Catholic Church there. In learning more about French history, Zithée begins to shift her focus from her own individual story to women in general, a feminist move that allows her an expanded view of her own life. In these two plays, Zithée gradually demonstrates a growing awareness that culture is not destiny. She needs the support of women, however, in order to fully realize a change within herself (or to impact others). Her interaction with Jeanne illustrates just that: the power of two women talking to each other, realizing that they have something in common with other women, even those across the ocean, from an entirely different cultural context.

Chabot and Redonnet point to an alternate vision of motherhood, one that acknowledges the harsh realities and grim situation of many women. Debunking the "myth of pious and pure French-Canadian women" (Mello), Zithée, bolstered by Jeanne's rebellious nature, now has more space to question this myth. Chabot holds the traditional family values up to a different litmus test, perhaps to focus more on a new future than return to an idealized (mythic) past that never existed. As scholar Leslie Choquette concludes, "Engaged in social issues, the author has a duty to contribute to the construction of the future. It is only by carefully considering all his values without exception will he be able to create something new, something better. Chabot thus rebels against the ideology of *survivance*, this vision turned towards the past that has dominated Franco-American discourse for more than a century" (119). Zithée gets a glimpse of what it might be like to dare to espouse new values to replace the old ones, even if she cannot yet envision her place in the creation of culture.

The audience can recognize that there is something healing about Zithée's connection to Jeanne: Zithée starts to see herself in a broader historical context, perhaps for the first time, as both a product and a creator of culture. Jeanne's strength and desire to be a "rebel" fortify Zithée and encourage her to think more broadly about mothers and women in general, in particular in relation to the church. Jeanne's strength and desire show the power of naming one's own reality and validating one's own experience. The possibility for a kind of transnational solidary among women emerges. Zithée's mother tongue, a local dialect, is spoken back to her by another earthy woman from France who speaks the same raw language and understands her plight. Jeanne and Zithée validate each other's culture, sense of self, and use of language to take the first steps to name their own realities as women, mothers, and French speakers and participate in the creation of culture. Zithée is able to transcend the reigning ideology of *survivance* and better understand herself as a mother and as a woman in a particular historical situation. Jeanne's seeing her may have saved her life.

NOTES

1. *No Trump* can be found in *Un Jacques Cartier errant: Trois pièces. Chère maman: Pièce en trois actes* was published separately.

2. The original monologue in French, titled "Calice" (or "Zithée"), was part of the "Sacrés monologues," a series of plays written in 2005–6 that were never published. We have the benefit of Chabot's own translation of this play into its English version, "A Life Lost." Its first performance was at the University of Maine at Orono in May 2006, followed by a performance in October 2006 at the University of Maine at Fort Kent. In "Sacrés monologues," "Yvonne" and "Mariette" also treat the subject of motherhood.

3. In their work, Langellier and Peterson note that Franco-American women "are voiceless when situated in United States, Maine, ethnic, and even Franco-American histories" (1).

4. In his 2002 interview with Leslie Choquette, Chabot spoke about being part of the bilingual generation. Children often did not speak English until the age of five and attended parochial schools (Choquette 119).

5. My translation. I am indebted to Grégoire Chabot and Jean-Claude Redonnet for reviewing my translations for this chapter. Redonnet was particularly helpful in understanding Jeanne Amiel's insertion of the Aranese language. All errors and omissions are, of course, my responsibility. All translations are mine unless otherwise stated.

6. Jean-Claude Redonnet's *Les monologues de Jeanne Amiel* was published in 2014. It was first performed in Amiel's own Pyrenees village, Fos, on July 14, 2014. More than

one hundred people from the village attended, and it was well received. Redonnet confirms that Jeanne Amiel is the same person in both the original monologue and the cowritten play "Jeanne et Osithée" (personal communication, Sept. 2016 and Jan. 2018). I am indebted to Jean-Claude Redonnet for our conversations on his great-grandmother and the cultural and linguistic context of her life.

7. Val d'Aran is a valley in the central Pyrenees that spans the border between Spain (Vielha e Mijeran, Generalitat de Catalunya) and France (Département de la Haute-Garonne). The valley was divided by the Treaty of the Pyrenees in 1659. Jeanne is a descendant of the Catalan families who fled to those mountainous regions after the Revolt of the Reapers (Els Segadors) against King Philip IV of Spain. They lived as day laborers, mountain farmers, with many men working as peddlers in northern France and southern Spain (Redonnet, personal communication, Jan. 2018).

8. This juxtaposition of French and Franco-American culture echoes Chabot's *Jacques Cartier Discovers America*, which offers a brief but enlightening encounter between Jacques Cartier reincarnated and Franco-Americans in a New England bar.

9. Aranese (Jeanne Amiel's native language) is a variety of Occitan in combination with Gascon and Catalan (Redonnet, personal communication, Jan. 2018). For additional reading, see "Aranese dialect," *Wikipedia*, 18 Jan. 2018, en.wikipedia .org/wiki/Aranese_dialect.

10. Jeanne completed her *certificat d'études primaires*.

11. Interestingly, as French Canadian communities became more settled in the United States, the birthrate decreased, as "large families were becoming more a liability and less an asset in the urban environment," in particular due to "stricter enforcement of child labor laws" (Roby 96).

12. I want to especially thank Rhea Côté Robbins for her groundbreaking and sustained work on the Franco-American Women's Institute, where I found many articles for this chapter. For more information on this resource, see http://www.fawi.net. Robbins founded this institute, which just celebrated its twentieth anniversary with the publication of *Heliotrope: French Heritage Women Create*.

13. For additional information about this migration and the complexities of the French Canadian or Franco-American identity in the United States, see Richard.

14. For general information on *les petits Canadas*, see Myall.

15. Chabot translated this play from French to English, with some minor changes. For additional information on Chabot's translations, see Pacini.

16. Comparing women to farm animals was a common literary motif. For example, Kevra discusses the "equation of cattle to little girls" (4) in Marie Claire Blais's *Une saison dans la vie d'Emmanuel* (1965).

17. For a discussion of the role of the priest in Franco-American culture and its continued influence, see Langelier 477.

18. *Making and Breaking the Rules* has an entire chapter devoted to issues of sexuality and contraception in Quebec in the early twentieth century, and Lévesque and Klein's conclusions could also be applied to French Canadians in New England: "The frequent denunciations issuing from the pulpit or from doctors' offices lead us to believe that certain more or less effective methods of contraception were in use, though, with the exception of *coitus interruptus*, these means were not easily come by" (83).

19. Jeanne speaks French with Aranese words mixed in (*aranais* in French): "Moi, Jeanne Amiel, je vous le dis tout haut! Ils m'aiment pas beaucoup au village. Même qu'ils m'appellent 'Jeanne la rebelle.' Moi, je suis une de ces femmes qui veulent que ça change, pour demain et pour jamais. On est pas là pour se monter le bourrichon entre nous! On est là pour la faire péter la vérité!"

20. "Eux-autres, les plus jeunes, y ont eu la chance de décoller d'icit pi de faire quèque chose. Moué qui sais pas lire pi écrire, chu resté pris icit."

21. There is a slight difference in the English translation of "Zithée" in this section. I have provided translated material that does not appear in Chabot's translation of the French. My translation appears in the first half, Chabot's in the second half: "J'ai marié mon Pierre à dix-sept ans. C'est comme ça que ça se faisait par chez nous. Si t'avais pas trouvé un homme à c't'âge-là, t'allais rester vieille fille pi passer ta vie seule . . . ou devenir soeur, pi passer ta vie dans un couvent. . . . La seule chose que j'ai fait c'est changer de maison. Une journée, j'travaillais comme une folle pour mon père pi ma mère. La journée d'après, j'travaillais comme une folle juste à côté presque, chez moué" (Chabot, *Zithée* 3).

22. "Hé, Madame, je te vois. Hé, tu vas pas te jeter dans le lac et nous revenir noyée, hein? Ne les écoute pas. Tu vois, ici, et chez vous où c'est que vous habitez, y sont pas tous des saints ces capelans de bénitier! Ils sont bien capables de te laisser sauter dans l'eau, parce que tu n'en peux plus de faire des petits à la chaine dans une usine d'enfer. Ah! Ils ont toujours les ongles propres, ces beaux Messieurs. Pas de terre dessous, Vaï, Y se tacheront pas la soutane eux! Y savent dire des choses, mais qu'ils sont mielleux quand ils t'embobinent."

23. For additional discussion of this topic, see Kevra.

24. "C'est comme son métier de nous les faire garder, pas d'aller faire un ange. Il les aime pas ces anges-là, l'homme de l'église! Mais là, celui de la dame de là-bas, le curé, c'est un hypocrite, un malfaisant qui te laisse faire des enfants jusqu'à que tu crèves à la fin."

25. "Ah, Madame, ça fait longtemps que j'écoute pas un mot qu'ils disent. C'est du monde qui ont jamais travaillé une journée de leur vie pi qui ont jamais eu de misère. . . . Qui viennent ramasser des patates avec nous autres pi manger d'la soupe mince avec nous autres."

26. "Ah, nos curés, on avait cru les mettre à la porte à la Révolution. On a même coupé le cou à certains. On leur a cassé leurs églises et bu leur vin de messe. *Bah, res a*

fa, Y sont revenus par le finestrou de derrière." *"Bah, res a fa"* could be translated from Aranese into English as "nothing worked" or "there is nothing to do."

27. "Mais faut dire que ça me surprend de t'entendre parler comme ça des prêtres. Vous êtes française ... et les français sont supposés être des vrais catholiques. Pas comme nous autres. Le curé nous a même dit que la France, c'est la fille ainée de l'église."

WORKS CITED

Alcoff, Linda. "The Problem of Speaking for Others." *Feminist Nightmares: Women at Odds*, edited by Susan Weisser and Jennifer Fleishner, New York University Press, 1994, pp. 285–309.

Almond, Barbara. *The Monster Within: The Hidden Side of Motherhood*. University of California Press, 2010.

Bouliane, Gretchen Richter. "Variations on a Theme: The Image of the Mother in Traditional French-Canadian History." I Am Franco American and Proud of It / Je suis franco americaine et fiere de l'être, edited by R.-C. Robbins, L. L. Petrie, K. M. Langellier, and K. Slott, manuscript, University of Maine, Orono, 1995, pp. 10–12.

Chabot, Grégoire. "Calice." Manuscript in the author's possession.

———. *Chère maman: Pièce en trois actes*. National Assessment and Dissemination Center for Bilingual/Bicultural Education, 1979.

———. "A Life Lost." Manuscript in the author's possession.

———. *Un Jacques Cartier errant: Trois pièces / Jacques Cartier Discovers America: Three Plays*. University of Maine Press, 1996.

———. "Zithée." Manuscript in the author's possession.

Chabot, Grégoire, and Jean-Claude Redonnet. "Jeanne et Osithée: Parallèles croisées." Manuscript in the author's possession.

Choquette, Leslie. "Portrait d'auteur @ Grégoire Chabot." *Francophonies d'Amérique*, vol. 13, 2002, pp. 119–23.

Cleary, Kate. "Survivance." Franco-American Women's Institute, http://www.fawi.net /ezine/vol3no4/cleary/Franco_American1.htm.

Gilbert, Paula Ruth, and Roseanna Lewis Dufault. Introduction. *Doing Gender: Franco-Canadian Women Writers of the 1990s*, edited by Paula Ruth Gilbert and Roseanna Lewis Dufault, Fairleigh Dickinson University Press, 2001, pp. 15–20.

Kevra, Susan K. "The Mechanization of Motherhood: Images of Maternity in Quebec Women Writers of the Quiet Revolution." *AmeriQuests*, vol. 4, no. 1, 2007, pp. 1–10.

Langelier, Régis. "French-Canadian Families." *Ethnic and Family Therapy*, edited by Monica McGoldrick, Joe Giordano, and John K. Pearce, 2nd ed., Guilford Press, 1996, pp. 545–54.

Langellier, Kristin. "Performing Family Stories, Forming Cultural Identity: Franco American Mémère Stories." *Communication Studies*, vol. 53, no. 1, 2002, pp. 56–73.

Langellier, Kristin, and Eric Peterson. "Voicing Identity: The Case of Franco-American Women in Maine." *Franco-American Women's Institute*, Fall 1998, www.fawi.net/ezine/pastezines/Volume2Number2and3.html#Langellier.

Lévesque, Andrée, and Yvonne Klein. *Making and Breaking the Rules: Women in Quebec, 1919–1939*. University of Toronto Press, 2010.

Mello, Tam'ara. "The Exploitation of Minority Mothers as Cultural Bodies: A View of French-Canadian and Black Mothers." *Franco-American Women's Institute*, Fall 2000, http://www.fawi.net/ezine/vol3no3/Mello.html.

Myall, James. "From French Canadians to Franco-Americans." *Maine Memory Network*, www.mainememory.net/sitebuilder/site/2122/page/3514/display?use_mmn=1.

Pacini, Peggy. "L'autotraduction chez Grégoire Chabot: Médiation, transmission, survie d'une communauté et d'une littérature de l'exiguité." *Glottopol*, vol. 25, Jan. 2015, n.p.

Redonnet, Jean-Claude. *Les monologues de Jeanne Amiel*. Sloane Intercultural, 2014.

Richard, Mark Paul. *Loyal but French: The Negotiation of Identity by French-Canadian Descendants in the United States*. Michigan State University Press, 2008.

Robbins, Rhea Côté. "Franco-American Women's Literary Tradition: A Central Piece in the Region's Literary Mosaic." *River Review / Revue Rivière*, vol. 5, 1999, n.p.

———. *Heliotrope: French Heritage Women Create*. Rheta Press, 2015.

Roby, Yves. *The Franco-Americans of New England: Dreams and Realities*. Septentrion, 2004.

4

Permissive Parenting

The Awful American Mother in
Nancy Huston's *Lignes de faille*

ALISON RICE

French-language author Nancy Huston's *Lignes de faille*, recipient of the prestigious Prix Femina in 2006, paints a bleak portrait of brilliant girls and boys who cannot escape their genetic predispositions. This ambitious work of fiction is divided into four lengthy chapters, each narrated by a precocious six-year-old member of the same family. All the six-year-olds hail from a diverse location and belong to a different generation. The book begins in 2004 with the voice of self-obsessed Sol, who remains unsupervised in his California home, surfing the internet for pornography and violent beheadings. The next chapter features the 1982 narrative of the lonely Randall, who longs for attention from his absent intellectual mother in New York or Tel Aviv. The third chapter is devoted to Sadie, who fervently wishes her young mother would put her singing career aside just long enough to sweep her away from her miserable life of feminine chores performed for her grandparents in their Canadian home in 1962. Finally, Kristina dreams that her sister will allow her to cuddle with the coveted doll she was given for Christmas in wartime Germany.

This novel thus proceeds in reverse chronological order to show in a complicated transnational tale, from one war to the next, how one family moves from girls fighting over dolls to boys engaging with internet porn. Permissive parenting in a variety of forms—across national borders and generational gaps—proves to wreak irreparable damage on the four children, who cannot escape their family faults, whatever the setting. But there is no doubt that the child with the greatest concentration of troubling characteristics is the Californian, and his narrative gives credence to the conviction that his American mother has unwittingly played a predominant role in creating such a problematic person.

The book opens with the story told by Sol, a boy so despicable that the novel was not distributed in the United States upon its completion in 2006. The *New York Times* review of the book came out two years later, in November 2008, and critic Susann Cokal was so repulsed by this character that she qualified him as "downright evil." What is particularly interesting is that this proud, obnoxious child is less off-putting to the French public than he is to American readers; one cannot help but wonder why there was no trouble with a publication in French in France, and why this work was lauded with such gusto in that version when it hadn't even gone to press in the original English version. According to the author's own analysis of the reception of her earlier publications, the novels that depict the "other side of the pond" tend to fare best on the opposite shore. In a series of essays titled *Nord perdu*, Huston affirms that the books she considered to be "very French" have always elicited a great deal of interest in Canada, whereas her "cowboys-and-Indians novel sold much better in France—never underestimate the power of exoticism!" (*Losing North* 39). It may have been that the character of the young boy wasn't as contentious in France because of this exotic aspect of his makeup. It is also possible that his American identity, his presumed predilections, his hatefulness itself was what made him a compelling character for French readers, particularly given his narrative's setting in 2004. The mentality and actions of the young boy are specifically tied to this explosive moment just following the American invasion of Iraq, during the early stages of a war that a large majority of the French population vehemently opposed.

The California child provides us with intimate insight into his self-conception in what we might call "Sol's soliloquy," a first-person set of reflections containing provocative language and conveying offensive attitudes.

When his mother is busy doing housework, he uses her computer to take in images of all forms of sex, as well as the devastating details of war. He provides ample descriptions of what he is able to view with a simple click: "You just have to download and you can get the girls being raped or screwed in the anus by horses or dogs or whatever else you want, click click click. . . . Mom almost never uses her computer and also she sings as she does the vacuuming so how could she possibly hear me clicking with my right hand on the mouse as I put my left hand on my crotch and start to rub" (Huston, *Fault Lines* 10–11). After an elliptical question ("did Dad . . . ?") followed by a sentence fragment without punctuation in the middle of the page ("good thing I'm a boy"), the narrative voice jumps directly to another scene without any textual transition:

> The corpses of Iraqi soldiers lying in the sand is one of my favourite things to click on. It's a whole slide show. Sometimes you can't even tell what body parts you're looking at. Torsos maybe? Or legs? They're sort of wrapped in rips and strips of clothing and they're lying in the sand, partially covered by the sand which has absorbed their blood, it's all very dry. You can see American soldiers standing around them, looking down at them and thinking *There but for the grace of God . . . was this a human being?* (Huston, *Fault Lines* 11)

These striking passages appear in the very early pages of the novel in a stream-of-consciousness narrative that later appears to reveal some of the reasons behind such unhealthy obsessions with bestiality and gore.

It might initially seem that this child is seeking gruesome entertainment because he doesn't receive enough attention at home. Surfing the web in search of sex and violence is the type of behavior one would more readily expect from a child with two working parents and no one to look after him in the afternoons. But what emerges in other portions of the novel is the portrait of a deeply devoted mother who is very involved in her child's upbringing. Indeed, she is self-sacrificing to a fault.[1] A flagrant example of one of the ways the mother, named Tess, ceaselessly caters to her only child's desires is found in her reaction to his demands when it comes to food. We learn from his matter-of-fact account that she indulges his every whim: "I'm actually never hungry and Mom is very understanding about this, she only gives me foods I like because they circulate with ease, yoghurt and cheese and pasta, peanut butter and bread and cereal, she doesn't insist on the whole vegetable-meat-fish-eggs aspect of eating, saying I'll get around to that when I'm good and ready for it" (Huston, *Fault Lines* 4). This is a mother who is forever cutting the crusts off the sandwiches she makes for her son without hesitating to question whether this is necessary or not. What she ultimately is feeding, despite her good intentions, is not the boy's stomach but rather his obsessions. He is overly concerned with every aspect of the digestive process, deliberately rehearsing each detail of his habits when it comes to chewing his food: he nibbles first, then wets the small pieces of soft bread with his saliva before swishing them up between his lips and gums, where he slowly allows them to dissolve in his mouth. He doesn't want to actually swallow them.[2] He indicates that he exercises caution and control with respect to everything that he allows in, in addition to everything that comes out: "I can't allow just anything into my body: my poop has to come out the right colour and consistency" (4). When his father mentions that he wonders how the boy will survive when he has to fend for himself the following year in the school cafeteria, it is clear that his mother has that step covered as well: "Mom says she'll pick me up and bring me home for lunch, that's what stay-at-home moms are for!" (4).

This description of Tess as a "stay-at-home mom" proves to be definitive when it comes to her relationship to Sol. Since she has no other title than this, no profession other than that of caring for the home and her son, this child has come to believe that he is of the utmost importance. Indeed, he is convinced that the world revolves around him. He places himself on a par with the two beings he sees as the supreme leaders of the world: "God and President Bush are buddies" (Huston, *Fault Lines* 5). And he is certain that he possesses divine powers himself: "I'm the Sun King, Only Sun and Only Son, Son of Google, Son of God, Eternal Omnipotent Son of the World Wide Web" (14). This power conferred on him is directly related to his mother's unwavering devotion: "www turned upside down is mmm: apart from My Miraculous Mother to whom I've allowed brief glimpses, no one has the vaguest notion of the brilliance, the radiance, the fabulous radioactivity in my brain that will one day transform the universe" (14).

This admiring maternal presence is essential to his delusions of grandeur; she is the ever-present spectator whose unconditional approval means that he is all that he believes himself to be. But the larger setting in which this microcosm of the home is found is a crucial component of the young boy's worldview, for he has taken on the attitudes that Huston perceives to reign in the United States in the twenty-first century; the child is the unattractive embodiment of many arrogant American assumptions at this point in time. The fact that Sol's religious convictions converge with his patriotic fervor makes his assertions about superiority particularly striking. He believes that God has endowed him with a superior body and mind because he has "high intentions for him," "otherwise I wouldn't have been born in the wealthiest state of the wealthiest country in the world, with the most powerful weapons system capable of blasting the whole human species to kingdom come" (4–5).

Sol's narrative underscores the role the mother plays in reinforcing his certainty that he is an exceptional human being who deserves special treatment. This becomes a point of contention when she varies mealtimes according to Sol's personal preferences and proves ready to serve him whatever he desires whenever he wishes. His parents have a disagreement one evening when Tess proves how willing she is to accommodate her son's demands:

> Or another time we were at home, they'd already had supper and I didn't feel like having any so I didn't join them at the table, and then we went upstairs to watch a non-violent family viewing film on TV together and in the middle of the film I started feeling a bit hungry so I asked Mom to bring me something to eat. She went down and got me a tray ready with milk and cookies, which I really appreciated because meanwhile she was actually missing the best part of the film, I said thank you but suddenly out of the blue Dad said in a loud voice: "Tess, it's time you stopped waiting on this child hand and foot. You're his *mother*, not his slave! Being his mother means that *you're* in power, *you've* got the authority, not *him*, for Christ's sake!" And Mom was so taken aback by his use of language especially the word Christ in vain that her hands were trembling when she set the tray down in front of me.
>
> "Let's talk about it later, Randall," she said. In the parent-child relationship course they probably said it wasn't a good idea for kids to sit in on their parents'

marital quarrels. Mom has taken all sorts of classes in meditation and positive thinking and relaxation and self-esteem, and she's gotten really good at it so later on in bed I heard them talking things over and trying to pinpoint exactly when the tension started rising in the course of the evening.

"Maybe it reminded you of a scene from your own childhood?" Mom suggested very gently. Dad grunted. "Or maybe, in a way, you're jealous because your own mom never took care of you the way I take care of Solly?" (Huston, *Fault Lines* 18–19)

It hits him where it hurts when Tess brings up her husband's upbringing, for Randall longed for his mother throughout his childhood, but Sadie was too busy to be with her only son. She was completely committed to her career as a scholar with expertise on the Second World War, as the six-year-old Randall explains in his narrative: "She gives lectures on evil in universities all around the country. Admittedly evil is a strange specialty to have and I don't know how to explain it so when my friends' mothers ask me what my mom does I just say she teaches History and is also working on a doctorate" (Huston, *Fault Lines* 84–85). The young Randall explains that his mother is the breadwinner in their family and that his father, a playwright whose work unfortunately hasn't met with much success, is the one who spends a great deal of time with him. His father is an excellent cook, but he raises Randall with little attention to regularity: "We shower when we feel like it, keep irregular hours, sometimes watch TV while we're having supper, drink Coke and spurt ketchup all over our food, not to mention things that can given you cancer like monosodium glutamate which is forbidden now even in Chinese restaurants" (85). This type of father-son relationship couldn't be further from the experience Randall knows with his Sol. Now he is the parent who has very little time for his son, commuting a great distance and working long hours in order to pay the high California rent while Tess remains in the home. Sol is aware that this arrangement is the result of a carefully considered choice: "Unlike my father, whose mom was away hectoring in universities all the time when he was little, I have an excellent mom who decided to be stay-at-home out of her own free will and not because it was women's destiny like in the olden days" (8). It is remarkable, and somewhat anachronistic, that Tess has opted to remain at home when Randall's mother had traveled the world pursuing professional goals, just as her mother, the celebrated singer, had done before her. This decision is of undeniable importance, given Huston's personal history.

When Huston evokes her childhood in interviews and essays, she inevitably mentions her mother's departure from their family home in Anglophone Canada when the future author was only six years old. In a recent autobiographical text, *Bad Girl: Classes de littérature*, the author revisits the choice her mother was apparently forced to make between serving as a full-time parent and pursuing her dream as an intellectual. According to this account, it was the father who demanded she be only one or the other: "Il lance donc à son épouse féministe un ultimatum: soit tu restes à la maison avec les enfants, soit je mets une vraie mère à ta place" ("He threw an ultimatum at his feminist spouse: either you remain at home with the children or I will replace you with a true mother") (Huston, *Bad Girl* 233).[3] This father figure in *Bad Girl* resembles Randall in *Lignes de faille*, for both knew the pain of an absent mother during their early years. It is likely that Huston's father sought to improve his children's lives by creating a stable home atmosphere with a mother who was present; indeed, when he issued this ultimatum, he had already ascertained that her mother's absence was negatively affecting the future writer, as the narrative voice of *Bad Girl* reveals: "Il n'a pas oublié les absences de sa propre mère pendant son adolescence. Finalement, les deux femmes ont fauté de façon assez comparable: en refusant de se contenter de leur rôle de mère, elles ont rendu leurs enfants malheureux" ("He hadn't forgotten the absences of his own mother during his adolescence. Finally, the two women had committed comparable faults: by refusing to find contentment in their role as mother, they had made their children unhappy") (235).[4]

What emerges in *Bad Girl* is the image of a child whose abandonment has led her to question her self-worth. She wonders if it was her own inadequacy that drove her mother to leave, naming the many skills she should have acquired in order to convince her mother to stay:

> Cela n'arrive jamais, qu'une mère quitte son enfant. C'est donc que l'enfant en question doit être nulle. Oui, tu mérites tout le malheur qui t'arrive, *bad*

girl, même si tu ne sais pas pourquoi. Peut-être est-elle partie justement parce que tu jouais mal du piano? ou parce que tu rotais trop fort, ou parce que tu ne savais pas lacer tes souliers avec un joli nœud? ou parce que tu mangeais trop de bonbons à la menthe? ou parce que tu n'as pas appris à lire à l'âge de deux ans? ou parce que tu as commis un autre péché, pire encore, mais tu ne sais plus lequel, tu as oublié. (Huston, *Bad Girl* 251)

That never happens. A mother doesn't leave her child. It must then be because the child in question is nothing. Yes, you deserve all of the misfortune that comes to you, bad girl, even if you don't know why. Maybe she left precisely because you play the piano poorly? Or because you would burp too loudly? Or because you didn't know how to tie your shoes with a pretty bow? Or because you ate too many mints? Or because you didn't learn to read at the age of two? Or because you committed another sin, even worse, but you don't know which one. You forgot it.

This self-deprecating series of questions that highlight the child's shortcomings in *Bad Girl* stands out in contrast to the self-aggrandizing discourse of Sol. Whereas the girl didn't learn how to read at an astonishingly precocious age, the boy did: "At kindergarten and elsewhere, I amaze everybody with my reading skills because Mom taught me to read when I was just a little baby" (Huston, *Fault Lines* 8). The mother who had little else to worry about than her son's advancement brought flashcards to his crib and drilled her infant for twenty-minute periods three times a day so that he learned to read at the same time he learned to speak. This parenting technique, along with many others, was the result of study and apprenticeship. Tess's vocation is a very involved one when it is represented through the eyes of her son.

Parents today have the option of enrolling in courses meant to enhance their ability to perform their roles as caretakers of and mentors to their children. Sol makes mention of his own mother's commitment to learning from others when it comes to her maternal duties: "Mom knows about all this stuff thanks to a course she took on parent-child relationships. It wasn't only about child-proofing, it was about all the other aspects, like how you should respect your children and listen to them and not treat them as if they were stupid idiots the way parents used to treat their children in the olden days" (Huston, *Fault Lines* 16). While this respect is hardly objectionable, it becomes harmful when the child is accorded too much control. For instance, Sol's parents are firmly in agreement that he should never be "slapped, spanked, or given any form of corporal punishment whatsoever" (19). This understanding led to a memorably hasty farewell that brought a family visit to an end when Sol's grandfather smacked him three times on the bottom after the boy had launched a wooden baseball bat into the air in a dangerous gesture of extreme frustration. After being reprimanded in this way, Sol threw a screaming fit that went on for an hour until his mother returned from her outing. A panicked Tess rushed to her yelping boy and, upon learning that he had received a spanking, set in motion a precipitous departure from her family's home. She refused to speak to her own father after his actions "until he sent her a written apology, along with the solemn promise never to hit me again," according to the son's speculation. Given the results brought about by his highly vocal protest, it is little wonder that the six-year-old Sol declares in capital letters: "I AM POWERFUL" (22).

There can be little doubt that the intentions behind these parenting choices are noble, but they certainly appear to be misguided, as well as exaggerated. Sol explains that his parents won't allow any corporeal punishment because his mother's readings have focused on books that demonstrate how "battered children turn into battering parents, molested children into pedophiles and raped children into pimps and prostitutes" (Huston, *Fault Lines* 19). His parents believe that the "important thing is you should always talk, talk, talk, ask the child why it misbehaved and give it the chance to explain itself before pointing out, as gently as possible, how it might be able to behave better the next time around. You should never hit it" (19). The use of the pronoun "it" seems unusual in this passage; it probably reflects the writer's distance from her native tongue, but it is probably also an indication of an attitude toward parenting that is not carefully attentive to the individuality, to the singularity, of the child.

What is difficult about properly responding as a parent to a child who has misbehaved is engaging in a conversation that allows for what Sara Ruddick has theorized under the term "maternal thinking," a reflectiveness that takes into account the many factors involved in raising children. The fact that Sol is a particularly bright child may mean that allowing him to explain himself will mean allowing him to outthink his parent and get away with a great deal more than he should. What makes Tess an awful mother is not her lack of attention to her son but the fact that she is not appropriately attentive to him. Catering to his every desire is not making him a more mature individual but is reinforcing selfish and self-centered forms of behavior that are making him close-minded and closed off to the world as a whole. Instead of opening up to intellectual conversation and well-informed formulations, the talk that Sol engages in with his parents is focused on petty personal goals. When he is confronted with a blemish on his face following a botched surgery to remove a birthmark, and when he finds himself at odds with a foreign culture on a family trip to Germany, Sol is not mentally equipped to meet these challenges.[5]

Since her mother left her traditional role as wife and mother in order to pursue a professional career, Huston has frequently grappled with the difficulties and touted the joys of engaging in intellectual work while parenting. The author's own life bears witness to the potential complementarity of the two activities: she has published over forty books and managed to raise two children with their father, renowned intellectual Tzvetan Todorov. Even though she has argued convincingly for the potential of human reproduction to contribute to the production of creative literary works in such publications as *Journal de la Création*, she has also shown herself to be attuned to the challenge of being a good parent and an effective writer. In an essay she contributed to the scholarly journal *Critical Inquiry* in 1995 carrying the evocative title "Novels and Navels," she addresses the potential conflict between the two professions: "Mothers tend to want everything to be beautiful for their children. They more or less force themselves to adopt an optimistic worldview in order to protect them, comfort them, and foster hope. Novelists may or may not have the same temptation—to put across a message of hope—but if they paint a world in which human existence is hunky-dory, their readers' response will be not hope but boredom. To write a meaningful story, one must be prepared to accept meaninglessness; face ugliness; describe horror; comprehend betrayal and loss" (711). Huston's own definition of literature as something that challenges our assumptions and provokes us to philosophize plays a part in these comments, as she maintains: "Real fiction—good fiction—must exercise our moral muscle, and if it tells us too clearly what is right and what is wrong, our moral muscle gets lazy and flabby" (710).

It is over ten years after writing these reflections in an essay form that the author portrays a particular mother-son relationship in fictional form in *Lignes de faille*, and it is my contention that the young Sol's shocking behavior and disturbing thoughts constitute a critique of a new trend of permissive parenting that Huston sees as specifically tied to the American way of life in the early 2000s. Huston's novel can be seen in many ways as a precursor to such publications as French philosopher Elisabeth Badinter's *The Conflict: How Modern Motherhood Undermines the Status of Women* (2010) and the American journalist Pamela Druckerman's *Bringing Up Bébé* (2011). Before these texts came to address the overwhelming sacrifices that women have recently been asked to make, in America first and foremost, but around the Western world by extension, Huston's work hints at the nonstop work of the American mother, Tess, who is eager to give up everything for Sol. Like so many other mothers feel obligated to do in the era of attachment parenting, she has unhesitatingly devoted herself to breastfeeding and caregiving, child-proofing and hovering, worrying and listening, and making herself constantly available around the clock. What Huston manages to show in a novel that recounts the stories of four generations is that those who benefited from the least parenting learned to cope in the most apparently successful ways, but he who has the most parenting, and in the most "traditional" manner of the stay-at-home mother, struggles inwardly in a dangerously pathological sense.

What appears to be wonderful and supportive parenting at first glance from the mother who is quick to fix food that is colorless and soft for her "fussy eater" (Huston, *Fault Lines* 25) to the mom and dad who "both kiss me and clap for me which is a family tradition they started when I said 'Amen' for the first time when I was a little baby and then they got into the habit of doing it at every gracetime so now it's become part and parcel of the ceremony" (24) is nothing but a veneer that hides sinister secrets for the child. These rituals do not replace the rigor that Sol needs. While "permissive parenting" is certainly not a term that ever appears in this novel, a glance at a website that quickly appears when one conducts an online search for this expression seems to describe the relationship in this family down to the last detail. According to psychologist Diana Baumrind, permissive parents "are more responsive than they are demanding. They are nontraditional and lenient, do not require mature behavior, allow considerable self-regulation, and avoid confrontation." Permissive parents have few rules or standards of behavior, and the rules they do enforce are often very inconsistent. Children raised in this environment often possess no self-discipline, have poor social skills, may be self-involved and demanding, and demonstrate insecurity due to the lack of boundaries and guidance.

These characteristics are certainly pertinent to Sol, who is deeply self-involved. Because of his working father's frequent absence from the home, he is also the embodiment, in many ways, of the boy described in Nancy Chodorow's 1978 study of gender identification and differentiation, *The Reproduction of Mothering: Psychoanalysis and the Sociology of Gender*. As Chodorow argues, "A boy must attempt to develop a masculine gender identification and learn the masculine role in the absence of a continuous and ongoing personal relationship to his father (and in the absence of a continually available masculine role model)" (280). It is important that the internet is the unfortunate tutor of the precocious child who has learned how to surf the web with ease, for it is there that he has found masculine role models in the most violent of settings. Chodorow explains that "[s]ociologically, boys in father-absent and normally father-remote families develop a sense of what it is to be masculine through identification with cultural images of masculinity" (280). Chodorow integrates into her analysis the idea that "boys are assumed to learn their heterosexual role without teaching, through interaction with their mothers," and Sol astutely shows us how he does define himself with respect to his mother but that he is not at all forthcoming with these personal definitions. This is in part because of his perception of his mother as a deeply sentimental being, in accord with her gender:

> Mom is very much against violence, she gets emotional about it which is only
> natural because women are always more emotional than men. She's just an

extremely positive person and I don't see any point in sullying her illusions. She supervises everything I watch on TV which means yes for "Pokemon" and no for "Inuyasha," yes for "Gummi Bears" and no for "The Simpsons." As far as movies go she says I'm still a bit too young for *Harry Potter* and *The Lord of the Rings*, which is unbelievable. I remember she didn't even want me to see *Bambi* when my friend Diane from kindergarten gave me the DVD for my fifth birthday, even if it's just an old cartoon she was afraid I'd be upset about the scene where Bambi's mother gets killed. She thinks I'm too young to know about death so I do my best to protect her. Last week we saw a dead sparrow at the edge of the road and she started stroking my hair and saying "It's all right, darling, he's in heaven with God now" and I clung to her leg and sobbed to make her feel better. (Huston, *Fault Lines* 13)

This indication of the incredible control that the mother exerts over her son's programming choices does help to refute some of the possible accusations that she has given herself over entirely to "permissive parenting." According to this account, she is inflexible about letting her child watch shows that she deems disturbing. But her overly conservative concerns about protecting him from any negative stories, whether they depict action and adventure or grief and loss, ultimately do him such a disservice that he seeks excitement elsewhere in much more deranged scenes of sexuality and violence. Of course, this is a powerful statement about the possibilities of the internet to influence children in our era. In contrast, Sol's father, Randall, his grandmother Sadie, and his great-grandmother Kristina adopted very different attitudes when they were afforded some leeway in their own early experiences. What becomes clear in all of their personal narratives, however, is that they crave regular and fruitful interaction with the parental figures in their lives and that while these three ancestors all longed for more exposure to their mothers, the opportunity to be with a mother at very great length, day in and day out, is not as blissful a situation for Sol as it might seem. What *Lignes de faille* makes clear is that well-intentioned parenting isn't enough to raise a fulfilled child and that adjustments must constantly be made for the individual who is being parented. Sol's story reveals that the pains of the past are passed on from one generation to the next, just as physical imperfections are, and that brilliant children might need the greatest accompaniment as they learn to navigate the web, and the world.

NOTES

1. It can be argued that sacrifice is integral to the maternal calling. In *Thérèse mon amour*, Julia Kristeva makes the following statement about the mother's relationship to the other: "[L]a mère vit de l'autre et agit pour lui. . . . Est maternelle la volonté de s'abandonner à la volonté de l'Autre pour fonder une nouvelle création" ("[T] he mother lives for the other and acts for him. . . . The will to abandon oneself to the will of the Other in order to found a new creation is maternal") (360). This translation from the French is mine.

2. Eating disorders play an important role in Nancy Huston's novels, figuring prominently in *Instruments des ténèbres* (1996) and *Dolce Agonia* (2001). In this text, it is noteworthy that the protagonist, who suffers from an obsession with food consumption, is a male child, and it is clear that the mother figure is enabling this unhealthy relation to nourishment.

3. This translation and those that follow from *Bad Girl* are mine; there is no existing English version of this text.

4. The autobiographical aspects of Huston's large corpus complement each other and invite critiques of her novels that draw from personal information provided in other textual contexts, as Kate Averis explains: "In a similar vein to much exiled women's writing, Huston encourages an autobiographical reading of the text through a protagonist who shares certain biographical traits with the author and the recurrence of themes and motifs drawn from Huston's explicitly autobiographical non-fictional texts" (174).

5. Like his mother, Sol has never set foot outside of the United States, and this trip to the German town where his grandmother spent her early childhood is destabilizing in many ways. The boy's reaction to a new country reveals his ignorance in no uncertain terms: "I don't like the road signs being in German, either. They feel like doors slamming in my face one after the other and I refuse to ask Grandma Sadie what they mean, I don't want ever to admit to any lack of knowledge and by the time I grow up everyone in the world will speak English or if they don't that's one of the laws I'll pass when I'm in power to make sure they do" (Huston, *Fault Lines* 63).

WORKS CITED

Averis, Kate. "The Formal Architecture of Identity in Nancy Huston's *Empreinte de l'ange*." *Francophères*, vol. 1, no. 2, 2012, pp. 171–84.

Baumrind, Diana. "What Is Permissive Parenting?" http://psychology.about.com/od/childcare/f/permissive-parenting.htm. Accessed 2 Jan. 2016.

Chodorow, Nancy. *The Reproduction of Mothering: Psychoanalysis and the Sociology of Gender*. 2nd ed. University of California Press, 1999.

Cokal, Susann. "Child's Play." *New York Times Sunday Book Review*, 31 Oct. 2008, http://www.nytimes.com/2008/11/02/books/review/Cokal-t.html?_r=0.

Huston, Nancy. *Bad Girl: Classes de littérature*. Actes Sud, 2014.

———. *Dolce agonia*. Actes Sud, 1996.

———. *Fault Lines*. Grove Press, Black Cat, 2008.

———. *Instruments des ténèbres*. Actes Sud, 1996.

———. *Lignes de faille*. Actes Sud, 2006.

———. *Losing North: Essays on Cultural Exile*. McArthur & Company, 2002.

———. *Nord perdu*. Actes Sud, 1999.

———. "Novels and Navels." *Critical Inquiry*, vol. 21, no. 4, 1995, pp. 708–21.

Kristeva, Julia. *Thérèse mon amour: Sainte Thérèse d'Avila*. Fayard, 2008.

Ruddick, Sara. *Maternal Thinking: Toward a Politics of Peace*. Beacon Press, 1995.

5

Lucie Joubert's Ironic Rejection of Motherhood in *L'envers du landau*

NATALIE EDWARDS

In the late twentieth and early twenty-first centuries, a variety of neologisms have appeared to describe women who choose to remain childless. Since terms such as "*non*mother" and "child*less*" imply a lack, several commentators have advanced alternatives to emphasize the choice made by this sizeable population. In English, the term "childfree" has existed since the 1970s and, although it now carries glib overtones, was originally intended as a reflection of the differences between the few who made this decision and the child-bearing majority.[1] The first academic researcher to survey this phenomenon, sociologist Jean Veevers, preferred the expression "childless by choice." More recently, Melanie Notkin proposes "other" and "otherhood," and French sociologist Charlotte Debest suggests the term "SEnVol," an abbreviation of "sans enfant volontairement" ("without children voluntarily"). The particularity of this word is its homonym *s'envole*, the third-person conjugation of the verb *s'envoler*, "to fly," "to fly away," or "to soar." Debest's term thus hints at the freedom and the lifestyle possibilities that the voluntarily childless may enjoy, yet it also fosters the stereotype of the hedonistic, egotistical childless woman. This chapter uses the term "voluntarily childless" as a means to emphasize that this lifestyle is a choice (especially as opposed to the traumatic experience of *in*voluntary childlessness) and to avoid any perception of superiority. The advent of these neologisms demonstrates the attention that the choice to remain childless is now attracting both in academic research and in popular culture.

Such scholarly enquiry into voluntary childlessness is a recent development. Early scholarship, which took place in the 1980s in the field of sociology, attempted to isolate the reasons for the choice and categorized women on the basis of their demographics, their education, their profession, and their social status. More recently, however, scholars have advanced more nuanced analyses that have implications for a historical appreciation of voluntary childlessness. Sociologist Rosemary Gillespie, for example, states that "the choices of women in the past have remained hidden. Being childfree has always been socially sanctioned for some groups, such as spinsters, widows, nuns, and nannies. Although these roles may have provided legitimacy for those who eschewed motherhood, they were defined by loss, self-sacrifice, and/or the nurturing of others' children. They failed to challenge, and even served to bolster, pronatalist cultural discourses that fused hegemonic femininity with motherhood" (133).

As Gillespie hints, both motherhood and nonmotherhood are discursively constructed concepts that alter according to culture and history. Several scholars have advanced similar arguments in order to counter the pronatalist discourse that they discern in contemporary Western societies. In *La révolution maternelle depuis 1945* (The post-1945 maternal revolution), for example, Yvonne Knibiehler builds on her previous work in the history of motherhood by arguing that practices of motherhood differ so greatly throughout history that successive "generations" of mothers can be defined. In *L'amour en plus* (*Mother Love*), Elisabeth Badinter points to seventeenth- and eighteenth-century French practices to argue that French society took a radically different approach to mothering from the pronatalist societies of the contemporary period. Psychoanalytic critics have also contributed to this debate, pointing to the different ways in which motherhood and nonmotherhood have been framed psychoanalytically over time. Jacques André and Catherine Chabert in *Désirs d'enfant* (Desire for children) and François Duparc and Martine Pichon in *Les nouvelles maternités au creux du divan* (New maternities on the couch) all attest to changing understand-ings of mothering and warn that contemporary pronatalist policies are psychologically damaging to mothers. In particular, psychoanalysts Isabelle Tilmant and Edith Vallée have both interrogated specifically voluntarily childless women. Tilmant interviewed both women and men in the early twenty-first century, and Vallée interviewed women in the 1970s and in the 2000s to compare their experiences. Both psychoanalysts conclude that the reasons for voluntary childlessness are manifold, and while they are often linked to the woman's mother, it is impossible to pathologize voluntarily childless women. As Vallée concludes, they give so many explanations that one single reason is not discernible; they simply experience what she terms a "nondesire" for children. The implication of these studies is that women who have felt no desire for children have always existed but that they have been silenced due to societal and historical constraints.

This chapter studies one of the first autobiographical expressions of the lack of desire for children. In English, recent works such as Nicki Defago's *Childfree and Loving It*, Aralyn Hughes's *Kid Me Not*, and Meghan Daum's *Selfish, Shallow, and Self-Absorbed* all present autobiographical accounts of voluntary childlessness. In French, texts such as Linda Lê's *À l'enfant que je n'aurai pas* (To the child I will not have), Jane Sautière's *Nullipare* (Nullip-arous), and Madeleine Chapsal's *La femme sans* (The woman without), all of which I discuss in my book-length study of voluntary childlessness, do likewise. In the case of Québécois literature, Lucie Joubert's landmark work *L'envers du landau: Regard extérieur sur la maternité et ses débordements* (2010) (The other side of the cradle: An outside perspective on motherhood and its spillover), the focus of this essay, brings attention to the consequences of voluntary childlessness in professional and nonprofessional contexts and looks set to spur broader discussion of this topic. The woman writer at the center of this essay is not necessarily a horrible mother, therefore, but she insists that she should *avoid* motherhood in order not to become one.

What is most interesting about *L'envers du landau* is that it does not conform to any standard genre; it is a self-reflexive essay that borrows from memoir and that incorporates both poetic elements and thorough academic research. I have argued elsewhere that it could be considered as a work of autocritography or personal criticism (Edwards, *Voicing*). Joubert is an academic based at the University of Ottawa. She specializes in Québécois women's writing and has studied at both the Francophone Université du Québec and the Anglophone McGill University. She has published extensively on contemporary women authors, including two books on humor and irony, two edited collections, and a series of articles and book chapters. In this chapter, I examine the ways in which Joubert constructs a narrative of self focused on her status as a voluntarily childless woman. I first examine the striking style of her writing, analyzing her irony as a form of self-deprecating defense at those who may chide her, rebuff her, or dismiss her arguments. I then study the ways in which she counters the stereotype of the selfish voluntarily childless woman.

Unsurprisingly, perhaps, given that Joubert has published academic analyses on the use of irony in literature, the tone of *L'envers du landau* is playful, comical, and disobedient. I use the term "disobedient" because Joubert is an academic who is obliged to write and publish her research, which necessitates an appropriate style. It is worth pointing out that French academic style, in which Joubert writes her scholarship, is particularly rigorous and standardized. In this text, however, Joubert plays with the style in which she regularly writes by developing a tone that melds comical self-reflection with analytical research. As Julie Rodgers writes, Joubert's "primary weapon in *L'Envers du landau* is her caustic use of humour, enacting a feigned awakening of the 'truths' of non-motherhood, as revealed to her by her culture and society" (84). For example, Joubert introduces and justifies her text thus:

> Il me manque un morceau. Je suis née, je vis et j'aurai vécu dépourvue de l'une des plus subtiles et mystérieuses parties de la mécanique féminine: l'envie de la maternité. Je n'ai pas d'enfant, n'en ai jamais voulu. . . . Tous les matins, je touche du bois; tous les matins, je dis merci. Mais voilà: depuis quelque temps, tout autour de moi me signale une fissure dans ce tableau trop beau pour être vrai. . . . Bref, j'ai l'impression de bien aller mais je suis dans un état épouvantable. (9)[2]

Joubert thus opens her text with self-reflection, highlighting that her text is clearly predicated upon her. Furthermore, she uses the first-person *je*, which is often greeted with disdain in French academic writing. Warren Motte, a scholar of French literature himself, regrets the paucity of academics who use "I" in their work: "[W]hy is it that we academics are discouraged from saying 'I'? What are we trying to hide? What lurks within us and threatens to erupt, unloosed by this 'I'? We are not dope fiends or outlaw bikers, utterly enslaved to our basest impulses. No. We are monkish folk for the most part, fully accustomed to keeping our ids in check" (185). Joubert, as can be seen from the opening lines of her text, is not afraid to follow Motte's advice, linking her experience directly to the subject matter of her book. The fact that she uses the first person to link her self and her academic writing in relation to a topic that has been as taboo as voluntary childlessness is even more striking. *L'envers du landau* thus constitutes a form of rebellion to academic mores, especially in French, and augurs nonconformism in both style and content.

A central part of the nonconformism of Joubert's text is the irony, which is clear from the opening lines quoted above. The end of the citation, in which she states that she feels perfectly well but is really in a terrible state, signals Joubert's intention to use humor in order to critique the treatment of voluntary childlessness in contemporary discourse. She proclaims that outsiders must know her better than she does herself and that she is not—and never will be—able to surmount the lack in her life that is the result of her short-sighted decision. Her playful, comedic assertions clearly belie more serious concerns as she writes of painful experiences in which she has been stigmatized as a result of her choice to remain childless. Research in this domain reveals that such experiences are shared by many women who have chosen childlessness. Sociologists Laurie Chancey and Susan Dumais's study of stigmatization of the voluntarily childless concludes that "stereotypes of the childfree held by the general population have been fairly consistent since the late 1970s, and they tend to be largely negative" (208). Joubert writes what many have experienced, therefore, and does so in a way that invites a light-hearted approach to a difficult situation. Carolyn Morrell, also a social scientist, discerns this approach as relatively common. She finds that the childless women with whom she has conducted interviews feel awkward when asked whether they have children, and many deflect this question through humor. She cites one who would reply, for example, "[O]h yes, we had kids but we sold them so we could travel" (77). Although the humor evident in this citation and in Joubert's work are different, the basis of the two is the same; it is often considered inappropriate for a woman to speak directly about a lack of desire for children, so many couch their feelings in humor. Maura Kelly suggests that childless women are now attempting to subvert stereotypes associated with them, and she isolates humor as one of the strategies that they develop to do so. This is not a wholly positive development, however, since many of the strategies that Kelly perceives may serve to entrench negative stereotypes. For example, she shows that some voluntarily childless women attempt to redefine their situation by discussing attitudes toward and practices of mothering, while some choose to lead people to assume that they will have children later or that they were physically unable to have them. Humor may serve to enable women to deflect questions about their choice but also belies the persistence of attitudes such as those identified by Chancey and Dumais. Although Kelly finds that attitudes toward the voluntarily childless are changing, this is more of an optimistic approach to future developments than an accurate account of recent times, especially in countries with a strong Catholic heritage that continues to influence discourse on motherhood.

Joubert's humor is thus related to propriety and to the way in which voluntary childlessness has traditionally been treated as taboo. Consequently, some readers may consider her writing style to be regrettable insofar as she may not challenge some of the prevailing approaches to the topic. Nevertheless, her text underscores that a humoristic writing style is all that is really available to her if she aims for her text to be greeted with approbation and to garner an audience. The ironic style that she develops is perhaps the most effective way of conveying her very serious message, since, as the sociologists' findings discussed above show, it conforms to readers' expectations of a voluntarily childless woman's self-representation. By incorporating passages of comedic self-reflection, Joubert personalizes the representation of voluntary childlessness by bringing her own experience into the text and writing a narrative of self with which readers may identify or disidentify. The very serious message that the text presents is argued very coherently on the basis of extensive academic research, but it is doubtful that it would have reached the same audience without its ironic style. The text is therefore a highly accessible volume with which a variety of readers can engage rather than a tightly argued academic argument that will circulate primarily in scholarly circles.

Simultaneously, Joubert's irony could be interpreted as deliberately self-deprecating. Her humor insists upon her humility: she is a highly successful academic, but her light-hearted, playful tone hints that she does not take herself or her arguments too seriously. For example, she recounts arriving at the family home for Easter when she had just submitted her doctoral dissertation and her two sisters had infants:

> Trois grossesses fort différentes, dont l'une, sinon ectopique du moins utopique, pour ainsi dire, que j'ai soulignée en arrivant à Pâques à la maison familiale avec un oreiller sous la chandail et en me tenant les reins à deux mains. Le bébé se présente bien, ai-je dit, mais il me tient réveillée la nuit. . . . Et alors que tous s'extasiaient sur les poupons, un jury scrutait attentivement les moindres travers de mon petit dernier. (36)[3]

By recounting how she played with her family by comparing her dissertation to a baby, she hints that her work may easily be considered unimportant when compared to the work of bringing a new life into the world, thus deliberately undercutting the severity of her argument. In this way, her style may be interpreted as anticipating the eye rolling of (male) fellow academics who would balk at the banality of her topic or those who would dismiss her arguments as middle-class navel-gazing. By presenting them comically, she invites her opponents not to take her too seriously, thus warding off any virulent critique, yet she allows sympathetic readers to engage with her ideas. In this way, Joubert's irony could be considered as a mechanism that she develops in order to find a balance between conveying her message and anticipating the backlash of her opponents. Overall, Joubert's irony is a powerful tool that enables her simultaneously to maneuver within a highly codified professional sphere and to show that the critique of pronatalist discourses on motherhood is no laughing matter.

The critique of pronatalist discourses is a key element of Joubert's text. Three of the five chapters are devoted to her research into journalism, film, and popular media and argue that the voluntarily childless are stigmatized and victimized routinely. In response, Joubert sets out to challenge the stereotypes of the voluntarily childless, and this sustained rebuttal becomes the focus of *L'envers du landau*. In the first book-length study of voluntary childlessness, *Childless by Choice* (1980), Veevers argued that stereotypes of the childless were particularly entrenched in five areas: morality, responsibility, marriage, sexuality, and normalcy. Several decades later, many of these categories find an echo in contemporary stereotypes: that voluntarily childless women are unable to develop successful long-term relationships with men, have difficult relationships with others, are professionally ambitious, are financially motivated, feel a gap in their lives, dislike all children, are hedonistic, are more individualistic, are less nurturing, are emotionally unstable, have dubious values, and are sexually promiscuous, for example. Joubert mentions many of these in *L'envers du landau*—Rodgers suggests she presents the voluntarily childless woman as "immature, ego-centric, child-hating, dysfunctional, and so on" (84)—but reserves her most sustained critique for the stereotype of selfishness.

Selfishness is perhaps the most obvious stereotype leveled at those who choose not to have children and is, most usefully for those who use it, very difficult to define. At a time of advanced capitalism, the semantic field of the word "selfish" is surely vast, yet it is still a justifiable critique of the voluntarily childless, as the famous cover of *Time* magazine devoted to the topic showed: a bronzed couple lie smiling dreamily on a beach with the words "The Childfree Life: When Having It All Means Not Having Children" hanging above them (Sandler). Such representations are one of the main targets of Meghan Daum's provocative collection *Selfish, Shallow, and Self-Absorbed: Sixteen Writers on the Decision Not to Have Kids*. As contributor Courtney Hodell states, "When you talk of not wanting children, it is impossible to avoid sounding defensive, like you're trying to prove the questionable beauty of a selfish and too-tidy existence. It is hard to come across as anything other than brittle, rigid, controlling, against life itself."

Joubert's assault on the term "selfish" is two-pronged. First, she discusses her professional activities at length, centering on her role as a feminist scholar and educator. Like Nancy K. Miller in *Getting Personal: Feminist Occasions and Other Autobiographical Acts*, she is unafraid to write of her pedagogical activity alongside her research, two domains that have traditionally been separated in academic writing. Throughout the text, she repeats that she is a feminist, that she been a militant feminist in the past, and that her feminist commitment is the foundation of her teaching. She provides glimpses into her classroom practice, describing techniques that she uses to convince her largely female student body that feminist thought is beneficial to them. Importantly, she highlights in these passages that she behaves in a way that could be labeled maternal yet chooses not to become a mother herself. She shows genuine and passionate concern for her students, which would defy any charge of "selfishness" that may be leveled against her. As an example, she writes of the female students who arrive in her classes dressed as sexualized objects: "[C]ette rivalité, dis-je souvent à mes étudiantes, est ma plus grande défaite comme militante: voir encore aujourd'hui, après toutes ces luttes, des filles se jauger entre elles comme des vaches de foire agricole" ("[T]his rivalry, I often say to my female students, is my biggest failure as a feminist: today, after all the battles, I still see girls sizing each other up like cows in a country fair") (Joubert 49). Her concern for her female students is evident, as she aims to provide them with alternative models of selfhood but regrets that she does not always accomplish this. Throughout the text, she provides glimpses of classroom situations in which she struggles to convince women of the need to resist constraining models of female identity. Such insights into Joubert's daily activity and her pedagogical practice are hard to reconcile with an image of a stereotypically selfish childless woman. Overall, she paints a portrait of herself as engaged in and committed to collective action that improves the lives of women: not just preaching equality from an imaginary ivory tower but actively promoting social change. While teaching is not an entirely selfless activity, Joubert's narrative portrays a voluntarily childless woman whose life choices clearly refute the facile charge of selfish, uncaring, and narcissistic.

In addition to Joubert's pedagogical practice, her critique of pronatalist discourse in Québec is an important element of her rebuff to the stereotype of the selfish childless woman. Rodgers underscores the importance of the context of Québec, since French Canadians have until recently maintained high birth rates in order partially to ensure their linguistic survival (80). The majority of Joubert's text is devoted to the exhaustive research that she has carried out into popular culture in Québec and her concern for the impact of the discourses that she discerns upon her society. She has amassed a wealth of evidence to convince her reader of the insidious place of pronatalist messages in Québécois society. As an example, she targets women's magazines that have recently shown a penchant for writing articles on celebrity adoptions, for photographing famous women with their infants, and for displaying pregnant celebrities on their front covers. Although Joubert states that "cela constitue en soi une révolution par rapport au temps où les stars cachaient soigneusement leur 'état' de peur de perdre d'éventuels contrats" ("this in itself constitutes a revolution compared to when stars carefully hid their "state" out of fear of losing potential contracts") (71), she underscores that these images promote a very limited model of femininity and female success:

> [E]en rendant la maternité glamour ou, si on n'en a pas les moyens, au moins cool, on réussit à convaincre les femmes qu'elles sont plus *sexy* dans leur rôle de mère, qu'elles peuvent être, elles aussi, une *yummy mummy* et qu'élever des enfants est la chose la plus facile du monde. La preuve: les stars en font à la demi-douzaine sans prendre un gramme! (71, emphasis in original)[4]

Again, her commitment to broader social concerns is evident, as she aims to highlight the negative impact of contemporary discourses upon the women and girls of her region. Her argument is not predicated upon self-centered reasons for childlessness; indeed, her self-narrative recedes to the background of the text for long sections. Instead, it is focused on her concern for Québec society as a collective. Her motivations do not adhere to the stereotypical model of selfishness, therefore, and serve to construct an alternative commentary based upon collective concerns.

Joubert's concern for contemporary Québec society is perhaps most apparent in her analyses of current discourses surrounding pronatalism. She explains that over the course of a year, she paid particularly close attention to cultural materials that represented motherhood in Québec. She assembles examples of these from a variety of sources, from low to high culture: blogs, political commentary, advertisements, women's magazines, radio interviews, television shows and journalism, for example. Although much of Joubert's text takes a universalist approach to voluntary childlessness, this section of the work focuses on Québec culture, mentioning journalists and celebrities by name to an audience who will likely be familiar with them. Her long list of examples include Radio-Canada's series *Les Parent*, Radio-Québec's *Toute une famille!*, to an episode of *Ça pourrait nous arriver* devoted to IVF that featured Céline Dion and Julie Snyder. In this way, Joubert emphasizes the contemporary aspect of her critique, highlighting how discourse has evolved in the last twenty years to raise the prestige accorded to mothers and motherhood. Her most stringent critique is aimed at journalists who have altered the perspectives from which they write. She quotes writers from reputable newspapers who write, for example, about "le papa en moi" ("the daddy in me") (Joubert 72) in a critique of journalists who used to concentrate upon political arguments but who now rely upon their status as parents in order to forge connections with their readers. In Joubert's characteristically caustic tone, she targets female journalists in particular. She cites several examples of women who write about their family circumstances in order to gain legitimacy for their writing. Well-known journalist for *La Presse* Marie-Claude Lotie is quoted at length, including attestations such as "comme toutes les mères du Québec, j'imagine" ("like all mothers in Québec, I imagine") (73), to which Joubert retorts, "[L]a journaliste se réclame de son *humanité*: elle est mère bien avant d'être reporter; cela fait plaisir au public" ("[T]he journalist emphasizes her *humanity*: she is a mother first and a reporter second; readers like that") (73). Joubert's implicit critique is that contemporary representations concentrate on the perceived centrality of motherhood to female identity and exclude all nonmothers, both voluntary and involuntary, in Québec. Joubert thus deftly counters the charge of selfishness aimed at nonmothers with evidence of exclusion, ignorance, and egotism from mothers themselves.

Overall, then, Joubert's text constitutes a highly crafted critique of pronatalist discourse in Québec that is nonconformist in both its style and its content. Its unsubtle blend of humor and research sets it apart from standard academic work and widens the audience that it will hopefully reach. The self-deprecating tone wards off harsh critique or dismissal, as Joubert is clearly aware of the precariousness of her position and anticipates the backlash against her arguments. She shows that it is still deemed inappropriate to discuss such unimportant things as motherhood or personal matters in academic discourse, yet her text underscores the need for such discussion both by mothers and by nonmothers. The way in which she specifically targets the negative stereotypes to which the voluntarily childless are subjected is a careful rebuttal to pronatalist discourse both in Québec and beyond. She testifies to a commitment to the collective throughout the text through her reflections on her interactions with female students and on her concern over the damaging consequences of pronatalist messages for Québécois society. This passionate call for action is penned by an individual on behalf of a collective, therefore, and is anything but selfish. Joubert's courageous text alters the lens in which nonmothering can be interpreted and changes the place of voluntary childlessness in literature: from fiction to autobiography, from sensation to critique, and from deviant to normal. Joubert's impassioned critique highlights that nonmothers are not necessarily horrible, that women who have been forced to be mothers can become horrible, and that women may decide perfectly reasonably not to become a mother because they suspect that they would be a horrible one.

NOTES

1. Margaret Movius explains the history of the term "childfree" in "Voluntary Childlessness, the Ultimate Decision," tracing how it was originally intended as a way of asserting childlessness as a choice at a time when contraceptives such as the pill were widely available for the first time.

2. "A bit of me is missing. I was born, I am living, and I will have lived deprived of one of the most subtle and mysterious parts of female mechanics: the desire for motherhood. I do not have a child, have never wanted one. . . . Every morning, I count myself lucky; every morning, I am grateful. But here we are: for some time, everything around me has been pointing to a crack in this picture that is too good to be true. . . . In short, I am under the impression that I am perfectly fine, but I am really in a terrible state." (All translations are my own.)

3. "Three very different pregnancies, one of which, if not ectopic, then at least utopian, so to speak, that I accentuated by arriving at Easter at the family home with a pillow under my jumper and with my hands on my hips. The baby is almost here, I said, and it keeps me up at night. . . . And while everybody was in raptures over the babies, a jury was attentively scrutinising every idiosyncrasy of my little one."

4. "By making motherhood glamorous, or for those who do not have the means, at least making it cool, women are successfully convinced that they are *sexier* in their role as mothers, that they too can be a *yummy mummy*, and that raising children is the easiest thing in the world. The proof: stars have tons of them without putting on a pound!"

WORKS CITED

André, Jacques, and Catherine Chabert, eds. *Désirs d'enfant*. Presses Universitaires de France, 2009.

Badinter, Elisabeth. *L'amour en plus: Histoire de l'amour maternel (XVIIᵉ–XXᵉ siècle)*. Flammarion, 1980.

———. *Mother Love: Myth and Reality; Motherhood in Modern History*. Macmillan, 1981.

Chancey, Laurie, and Susan A. Dumais. "Voluntary Childlessness in Marriage and Family Textbooks, 1950–2000." *Journal of Family History*, vol. 34, no. 2, 2009, pp. 206–23.

Chapsal, Madeleine. *La femme sans*. Fayard, 2001.

Daum, Meghan, ed. *Selfish, Shallow, and Self-Absorbed: Sixteen Writers on the Decision Not to Have Kids*. Picador, 2015.

Debest, Charlotte. *Le choix d'une vie sans enfant*. Presses Universitaires de Rennes, 2015.

Defago, Nicki. *Childfree and Loving It!* Matrix Digital Publishing, 2007.

Duparc, François, and Martine Pichon, eds. *Les nouvelles maternités au creux du divan*. In Press, 2009.

Edwards, Natalie. "Obliged to Sympathise: Infanticide in *Il y a longtemps que je t'aime* and *A perdre la raison*." *Australian Journal of French Studies*, vol. 52, no. 2, 2015, pp. 174–87.

———. *Voicing Voluntary Childlessness: Narratives of Non-mothering in French*. Peter Lang, 2016.

Gilbert, Paula Ruth. *Violence and the Female Imagination: Quebec's Women Writers Reframe Gender in North American Cultures*. McGill-Queen's University Press, 2006.

Gillespie, Rosemary. "Childfree and Feminine: Understanding the Gender Identity of Voluntarily Childless Women." *Gender & Society*, vol. 17, 2003, pp. 122–36.

Hirsch, Marianne. *The Mother/Daughter Plot: Narrative, Psychoanalysis, Feminism*. Indiana University Press, 1989.

Hodell, Courtney. "Babes in the Wood." *Selfish, Shallow, and Self-Absorbed: Sixteen Writers on the Decision Not to Have Kids*, edited by Meghan Daum, Picador, 2015, pp. 11–30.

Hughes, Aralyn. *Kid Me Not: An Anthology by Child-Free Women of the '60s Now in Their 60s*. Violet Crown Publishers, 2014.

Jacob, Suzanne. *L'obéissance*. Les Éditions du Boreal, 1991.

Joubert, Lucie. *L'envers du landau: Regard extérieur sur la maternité et ses débordements.* Triptyques, 2005.

Kelly, Maura. "Women's Voluntary Childlessness: A Radical Rejection of Motherhood?" *Women's Studies Quarterly*, vol. 37, no. 3–4, 2009, pp. 157–72.

Knibiehler, Yvonne. *La révolution maternelle depuis 1945.* Perrin, 1997.

Knibiehler, Yvonne, and Catherine Fouquet. *L'histoire des mères du moyen âge à nos jours.* Montalba, 1980.

Lê, Linda. *À l'enfant que je n'aurai pas.* NiL, 2011.

Miller, Nancy K. *Getting Personal: Feminist Occasions and Other Autobiographical Acts.* Routledge, 1991.

Morrell, Carolyn. *Unwomanly Conduct: The Challenges of Intentional Childlessness.* Routledge, 1994.

Motte, Warren. "I, Me." *Contemporary French and Francophone Studies*, vol. 18, no. 2, 2014, pp. 184–90.

Movius, Margaret. "Voluntary Childlessness, the Ultimate Decision." *Family Coordinator*, vol. 25, no. 1, 1976, pp. 57–63.

Notkin, Melanie. *Otherhood: Modern Women Finding a New Kind of Happiness.* Seal Press, 2015.

Rodgers, Julie. "On the Margins of Motherhood: Choosing to Be Child-Free in Lucie Joubert's *L'Envers du landau.*" *Women: A Cultural Review*, vol. 29, no. 1, 2018, pp. 75–96.

Sandler, Lauren. "The Childfree Life: When Having It All Means Not Having Children." *Time*, 12 Aug. 2013, http://content.time.com/time/subscriber/article/0,33009,2148636,00.html.

Sautière, Jane. *Nullipare.* Verticales/Gallimard, 2008.

Tilmant, Isabelle. *Ces femmes qui n'ont pas d'enfants: La découverte d'une autre fécondité.* De Boeck, 2010.

Vallée, Edith. *Pas d'enfant, dit-elle: Les refus de la maternité.* Imago, 2005.

Veevers, Jean E. *Childless by Choice.* Butterworths, 1980.

6

Voicing Shame

From Fiction to Confession in the Work of Marguerite Andersen

LUCIE HOTTE AND ARIANE BRUN DEL RE

Nearly every mother has at one time or another felt unequal to her task. This feeling of being a bad mother surfaces whenever a woman is unable to meet society's expectations of her as a mother. Indeed, since the eighteenth century, our relationship to motherhood has evolved (see Badinter) and has led to the romanticization of motherhood, which "has divided mothers into the categories of either the naturally good or pathologically bad. This has meant that mothers felt an exaggerated guilt over the slightest feeling of aggression or impulse toward violence against their children" (Lachance Adams 12).

Although loving and devoted to their children, mothers must nevertheless consider their own needs. The tension between the needs of their children and their own has resulted in what many researchers—psychologists and philosophers alike—call "maternal ambivalence," that is, "mothers' simultaneous desires to nurture and violently reject their children" (Lachance Adams 4). While it is true that not all mothers will violently reject their children, it is nonetheless a fact that this feeling of ambivalence, which "results from the mother's efforts to achieve both intimacy and separation in relation to their children" is more common than most women would dare confess (4). How might one express the shame and guilt that haunt women who embrace their own needs to the real or imagined detriment of their children's well-being?

The work of Franco-Ontarian writer Marguerite Andersen, inspired by her own life, seeks a way to express this shame and guilt.[1] These two emotions, which are the driving force behind her work, have various origins: Nazism and her German citizenship, her unfettered sexuality, and her relationships to her mother and to her children. The latter source of shame will be the subject of our analysis of the literary genres Andersen uses. We will begin with an introduction to Andersen's work and her use of different literary genres, from her first novel, *De mémoire de femme* (1982), subtitled *Récit en partie autobiographique*, to her most recent, *La mauvaise mère* (2013), labeled as "confessions."[2] We argue that this progression from fiction to confession allows the writer to finally declare her failings as a mother. To support this claim, we will analyze the ways in which she recounts her negligence toward her children, especially her sons. This literary analysis will reveal her self-imposed inability to see her performance of motherhood as equal to that of her mother's. Writing thus becomes a means to confess, to seek exoneration, and to do penance.

A Woman and Literary Genres

In her 1997 article on Andersen's second literary piece, *L'autrement pareille*, Katherine Lagrandeur argued that Andersen had chosen distinct genres for her first two books—the first a novel of autobiographical inspiration and the second of poetic prose—"comme si [elle] avait eu besoin de plus d'un genre pour bien faire le tour de son sujet" ("as though [she] had needed more than one genre to address the topic completely") (92). Lagrandeur's insight has since turned out to be accurate. Indeed, Andersen's writing process, from her first "partly autobiographical narrative" to her most recent "confessions," inspired her to rely on multiple literary genres. Of the thirteen nonacademic works she authored, seven are clearly inspired by her own life.[3] In these books, Andersen recalls identical episodes of her life, adding details and modifying others, so that the reader experiences a multidimensional account of these memorable events. Her characters also change names from one book to another: the sons, for instance, are called Dominique and Claude in *De mémoire de femme*, then Christian and Marcel in *Parallèles*, Sébastien and Bertrand in *La vie devant elles*, and Michel and Martin in *Le figuier sur le toit* and *La mauvaise mère*. Each book is labeled as a distinct genre: *De mémoire de femme* bears the notations "partly autobiographical narrative" and "novel"; *L'autrement pareille* is listed as "poetic prose" in the author's subsequent publications; and *Bleu sur blanc* is characterized as "poetic narrative" or "poetic prose."[4] Other examples include *Parallèles*, a "documentary fiction" according to the title page but a "novel" according to the book cover; *Le figuier sur le toit* and *La vie devant elles*, both identified as "novels" and "narratives"; and, finally, *La mauvaise mère*, labeled as "confessions." These labels illustrate discomfort with the truth and the telling of "true" or "lived" stories, as well as a constant desire to explicitly affirm the veracity of the story.[5]

From one book to another, the author seems to be increasingly at ease speaking with her autobiographical voice and addressing the shameful origins of her writing in a clearer and clearer manner. Of her evident shame at being German, Michel Lord remarks: "[L]e pays et le paysage familier sont devenus après les crimes nazis le symbole absolu de l'Altérité maléfique même, une altérité rendue encore plus insupportable par le fait que le pays a été l'objet d'un amour intense. La honte du sujet pour cet objet maintenant tenu à distance est si intense qu'elle ne cesse de hanter sa psyché souffrante. Pâtir incessamment devient alors le lot de Marguerite Andersen et de tous ses alter ego, eux-mêmes autres dans un monde où le pays d'origine est devenu objet de rejet" (116).[6] Yet the most pernicious shame, which only explicitly appears in her most recent work, is that of having been a "bad mother."

In her first "novel," not yet able to reveal herself, Marguerite Andersen oscillates between fiction and truth. She recounts bits of her life under the cover of fiction.[7] The similarities between the protagonist, Anne Grimm (whose name alludes to the Brothers Grimm and therefore to another storyteller with whom she shares a last name, Hans Christian Andersen), and the author are numerous. Both are of German origin, grew up under Hitler's regime during World War II, were married three times, had three children, lived on three continents (Europe, Africa, North America), and spoke three languages (German, French, and English). The narrative structure testifies to her reluctance to speak, as shown by her use of multiple narrative voices and viewpoints.

The advantage of the partly autobiographical narrative lies in the ability to speak without taking full responsibility for what is said. The same goes for poetic prose or poetic narratives, whose fragmented and allusive forms succeed in evoking scenes, emotions, and moments through silence rather than speech. Marguerite Andersen establishes what Johanne Melançon coined "un pacte de sincérité" ("a sincerity pact") (144). Andersen thus uses poetic prose to allow her to speak and not speak, to reveal while hiding, and "se dire . . . peut-être même avec plus de 'vérité' qu'une autobiographie parce que plus près des émotions" ("to express herself . . . with possibly even more 'truth' than an autobiographical work, as it is more in touch with emotions") (Melançon 154). *Parallèles: fiction documentaire* and *Le figuier sur le toit* similarly demonstrate ambivalence between fiction and reality, revealing and covering, fiction and documentary.

Each of her works arises from a different writing project presented by Andersen's alter egos. Most often, she is taking stock of her life without telling everything. In *De mémoire de femme*, Anne immediately notes: "Je ferai un tri, je ne noterai pas n'importe quoi, mais seulement ce que j'ai vécu de plus valable" ("I will sort through. I will not record just anything, but only the most valuable of what I've lived") (26). This will to testify to personal experiences and to revisit the significant stages of her life is emblematic of Andersen's work. *L'autrement pareille* emerges from the painful void she experienced when her grown daughter left her. "Adultement" ("Adulting") (62), as the narrator calls it, is described as a second, more painful childbirth. Absence, as Lagrandeur points out, is at the heart of the writing process:

C'est l'absence qui parle le plus fort tout au long de ce livre laconique: absence de ponctuation à certains endroits, absence de verbes à d'autres, et surtout (ce dernier phénomène parcourt paradoxalement l'ensemble du livre) absence de texte. . . . Aussi la narratrice tisse-t-elle des espaces, des vides, des silences dans le même geste par lequel elle tente de créer quelque chose de tangible, ou plutôt, c'est grâce au silence que la narratrice communique avec l'Autre. C'est peut-être la page la plus brève qui en dit le plus long à ce sujet: "Je suis nue et j'écris." (94)[8]

The same applies to *Bleu sur blanc*, which serves to "relive" (8) and "célébrer ce qui reste en [elle], aujourd'hui, de la Tunisie" ("celebrate what is left within [her], today, of Tunisia") (7), where she spent seven years of her life (1946–53) and gave birth to her two sons. However, the book is presented as incomplete: "Pourtant je n'ai pas tout dit. Il me semble que moi, mon corps, tout mon être est secrètement imbibé de mes années tunisiennes. Je peux en parler, mais pas pendant très longtemps" ("Yet, I have not said it all. It seems that I, my body, my whole being is secretly soaked in my Tunisian years. I can speak of it, but not for long") (79). In *Parallèles*, writing also facilitates the reliving of the past of a deceased friend. Nevertheless, the author decides to tell all, even if she must imagine what she does not know:

> C'est au moment des funérailles que j'ai pris la décision de conter un jour l'histoire de Lucienne. Puis l'idée me vint de mêler ma vie à la sienne, pour ne pas la laisser seule; elle avait peur de la solitude. Et parce que je ne sais pas écrire sans m'impliquer. Par vanité ? Par un désir de participation et de contrôle ? Je ne sais pas. En tout cas, ce livre sera à la fois document et fiction, invention, biographie et autobiographie. . . .
>
> Deux personnages plus ou moins fictifs, leurs vies revues et corrigées, complétées. (10–11)[9]

Le figuier sur le toit further acknowledges its link to shame and guilt, which might explain the author's decision to return to the "novel," even if the protagonist shares her name: "Un jour, se dit Marguerite, je m'y prendrai. Je veux y voir clair, une fois pour toutes. J'irai visiter mes origines, examiner les actions de mes ancêtres, me laver, si nécessaire, non, me repentir de leur culpabilité si jamais il y en a. La dire dans un livre" (30).[10]

It is, however, in *La mauvaise mère* that this link becomes explicit. From the outset, the narrator explains to her son that she was a bad mother:

> —Michel, laisse-moi parler, que je te le dise, que je te le montre, tu verras que j'ai raison, ne m'interromps pas, j'ai besoin de confesser mes erreurs, mes regrets, d'y regarder de près, il faut que je passe par cette porte étroite, je te jure qu'après on n'en parlera plus. Je sais, vous voulez croire que la vie est toujours plaisante, les familles nucléaires, comme on dit, heureuses, les enfants

intelligents, et en bonne santé, le monde, presque parfait . . . et toutes les mères, bonnes . . . (9–10)[11]

Later on in the conversation, Marguerite clarifies the objectives of her writing project:

—Cette fois-ci, je ne m'attarde pas à raconter des détails historiques. Il s'agit d'émotions plus ou moins floues, de faits réduits à leur plus simple expression. En choisissant toujours le plus sensible. Comme si je prenais des notes. Poésie et prose . . . Avec ou sans ponctuation . . .

—. . . un exercice de style?

—Ah non!

—Une nouvelle méthode d'autotorture?

—Non plus.

—Quoi alors?

—Une sorte de quête plutôt . . . Comme tous mes livres. Comme beaucoup de.

—Quête de la transparence?

—Tâtonnements . . . Les mots qui manquent . . . Les mots qu'on n'a pas dits . . . (MM 11)[12]

Thus, from one book to another, Andersen moves away from fiction and chooses literary genres (narrative, confession) that align more with autobiography. This mechanism proves necessary to expiate her wrongdoings. For her confessions to be effective, she cannot hide behind the veil of fiction. She wants to acknowledge her wrongdoings. As far as one can tell, this is likely the reason why the characters' names in her later novels, although fictional, tend to remain unchanged.

A Woman and Her Mother

Marguerite Andersen's concerns with regard to motherhood and women's conditions lie at the heart of her first scholarly work, *Mother Was Not a Person* (1972).[13] Such a title, which evokes Canada's Persons Case, might echo her own life—at the time, she was already a mother of three.[14] However, the title might also echo her own mother's life, whose fictional names are Marthe, Martha, or Maria.[15] Referred to as "Ma" "[pour] éviter d'évoquer la

Marthe du Nouveau Testament, soumise et bonne menagère" ("[to] avoid the reference to Martha from the New Testament, the submissive, good housewife") (FT 20–21), the character is nevertheless depicted as the ideal mother, though only minimally emancipated.[16] In *Le figuier sur le toit*, the narrator describes her mother as an "authentique Mère Courage, capable de soutenir les autres sans jamais se plaindre, sans jamais montrer les effets du stress qu'elle a dû ressentir" ("true Mother Courage, able to support others without ever complaining, without ever revealing the effects of stress on what she must have felt") (205). Because she is so devoted to her family, she appears to find fulfillment only in motherhood. The narrator thus wonders why her mother never joined feminist groups and concludes that she must have lacked confidence: "C'est aussi qu'elle se croit femme sans qualités et surtout sans savoir" ("She thinks herself a woman of no qualities, and above all of no knowledge") (FT 133). The narrator also concludes that her mother was overwhelmed by her duties as mother, wife, and housewife:

> [E]lle devient la femme d'un homme très occupé qui s'attend à ce qu'elle prenne la responsabilité du reste. Ce reste: un enfant qui demande qu'on s'occupe de lui, un mari qui veut la même chose, un deuxième enfant, des commissions à faire, des repas à préparer, un appartement à entretenir—avec l'aide d'une bonne, mais quand même—, de la lessive à laver, rincer et à faire sécher, du linge à repasser, tant de chemises, de caleçons, de mouchoirs, de chemises de nuit, de nappes et de serviettes de table, sans mentionner les draps et les taies d'oreiller, les serviettes de bain et les torchons de cuisine. . . . Comment une femme, même si elle a une bonne, peut-elle prendre soin de tout cela et de tout ce qui a été omis sur cette liste? (FT 136, see also 133)[17]

When Ma attempts to confront her father about his Nazi leanings, he chastises her and blames her emotion on her "cœur de femme" ("woman's heart") (FT 146). While she manages to take a few political stands, such as shopping in Jewish-owned stores (FT 146), listening to the forbidden BBC radio (FT 234), and refusing to allow her daughter to walk around holding a Nazi flag (DMF 84), she only ever does so in her capacity as mother and housewife, her priorities. As for the narrator, she plans an altogether different future for herself, which will come true thanks to her mother's help.

All the texts selected for this analysis show the mother's dedication to her daughters even when they have become adults and, in turn, mothers. She prepares her youngest daughter's wedding trousseau (DMF 93–94). When the couple divorces, she coordinates everything so that her daughter can join her (DMF 117–18). During the war, she would move heaven and earth to feed her family (DMF 119–20; FT 234). When Marguerite lives in Tunisia with her second husband, Ma comes to her rescue: aware that her daughter is unhappy, she sends her a plane ticket for London, where the rest of the family resides (MM 37 / BM 29; P 133; DMF 126).[18] Some years later, Ma even goes to Tunis to support her daughter through the delivery of her second son (DMF 44; FT 244). She then takes care of the children to allow her daughter to go to school (DMF 146; BSB 31; FT 244). Later on, she provides her with contraceptives to avoid another pregnancy (P 144).[19] Ma is not only a good mother but also a good grandmother. Her behavior toward her grandchildren is just as irreproachable: "La grand-mère allemande, Marthe, était belle et douce. Elle ne donnait pas de coups ni ne prononçait de menaces" ("The German grandmother, Marthe, was beautiful and gentle. She never hit nor did she threaten anyone") (LVD 29).

Faced with such devotion, Marguerite, the character, feels like a bad daughter because she was unable to give back to her mother as much as she received. Guilt gnaws her to the bone so much so that it is found in every text where the mother appears. It usually appears after the announcement of her mother's death, when the narrator, who lives in Canada, prepares to move to Ethiopia. In *De mémoire de femme*, the narrator blames herself for not going to her mother's bedside:

> Ma mère se meurt dans une ville que je ne connais pas, je n'irai pas au cimetière, je pleure dans la pénombre d'un cinéma où Amédée m'a amenée parce qu'il ne veut pas voir le spectacle de mes larmes. Ma mère n'existe plus, la mer Baltique a chaviré, je ne verrai plus ni l'une ni l'autre, . . . je ne me suis pas assez occupée d'elle, je ne lui ai pas écrit assez souvent, je ne lui ai pas porté secours, c'est à contrecœur que je l'ai accompagnée dans ses promenades sans espoir, au temps de sa paralysie, je suis au cinéma et non au cimetière, je ne peux plus rien pour elle, j'aurais dû lui dire combien je l'aimais . . . (303)[20]

In *Parallèles*, the narrator feels particularly guilty for her frivolity and selfishness:

Mais ma mère est morte sans que j'aie pu me déculpabiliser de ce que je lui ai fait. Ah non, je ne me dis pas matricide, mais il reste que, quand ma mère malade, paralysée, avait besoin de moi, je n'ai pas sacrifié ma propre vie, non, je suis partie au Canada avec mes fils, j'ai pris des amants, fait des études, et n'ai pas assez souvent écrit à ma mère qui se lamentait de ce manque d'amour. . . . Égoïste . . . (216)[21]

Neither confession in writing nor the passing of time allows the narrator to be at peace with herself. Fifty years after her mother's death, she still wishes she had been at her bedside: "Et qui l'a soutenue à son tour? . . . Où étais-je à l'époque? Où était Eva? Nous étions toutes les deux au Canada, pendant que Mère Courage se désespérait à Berlin devant son corps épuisé lui faisant défaut" ("And when it was her turn, who supported her? Where was I at that time? Where was Eva? We were both in Canada, while Mother Courage despaired in Berlin, her exhausted body failing her") (FT 205).

Finally, in *La mauvaise mère*, the narrator tries to justify her absence yet fails to find valid reasons to stop feeling guilty:

De plus en plus paralysée, Marthe se meurt à Berlin,
je devrais y aller, tout de suite, mais ne sais pas
comment faire pour inscrire cette obligation non,
cette nécessité, ce désir à la liste des obligations,
enseigner, examens de fin d'année à préparer et à
corriger, bulletins de notes à écrire, le déménagement
de Martin à organiser, notre départ pour l'Afrique . . .
Égoïste, pragmatique, je ne cours pas vers ma mère,
n'entre pas dans sa chambre d'hôpital, ne lui tiens pas
la main, ne vis pas la mort de celle qui m'a toujours
secourue.
Marthe est morte.
Je sanglote. (136)[22]

As far as Marthe/Martha/Maria is concerned, the narrator feels not only like a bad daughter but also like a bad mother. In *The New Don't Blame Mother*, Paula J. Caplan shows how the roles of mother and daughter are intimately bound by the myth of the nurturing mother: "A mother is supposed to train her daughter to be a nurturer, in accordance with the nurturance myth. She believes the myth that a perfect daughter is the measure of a good mother: what more tempting place to begin that by training her daughter to take care of her mother, her closest companion? . . . A daughter who takes good care of her mother will be well prepared to fit the ideal: a woman who can nurture her husband and sons" (81).

Following this logic, a bad daughter is inevitably a bad mother. Andersen herself perpetuates this discourse:

> Fille minable.
> J'ai perdu ma mère,
> un fils en France
> un autre au Canada
> moi à la dérive
> courant l'aventure . . . (MM 137; see also DMF 343)[23]

If she feels inept to take care of her sons, it is always in relation and comparison to her mother's maternal abilities. In *La mauvaise mère*, recounting the delivery of her second son, which Ma attended, she writes: "Marthe, la bonne mère, l'excellente mère venue / comme elle l'avait promis, me tient la main" (41) ("Martha, the good mother, the excellent mother, who has / come as she promised, holds me by the hand" [BM 33]). Yet she uses much harsher words to describe herself on the previous page: "Moi, mère irréfléchie, écervelée" (MM 40) ("Me, the thoughtless and featherbrained mother" [BM 32]). This self-punishing comment only serves to blame herself. By constantly depicting Ma as a perfect model of motherhood and thus inviting a comparison between the two individuals, Andersen forces the reader to see the narrator as nothing but a bad mother.

A Woman as Bad Mother

The mother figure looms over the entirety of Andersen's oeuvre, since she is the one who encouraged her to learn French, which became her adopted language, her writing language. She is also the model of motherhood that the narrators use to assess their lives, in particular, the ways they behaved with their own children. Andersen's alter egos do not, at first, wish to become mothers. There are, at times, references to imagined abortions (DMF 135; P 126; MM 17 / BM 9), if not to real abortions (P 145; MM 108 / BM 100). These alter egos became pregnant either out of wedlock or after submitting to a violent husband, only to be obliged to live with him again (P 134; MM 39–40 / BM 31–32). The fear of motherhood haunts them constantly, all the more given their inability to prevent pregnancies (P 144). Only the daughter is desired and planned (DMF 304; MM 144–45 / BM 137–38). The narrator even calls her "l'enfant du désir" ("the child of desire") (DMF 306). As such, although Marguerite brings up her wrongdoings toward her daughter in *La mauvaise mère*, her shame and guilt arise for the most part from her relationship with her two sons.

Three elements contribute to her feeling like a bad mother. First, it comes from the disgust that she feels toward herself. In Tunisia, as a battered woman, she has no self-esteem and sees herself as an abject being:

> Puis la violence.
> Les coups.
> Les insultes.
> —Salope! Putain! Putain de boche!
> Se taire. Ne pas pleurer. Ne pas gémir. Ne pas réveiller les enfants.
> La honte. La honte d'être si faible, si lâche, d'être une femme battue.
> Se sauver? Mais où? Pour dire?
> —Il m'a battue . . .
> À qui le dire?
> —Qu'est-ce que c'est, maman? Cette tache bleue sur ton visage?
> —Je me suis cognée, t'en fais pas, mon chou. Ce n'est pas grave.
> Faible. Lâche. Incapable d'agir. (MM 69–70)[24]

In this context, the narrator can't help but have mixed feelings for her children. If it weren't for them, she would certainly leave. But the texts never evoke this reality in an explicit manner. In fact, the narrators—even in *Bleu sur blanc*—refuse to even address the question. In the introduction, titled

"Conversation avec É. . . , ma petite-fille," Andersen says that she will not speak of the pain she experienced in Tunisia.

Usually, the narrators focus instead on their efforts to be good mothers and wives (see P 143–44). In this instance, however, the violence Andersen endured prevented her from being fully dedicated to her children:

Il faut juste que je sois là
présente
disponible
à tout moment.
Or, il y a un vide quelque part.
Mes enfants, le soleil, la mer, et mille petites choses, je les aime,
mais quelque part
tout près il y a ce vide
qui brûle, fait mal, assourdit, aveugle, insensibilise.
Vide où?
Vide de quoi?
Je lis pour le meubler. Un livre après l'autre.
Pêle-mêle . . .
Mme Bovary n'aime pas trop sa fille.
Est-ce possible de ne pas aimer ses enfants? (MM 73–74)[25]

In *La mauvaise mère*, the narrator reflects on the shame she felt from her inability to defend her sons, especially when her husband beats the one with a learning disability:

Une bonne mère, n'aurait-elle pas protégé son fils?
Ai-je peur pour moi-même?
Une bonne mère, n'aurait-elle pas su faire comprendre à son fils que l'école
     est une chose utile et nécessaire?
Suis-je une mère suffisamment bonne quand, les coups et les cris ayant cessé,
     je prends l'enfant dans mes bras?[26] Que je lui essuie les joues des larmes
     douloureuses? Caresse doucement ses fesses meurtries?
Ou bien suis-je tout simplement lâche?
J'aurais dû obéir à ses sanglots, à ce cri

—Maman !
saisir la ceinture, me jeter dans la bataille, hurler
—Arrête!
à l'homme violent
défendre mon fils. (MM 56–57)[27]

Shame also emerges from a second, more pernicious source. Sick and defeated, the narrator of several texts resorts to asking for help from her parents. Her mother sends her a plane ticket so she can fly to Germany and receive medical attention. Just one ticket. She thus leaves her children behind with their father and goes back to her parents. In this instant, as she abandons her children, she comes to fully identify as a bad mother. In *Parallèles*, Andersen writes:

Si les morts ne me reprochent rien, je m'en charge très bien moi-même. Ainsi, je ressens quelquefois des bouffées de chaleur qui ne sont point provoquées par la ménopause depuis longtemps passée. Non, la culpabilité, voilà ce que c'est. Les maris quittés, les fils temporairement abandonnés, la mère, elle surtout.

Car il fallait quitter les maris qui me brimaient, abandonner les enfants que le Nord-Africain et le manque d'argent m'interdisaient d'emmener. D'ailleurs je les ai récupérés peu après. Mais ma mère est morte sans que j'aie pu me déculpabiliser de ce que je lui ai fait. (P 215–16)[28]

Although she tries to convince herself that she is not so bad after all because she regained custody of her children, she does not quite succeed, so much so that this episode comes back in several of her texts:

Bref, il y a eu une grande dispute, puis, tout à coup, j'ai dit que je partais. Bagarre. Toute une nuit, il m'a battue, il voulait me prendre mon passeport que j'avais caché.

Télégramme à ma mère, miracle, elle m'envoie un billet d'avion. Comment fait-elle, où trouve-t-elle l'argent? *Un* billet. Je dois laisser les enfants ici.

1954. Berlin. Les enfants sont avec moi, grâce aux événements politiques. La lutte des Tunisiens pour l'indépendance de leur pays a fait peur à leur père, du coup il m'a envoyé les petits. Il faut absolument que je me trouve un appartement, nous ne pouvons pas rester à l'infini avec mes parents. (P 145)[29]

J'ai quitté la Tunisie en 1953. Sans les enfants que leur père gardait en otage. Épuisée par un mariage qui ressemblait à un emprisonnement, femme battue incapable de me défendre sur place, j'ai été cherché à Berlin l'aide de mes parents.

C'est au moment de l'Indépendance qu'on m'a permis de reprendre mes fils, en décembre 1955, alors que leur père devenait, à son tour, une personne déplacée. (BSB 75)[30]

Plus tard—un an, deux ans, Sébastien Boutier ne veut pas faire le compte—, la mère absente est venue les chercher. C'était au moment des vacances de Noël. Elle est arrivée en avion, avec un sapin attaché à sa valise. Il faut être folle pour faire des choses pareilles. Dans la valise, il y avait de quoi le décorer. Des biscuits de Noël, en forme d'étoiles, de lunes et de cœurs. Des bougies. Ils ont eu du mal à le monter, à le mettre debout, finalement un gros vase en cuivre a fait l'affaire. Elle était jolie, la chambre d'hôtel. Ils ont même chanté des chansons de Noël en allemand: Oh Tannenbaum, oh Tannenbaum … "Je vous emmène en Allemagne, chantait-elle, victorieuse. À Berlin. Chez moi." Le père semblait content de se débarrasser des deux garçons. C'était l'époque de l'indépendance de la Tunisie et il ne savait pas encore où il allait être muté. (LVD 28)[31]

La mauvaise mère opens on this traumatic episode:

—Ah non, Marguerite, vraiment, tu te tracasses pour rien. Pourquoi faut-il tout à coup proclamer que nous avons souffert de cette vie … comment dirais-je … mouvementée que tu nous as fait mener?

—Je vous ai fait vivre dans six pays, sur trois continents. Toi, tu aimais …

—On a vu du pays.

—Disons-le carrément:

À un moment, je vous ai abandonnés. Laissés. Et vous étiez petits.

—Nous avons survécu.

—Un an et demi. Nous sommes restés séparés pendant un an et demi.

—C'est vrai. Mais, toi, une mauvaise mère? (MM 9)[32]

In addition, Andersen's texts deal with two more scenes of abandonment that affect each of her sons. In *De mémoire de femme* and *La mauvaise mère*, the protagonist, Anne/Marguerite, immigrates to Montréal with her older son, leaving the youngest in France with his father. Indeed, before she leaves for Canada, she agrees to let her sons see their father one last time (MM 98–100 / BM 90–92; DMF 154). However, the father then refuses to let them go:

—Je les garde, m'écrit leur père dès leur arrivée chez
lui, ils ne retourneront pas en Allemagne.
Larmes.
Désespoir.
Colère.
Est-ce possible d'être aussi naïve? (MM 99)[33]

In both instances, Anne/Marguerite manages to reclaim the older son, but the younger son will not join her for several years. On her way to Ethiopia, she stops for a visit and learns that his father beats him, and she decides to take him away (MM 138–39 / BM 131–32; DMF 188). At that moment, the protagonist is thus separated from her other son, who chose to stay in Canada (MM 132–33 / BM 125–26; DMF 186). In *Parallèles*, however, the narrator moves to Montréal with both of her sons (P 152).

For Andersen, the worst crime a mother can commit, other than actually hurting or killing her children, is to abandon them. These occurrences are the primary reasons why she considers herself a "bad mother." There are, of course, other moments when the main character of the book prioritizes her well-being before that of her children, especially when she is in a relationship with Amédée, whom she loves madly and whose desires she satisfies before those of her children. In fact, she rents an apartment with no suitable space for her son (DMF 176; MM 128–29 / BM 121). Once more, subjugated to a man's will, though this time for love, she is so overwhelmed by her own needs and desires that she forgets her son's (see MM 127, 130 / BM 120, 122–23). Recalling these events later in life contributes to the narrator's shame and guilt of having been a bad mother.

Conclusion

Admittedly, the narrators do not depict themselves in an altogether negative manner. They are not genuinely "horrible mothers"; they are simply "bad mothers." Indeed, they enjoy spending time with their children, even in Tunisia, where the husband is violent and forces them to live in poverty (see BSB 45, 52). They do try to be good mothers:

> Je me reprends.
> Me prends en main.
> Je ne veux plus vivre malheureuse.
> Je me couche de bonne heure afin d'être en forme le lendemain,
> me lève tôt, réveille les enfants,
> ils vont à l'école, joyeux, ne manquent de rien.
> Je suis la bonne mère.
> Je cours enseigner, étudier,
> je serai de retour à l'heure où ils rentreront joyeux.
> Je ris avec eux
> de leurs folies
> de leurs bêtises
> de ce qu'ils me racontent.
> Vite, un goûter de fruits, des dattes peut-être, des biscuits.
> Ils s'en vont jouer avec les enfants du quartier puis rentrent dîner.
> Je suis la mère nourricière,
> je les embrasse, ils s'endorment contents. (MM 71)[34]

Yet the feeling of having been a bad mother is overwhelming and is at the heart of Andersen's writing process. Andersen could certainly relate to Annie Ernaux, who explains about her writing: "Le lieu d'où j'écris, qui m'apparaît de plus en plus, c'est la mémoire de la honte" ("The place from where I write, which becomes clearer and clearer, it's the memory of shame") (314). However, unlike Ernaux, she does not engage in "écriture-cilice" ("hair shirt writing"), where writing is used as a means of repentance (see Hotte). Rather, she writes to reveal, to unveil, to confess in order to make room for self-forgiveness. Andersen's work gives priority to "self-blame." Her addresses to her sons and her daughter, even to her granddaughters in *La vie devant elles*, allow her to forgive herself to the extent that they do not hold a grudge. At times, her children do not even remember the wrongdoing for which she blames herself. In fact, as they are portrayed, her children do not seem to be resentful, except for Dominique, in *De mémoire de femme*, who criticizes Amédée's domineering attitude toward her mother.

In the end, Andersen's narratives, her books of accounts and records, turn out to be quite positive:

JAMAIS JE N'AI PENSÉ QUE NOUS NE NOUS AIMIONS PAS

. . . .

Car bien sûr
il y a eu des moments heureux dans notre vie vécue ensemble:
les plages tunisiennes
si blanches
la cueillette de cyclamens
sur le Boukornine
nos marches à travers le Grunewald
les arbres fruitiers dans le jardin de mes parents
la danse sur le gazon glacé de Grand Forks
les fêtes de Noël
la vie joyeuse à Montréal
la révolte des étudiants et des profs à Loyola
la neige
la sloche
et la chaleur de l'été
tous les repas pris
les fruits
les sourires
le vin bu
les voyages en bateau, en train, en voiture et en avion nos rires.
Ce qu'on appelle les petits bonheurs quotidiens . . .
Jamais je n'ai pensé que nous ne nous aimions pas. (MM 178–79)[35]

The writer, however, like her alter egos, struggles to convince herself she is not so bad, as though the confession that unfolds in *La mauvaise mère* failed to fully expiate her sins. Indeed, this book ends with another occurrence of blame: Marguerite blames herself for covering up her daughter's homosexuality instead of supporting her and welcoming her partner into the family (MM 194–96 / BM 190–92). For Andersen to finally achieve peace once and for all, she might benefit from autobiography. The truth that the autobiographical pact demands (see Lejeune) would prevent her from hiding behind the mechanisms of fiction; she would be accountable for her every word. The evolving nature of her works, slowly moving away from fiction, might indicate a step in that direction.

Translation by Loïc Bourdeau and Didier Pilon

NOTES

Loïc Boudreau would like to thank Saphire Wolven for her help in translating parts of this article, as well as her overall input throughout the process.

1. Born in 1924, Andersen grew up in Germany, where she learned French as a child. She moved to Canada in 1958 and received a PhD in French literature from the Université de Montréal in 1965. Andersen eventually settled in Ontario, where she worked as a professor at the University of Guelph. During a sabbatical leave she turned to fiction.

2. In this chapter, English citations come from Donald Winkler's 2016 translation, *The Bad Mother* (BM). For more clarity, we chose to include references to both the original work in French and its English counterpart.

3. In *L'homme-papier*, *La soupe*, and *Conversations dans l'interzone*, the autobiographical ("l'autobiographique," to use Louise Dupré's terminology) is not as obvious and easy to pinpoint. The same goes for Andersen's collections of short stories: *Courts métrages et instantanés* and *Les crus de l'esplanade*. This contribution focuses solely on works in which the autobiographical plays a central role in the narrative structure: *De mémoire de femme* (DMF), *L'autrement pareille* (LP), *Bleu sur blanc* (BSB), *Parallèles* (P), *Le figuier sur le toit* (FT), *La vie devant elles* (LVD), and *La mauvaise mère* (MM). For Dupré, "L'autobiographique . . . renvoie à une matière, à un contenu relatif à l'expérience personnelle que l'auteur cherchera à dissimuler ou, au contraire, à mettre en relief par une stratégie discursive visant à produire des effets référentiels sur le lecteur" ("the autobiographical . . . refers to a matter, a content that pertains to the writer's personal experience, which she or he will attempt to hide, or on the contrary to bring forth, through a discursive strategy aiming at creating referential effects for the reader") (68).

4. The title page includes "poetic prose," but in the "Other Works by This Author" section that appears in *La vie devant elle* and *La mauvaise mère*, it is listed as "poetic narrative."

5. The inscription "novel" in *Le figuier sur le toit* is quite surprising and erroneous. Such an anomaly might, however, be justified by Andersen's temporary change

of publishers. Éditions L'Interligne, which publishes this "novel," organizes its texts by genre. The "Vertiges" collection to which *Le figuier sur le toit* belongs is dedicated to novels.

6. "[T]he country and the familiar landscape have come to symbolize, after Nazi war crimes, the epitome of maleficent Alterity, rendered even more unbearable by the fact that the country was once the object of strong affection. The individual's shame for this now-rejected object is so intense that it ceaselessly haunts her suffering psyche. To suffer thus becomes Andersen's and her alter egos' burden. They too are others in a country where the homeland now instills nothing but rejection."

7. For instance, in *La vie devant elles*, Marguerite tells her granddaughter Ariane how she used to masturbate in the empty Berlin metro. She refers to this event in other works (DMF 241; P 142). She only ever confides in Ariane when the latter insists, first arguing: "Ce ne sont pas des histoires à raconter. On peut mettre des trucs comme ça dans un roman, puis les gens croient que c'est de la fiction" ("These aren't stories to tell. You write things like that in a novel, and people assume that it's fiction") (LVD 142). Fiction gives her the tools to express herself freely.

8. "Throughout this laconic book, absence speaks volumes: the lack of punctuation in certain passages, the lack of verbs in others, and especially the lack of text (which paradoxically run through the entire book).... The narrator weaves spaces, gaps, and silences in the same gesture with which she attempts to create something tangible. Or rather, through her silence, the narrator communicates with the Other. The shortest page perhaps speaks loudest: 'I am naked and I write.'"

9. "It was at the funeral that I decided to recount one day the story of Lucienne. Then it occurred to me to blend my life to hers, so as not to leave her alone; she was so afraid of being lonely. And since I do not know how to write without involving myself. Out of pride? From a willingness to participate or to control? I don't know. At any rate, this book will be document and fiction, invention, biography and autobiography, all at once....

Two characters, more or less fictitious, their lives reviewed and corrected."

10. "One day, thinks Marguerite, I'll give it a shot. I want to make sense of it, once and for all. I'll visit my origins, examine my ancestors' actions, wash myself, if necessary, no, do penance for their guilt, if ever there was some. I'll tell it in a book."

11. "Michel, let me have my say, let me tell you, let me show you. You'll see I'm right—and don't interrupt. I have to admit my mistakes, things I'm sorry for. I have to look them straight in the eye; I have to get through that narrow door. And I promise this will be the last you'll hear of it. I know . . . you want to believe that life's always rosy, with nuclear families, happy families, bright, healthy children, a world that's close to perfect—and all the mothers are good, but—" (BM 1–2).

12. "'This time I'm not going to get bogged down in historical details. It's all about feelings, hard to define, about facts reduced to their simplest expression. And always the most pertinent. As if making notes. Poetry and prose, with or without punctuation—'

    'So . . . a stylistic exercise?'

    'Not at all!'

    'A new form of self-torture?'

    'Not that either.'

    'What then?'

    'More like a quest. Like all my books. Like many [books].'

    'A quest for transparency?'

    'Gropings . . . words that escape me . . . words unsaid—'" (BM 3).

13. Selling six thousand copies across Canada (making it an instant best seller), this book originates from an interdisciplinary class (Women in Modern Society) that Andersen taught at the Loyola College (now part of Concordia University, Montreal).

14. Up until 1929, women were not allowed to sit in Canada's Senate because they were not considered "people" according to the British North America Act (known today as the Constitution Act of 1867), which established the Canadian Confederation. The Persons Case refers to a constitutional case put forward by a group of women, the "Famous Five," who fought for women's rights.

15. In *De mémoire de femme*, the daughter is named Marthe.

16. Ironically, in French, the nickname "Ma" recalls the word *maman*, which in the end prevents the character from escaping her maternal role.

17. "[S]he became the wife of a very busy man who expected her to take care of the rest. This rest: a child who asks what we take care of him, a husband who wants the same, a second child, shopping to do, meals to prepare, an apartment to clean— with the help of a maid, but still—, laundry to wash, rinse and put to dry, clothes to iron, so many shirts, underpants, handkerchiefs, nightdresses, tablecloths, and napkins, without mentioning sheets and pillowcases, bath towels and kitchen towels. . . . How can a woman, even with a maid, take care of all this and everything else that was omitted from this list?"

18. This episode occurs once more in *De mémoire de femme*: the narrator's mother manages to save enough money to fly her and her youngest son, Claude. The oldest son, Dominique, stayed with his father: "Pierre refusait de la laisser partir avec les deux, de crainte qu'elle ne rentre pas" ("Pierre refused to let both of them go, for fear she would not come back") (DMF 141).

19. In *De mémoire de femme*, before her daughter's first marriage, the narrator's mother "résolut de l'envoyer chez le médecin" ("resolved to send her to the doctor") to learn about contraception (DMF 102).

20. "My mother is dying in a city that I don't know, I won't go to the cemetery, I'm crying in the gloomy movie theater where Amédée took me because he doesn't want to see the show of my tears. My mother no longer exists, the Baltic Sea capsized, I'll never see either again. . . . I didn't take care of her enough, I didn't write to her often enough, I didn't help her, I only reluctantly accompanied her on her hopeless walks, in her time of paralysis, I'm at the movie theater, not the cemetery. There's nothing I can do for her now, I should have told her how much I loved her."

21. "My mother died before I could rid myself of my guilt for what I've done to her. Oh no, do not say matricide, yet, while my mother was sick, paralyzed, and needed me, I didn't sacrifice my life, no, I left for Canada with my sons, I had lovers, I studied, and I didn't write often enough to my mother, who lamented this lack of love. . . . Selfish . . ."

22. "Increasingly paralyzed, Martha dies in Berlin. I ought to go,
    right away, but I don't know how to fit this obligation, no,
    this necessity, this desire, into the long list of my obligations:
    teaching, end-of-year exams to prepare and correct, report
    cards to write, Martin's move to organize, our departure for
    Africa . . . A pragmatic egoist, I do not rush to my mother's
    side, I do not enter her hospital room, I do not hold her
    hand, I am not there for the death of the one who was
    always there for me.
    Martha is dead.
    I weep." (BM 129)

23. "Pathetic creature.
    I've lost my mother,
    one son in France,
    another in Canada
    myself adrift
    chasing after adventure . . ." (BM 130; see also DMF 343)

24. "The violence.
    Blows.
    Insults.
    'Bitch! Whore! Fucking Kraut!'
    Say nothing. Don't cry. Don't moan. Don't wake the
    children.
    Shame. Shame at being so weak, so cowardly, of being a
    battered woman.
    Run away? But where? To say?
    'He beat me . . .'

To say it to whom?
'What's that, mama? That blue mark on your face?'
'I bumped into something, don't worry, my love. It's
nothing serious.'
Weak. Cowardly.
Helpless to act." (BM 60–61)

25. "I have to be there
    present
    available
    at all time.
    But there's a void somewhere.
    My children, the sun, the sea, and a hundred little things,
    I like them,
    but somewhere
    very near
    there is this void
    that burns, hurts, deafens, blinds, numbs.
    A void where?
    Empty of what?
    I read to fill it. One book after another.
    Pell-mell . . .
    Madame Bovary doesn't like her daughter very much.
    Is it possible not to like one's children?" (BM 64–65)

26. Marguerite Andersen probably alludes here to D. W. Winnicott's "mère suffisam-
    ment bonne" ("good-enough mother"), to which she also refers in a documentary
    on *La mauvaise mère*. See Alisa Siegel, *Good Enough*, a documentary on Marguerite
    Andersen, *The Sunday Edition*, CBC Radio One, 23 Mar. 2014, http://www.cbc
    .ca/player/AudioMobile/Sunday%2BEdition/ID/2443512448/. According to
    Winnicott, famous British pediatrician and psychoanalyst, "The good-enough
    mother . . . starts off with an almost complete adaptation to her infant's needs,
    and as time proceeds she adapts less and less completely, gradually, according to
    the infant's growing ability to deal with her failure" (15).

27. "Would a good mother not have protected her son?
    Am I afraid for myself?
    Would a good mother not have known how to make her son
    understand that school is a useful and necessary thing?
    Am I a good enough mother when, the blows and cries
    having stopped, I take the child in my arms? When I wipe

his sorrowful tears from his cheek? And gently caress his
bruised bottom?
Or am I simply a coward?
'*Mama!*'
Seize the belt, throw yourself into the fray, scream
'Stop!'
at the violent man.
Defend your child." (BM 48)

28. "If the dead don't blame me, I do it quite well myself. And so, I sometimes feel hot
flashes that aren't symptoms of my long-past menopause. No, it's the guilt. The
husbands I left, the sons I temporarily abandoned, the mother . . . especially her.

   Because I had to leave the husbands who violated me, and abandon the children that the North African and the lack of funds forbade me to take. Besides, I
recovered them soon after. But my mother died before I could rid myself of the
guilt for what I've done to her."

29. "In short, there was a big argument, and, all of a sudden, I said I was leaving. We
fought. He beat me the whole night. He wanted to take my passport that I had
hidden.

   I telegraph my mom and, by some miracle, she sends me a plane ticket. How
does she do it, where does she find the money? *One* ticket. I have to leave the
kids behind.

   1954. Berlin. The kids are with me, thanks to the political events. The Tunisians'
struggle for their country's independence scared their father, so he sent them over.
I absolutely have to find an apartment; we can't stay with my parents forever."

30. "I left Tunisia in 1953. Without the kids that their father held hostage. Exhausted by
a marriage that seemed like imprisonment, a beaten woman incapable of defending
myself on the spot, I went to Berlin to seek my parents' help.

   I regained custody of my sons at the time of Independence, when their father
was also displaced."

31. "Later—one year or two, Sebastien Boutier doesn't want to keep count—the
absent mother came to get them. It was during the Christmas holidays. She came
by plane, a Christmas tree tied to her suitcase. You have to be crazy to do that. The
suitcase carried ornaments. Star-shaped, moon-shaped, and heart-shaped Christmas
cookies. Candles. They had a hard time putting it up, but a huge copper vase did
the trick. The hotel room was nice. They even sang German Christmas songs: Oh
Tannenbaum, oh Tannenbaum . . . 'I'm bringing you to Germany. To Berlin. My
home.' The father seemed pleased to get rid of the two boys. It was during the
Tunisian independence and he didn't know where he would be moved."

32. "'Really Marguerite, you're getting all worked up over nothing. Out of nowhere you're insisting that we've suffered from this—how should I put it—unorthodox life you led us?'

'I made you live in six different countries, on three continents. You liked that, but...'

'We saw the world.'

'Yes, but let's be frank: at one point I abandoned you. I left you. And you were small.'

'We survived.'

'A year and a half. We were separated for a year and a half.'

'That's true. But a bad mother—you?'" (BM 1)

33. "'I'm keeping them,' their father writes me once they've
arrived. 'They'll never go back to Germany.'
Tears.
Despair.
Anger.
How could I have been so naïve?" (BM 91)

34. "I pull myself together.
I take myself in hand.
I don't want to live unhappy.
I go to bed early so as to be in form the next day,
get up early, wake the children,
they go to school, happy, lacking for nothing.
I am the good mother.
I run off to teach, to study,
I'll be back home when, happy, they return.
I laugh with them
at their pranks
at their silliness
at what they tell me.
On the fly,
a snack of fruits, of dates perhaps, of biscuits.
They go out to play with the neighborhood children
and come home for dinner.
I am the nurturing mother,
I kiss them, they go to sleep happy." (BM 62)

35. "NEVER DID I THINK WE'D NOT LOVE EACH OTHER
. . . .
Because of course

there were happy moments in the life we shared:
the Tunisian beaches
so white
Gathering cyclamens
on Mount Boukornine
our walks through the Grunewald
the fruit trees in my parents' garden
dancing on the icy Grand Forks lawn
Christmas celebrations
the joyous life in Montreal
the revolt of students and professors at Loyola
the snow
the slush
and the summer heat
all the meals
fruits
smiles
wine
the boat trips, train trips, car and plane trips
our laughter.
What one calls everyday happiness . . .
Never did I think we'd not love each other." (BM 173–74)

WORKS CITED

Andersen, Margret. *Bleu sur blanc*. Prise de parole, 2000.

———. *Courts métrages et instantanés*. Prise de parole, 1991.

———. *De mémoire de femme: Récit en partie autobiographique*. 2nd ed. L'Interligne, 2002.

———. *Doucement, le bonheur: Roman*. Prise de parole, 2006.

———. *La mauvaise mère*. Prise de parole, 2013.

———. *La soupe*. Prise de parole, 1995.

———. *L'autrement pareille*. Prise de parole, 1984.

———. *La vie devant elles*. Prise de parole, 2011.

———. *Le figuier sur le toit*. L'Interligne, 2008.

———. *Les crus de l'Esplanade: Nouvelles*. Prise de parole, 1998.

———. *L'homme-papier*. Édition du Remue-ménage, 1992.

———, ed. *Mother Was Not a Person*. 2nd ed. Black Rose Books, 1974.

———. *Parallèle: Fiction documentaire*. Prise de parole, 2004.

Andersen, Marguerite, and Paul Savoie. *Conversations dans l'interzone: Roman*. Prise de parole, 1994.

Badinter, Élisabeth. *L'amour en plus: Histoire de l'amour maternel (XVIIᵉ–XXᵉ siècle)*. Flammarion, 1980.

Caplan, Paula J. *The New Don't Blame Mother: Mending the Mother-Daughter Relationship*. Routledge, 2000.

Dupré, Louise. "*Le lièvre de mars*, de Louise Warren: Vers une réalité 'virtuelle.'" *Voix et Images*, vol. 22, no. 1, 1996, pp. 67–77.

Ernaux, Annie. "La honte, manière d'exister, enjeu d'écriture." *Lire, écrire la honte*, edited by Bruno Chaouat, Presses universitaires de Lyon, 2007, pp. 307–19.

Hotte, Lucie. "Retour aux origines: Le discours mémoriel dans trois textes d'Annie Ernaux." *La parole mémorielle des femmes*, edited by Linda Cardinal and Lucie Hotte, Éditions du Remue-Ménage, 2002, pp. 139–55.

Lachance Adams, Sarah. *Mad Mothers, Bad Mothers, & What a Good Mother Would Do: The Ethics of Ambivalence*. Columbia University Press, 2014.

Lagrandeur, Katherine. "*L'autrement pareille* de Marguerite Andersen: (s')écrire (en) silence." *Postures scripturaires dans la littérature franco-ontarienne*, edited by Lucie Hotte and François Ouellet, special issue of *Tangence*, vol. 56, Dec. 1997, pp. 91–101.

Lejeune, Philippe. *Le pacte autobiographique*. Seuil, 1975.

Lord, Michel. "Altérité et dialogisme chez Marguerite Andersen." *Écrire au féminin au Canada français*, edited by Johanne Melançon, Prise de parole, 2013, pp. 105–24.

Melançon, Johanne. "*Bleu sur blanc*: Une écriture au plus près de soi." *Écrire au féminin au Canada français*, edited by Johanne Melançon, Prise de parole, 2013, pp. 141–59.

7

The Transgressive Mother in Nancy Huston's *Bad Girl: Classes de littérature*

SUSAN IRELAND AND PATRICE J. PROULX

> As readers our duty is to go beyond our own limitations and expectations to grasp what is archaically common in these experiences, to acknowledge what is sometimes seen as unacceptable in motherhood and mothering, what is usually deemed unthinkable and thereby untellable, because it violently denies our comforting representation of the good mother.
>
> PASCALE SARDIN

Personal experience and a critical engagement with feminist issues have led Canadian writer Nancy Huston to privilege an exploration of the maternal figure in many of her fictional and nonfictional texts. Themes such as pregnancy, abortion, miscarriage, motherhood, and (pro)creation recur throughout her oeuvre and take a variety of forms, ranging from the rejection of motherhood by the protagonist in *La virevolte* (1994), who leaves her two children in order to pursue her career as a dancer, to the "helicopter" mother in *Lignes de faille* (2006), whose excessive valorization of her role as mother threatens her own identity and that of her child. In similar fashion to the two daughters in *La virevolte*, Huston was abandoned at the age of six by her own mother, who left her family in order to engage more fully in intellectual endeavors rather than limiting herself to the traditional role of "housewife." The significance of this abandonment for Huston's personal and creative life is evident in her assertion that "[q]uatre-vingt-dix pour cent de [son] oeuvre littéraire est contenue dans ce seul après-midi" ("[n]inety percent of [her] literary oeuvre is contained in that one afternoon") (*Bad Girl* 236), that of her mother's departure.

Born in Calgary, Alberta, in 1953, Huston spent her formative years there before moving to the United States, attending high school in New Hampshire and then undertaking French studies at Sarah Lawrence College in New York. Given the opportunity to study in Paris, she moved to France in 1973 and settled there for more than three decades.[1] Indeed, Huston explicitly connects the renunciation of her native tongue to the fact that her English-speaking mother left her family when the author was a young girl: "Donc, en matière de langue maternelle, quand j'avais six ans, elle a disparu. Ma mère. Avec sa langue dans sa bouche" ("So, as far as my native language is concerned, when I was six, it disappeared. My mother. With her tongue/language in her mouth") (*Désirs et réalités* 232). While Huston has often expressed a feeling of indifference or antagonism toward her native land as a means of distancing herself from a painful childhood and from a country she at one time considered lacking a history, she has nevertheless returned repeatedly to North America via her writing, exploring through her textual production what she found difficult to understand and forgive in her mother's actions. Significantly, Canada played a prominent role in *Cantique des plaines* (1993), initially written in English as *Plainsong* (1993), and it also served as part of the geographical setting in *Danse noire* (2013).[2] The creation of other works, most notably the aforementioned *La virevolte*, was cathartic for Huston in the sense that it enabled her to come to terms with the absent mother figure in her life and to reach an understanding vis-à-vis her own loss and the loss of family suffered by her mother.

In this chapter, which centers on Huston's semi-autobiographical *Bad Girl: Classes de littérature* (2014), one of her most recent and most intimate texts, we will examine the violation of the prescribed norms for motherhood in 1950s Canada, focusing in particular on how Huston depicts the cultural and societal pressures that lead a woman to abandon her children, while at the same time positing that her mother was a "pionnière du féminisme" ("pioneer of feminism") (Trapenard). Throughout the text, the recounting of the adult narrator's life as an unborn fetus foregrounds the price that she pays for her mother's transgression: her decision to favor her own intellectual life over societal expectations regarding a woman's role as wife and mother. The text thus provides a compelling illustration of a woman's rebellion against the reality described by Adrienne Rich, who observes that "[i]nstitutionalized motherhood demands of women maternal 'instinct' rather than intelligence, selflessness rather than self-realization, relation to others rather than the creation of self" (42). At the same time, the fragmented nature of the narrative, with its short vignette-like chapters, forcefully conveys the dislocation of the self experienced by the narrator, whose mother's behavior causes her to see herself as the titular "bad girl." The narrator also suggests, however, that the daughter eventually comes to understand that her "mauvaise mère" ("bad mother") (Huston, *Bad Girl* 233) was "en avance sur son temps" ("ahead of her time") (133). Paradoxically, then, the narrator portrays the traumatic experience of being an unwanted child as the impetus behind her coming to writing and as a continuing source of creativity.

This unconventional narrative, in which the narrator speaks to her fetal self during the gestation period, highlights the vulnerability of the undesired, unborn child. The prominent use of the second-person singular and the importance of intertextuality in Huston's work are established in the opening lines of the text, where the narrator first addresses her embryonic self, naming it Dorrit: "*Toi*, c'est toi, Dorrit. Celle qui écrit. Toi à tous les âges, même avant d'avoir un âge, avant d'écrire, avant d'être un soi" ("*You*, it's you, Dorrit. The one who writes. You at every age, even before you have an age, before you write, before you have a self") (*Bad Girl* 11).[3] In this fashion, Huston creates an *autobiographie intrautérine*, an innovative form of life writing that offers an account of the past but presents much of it in the future tense as the narrator relates the story of her family to Dorrit and reveals the formative events that will shape her life and her identity after she leaves the womb. In fact, this narrative is continually grounded in the corporeal; as the narrator reminds us early in the text, "Pour l'instant, tu n'es qu'un petit tas de cellules qui passent leur temps à se diviser c'est-à-dire à se multiplier dans l'utérus d'Alison" ("For the moment, you're just a little cluster of cells that spend their time splitting, multiplying in Alison's uterus") (14). In addition, Huston links her use of the vocative to the all-important missives she received from her mother after she had left the family. As she puts it in *Bad Girl*, "Ses lettres t'aideront à rester en vie, et quand, plus tard, tu te mettras à écrire des livres, la deuxième personne sera toujours celle que tu préfères" ("Her letters will help you stay alive, and when you later begin to write books, the second person will always be your preferred form") (254). Indeed, the format of the narrative gives the textual impression of a letter written to oneself, "un soi-même pour qui tout est encore à venir" ("a self for whom everything is yet to come") (De Balsi 14).

As suggested above, the figures of the transgressive mother (Alison) and the undesired fetus (Dorrit) constitute the center of this intrauterine autobiography. The subversive nature of the mother's actions—her rejection of traditional gender roles—is underscored by the narrator's pejorative delineation of 1950s Canada, which is portrayed as a period when women were expected to return to the "putains de foyer" ("goddamn households") (Huston, *Bad Girl* 134) that many of them had abandoned during World War II, when they came to appreciate a newfound sense of independence outside the home. As the narrator ironically forewarns her unborn self, "Comprends-tu Dorrit, tu vas naître à une époque vraiment nulle" ("Understand, Dorrit, you're going to be born during a truly worthless era") (134). Alison's own mother embodied the sanctioned role of wife and progenitor, which was predicated on the disjunction between motherhood and self-fulfillment and is presented as a negative model, the incarnation of the role of victim the daughter wishes to reject. Rich attributes this matrophobia to the daughter's fear of becoming her mother and thereby replicating the cycle of victimization. For the daughter, then, liberating herself from the cycle will entail a form of "radical surgery" (Rich 236), severing her ties with her mother. Indeed, Alison reacts strongly to the norms of her day, which she perceives as reducing women to their maternal function: "A regarder sa mère parfaite vaquer ainsi à ses obligations quotidiennes, les lèvres serrées, réprimant toujours ses propres ambitions et talents, ta mère jurera de ne pas lui ressembler, plus tard. Jamais au grand jamais elle ne mettra les besoins et désirs des autres avant les siens. . . . Voilà. Les éléments du drame sont en place" ("Watching her perfect mother go about her daily obligations, lips pressed tightly together, constantly repressing her own ambitions and talents, your mother will swear not to become like her, later. Never ever will she put the needs and desires of others before her own. . . . There you have it. The elements of the drama are in place") (Huston, *Bad Girl* 97).

The drama evoked at the end of this passage, Alison's decision to abandon her own children in order to avoid becoming like her mother, comprises her form of "radical surgery" and serves to illustrate Rich's contention that "[t]he loss of the daughter to the mother, the mother to the daughter, is the essential female tragedy" (237). Indeed, it is Alison's concern with giving her life meaning and her conviction that motherhood alone will not lead to self-realization that make her "un prototype de la Femme moderne" ("a prototype of the modern Woman") (Huston, *Bad Girl* 135).

The tension between motherhood and self-fulfillment is borne out in the depiction of Alison's struggle to envision herself mother to a second child. She finds the idea of having another child so oppressive that she views the new pregnancy as "un problème" ("a problem") (Huston, *Bad Girl* 17), "une mauvaise nouvelle . . . plus mauvaise à chaque instant" ("bad news . . . worse every moment") (18). Subsequently, she desperately endeavors to provoke a miscarriage by jumping up and down, an action that is strongly emphasized in the text through the repetition of the verb *sauter*: "[E]lle saute et saute et saute et saute et saute" ("[S]he jumps and jumps and jumps and jumps and jumps") (25). In contrast, her husband, Kenneth, while also initially upset about this additional pregnancy, nonetheless favors a patriarchal model of the family and wants his wife to conform to his expectations of what constitutes a "good" mother. In *Narratives of Mothering*, Gill Rye observes: "The stereotype of the 'good mother' may be culturally and historically contingent, but it is nonetheless powerful. In the West, the 'good mother' has been linked throughout the twentieth century to the nuclear family" (99).

Kenneth himself greatly resented the fact that his mother was absent during much of his adolescence, as she traveled to work in a neighboring town each week to provide for her husband and children, and he sees Alison as having "fauté" ("transgressed") (Huston, *Bad Girl* 235) in a similar way to his own mother. For him, the fact that the two women deviated from societal norms "en refusant de se contenter de leur rôle de mère" ("by refusing to be satisfied by their role as mothers") (235) caused the unhappiness of their children. Viewing his own father as having been "dévirilisé" ("emasculated") (94) as a result of his wife's behavior, he swears to never find himself in the same situation, and he clearly articulates his vision of a traditional family structure with the Father at the center, as master of the House: "Son épouse à lui se tiendra au carreau. Il sera le roi et le maître de son foyer; elle, restera à la maison comme une femme normale" ("*His* wife will watch her step. He will be the king and master of the household; *she* will stay at home like a normal woman") (94). Within this patriarchal conception of what Huston has elsewhere referred to as the "roman familial" ("family plot") (*Journal* 203), Alison represents the bad mother, an idea reinforced by the accumulation of a series of negative modifiers chosen to depict her through Kenneth's eyes as unfeminine and unnatural: "la mauvaise mère, l'assoiffée de diplômes, la femme anormale, ambitieuse, dévorée par l'envie du pénis" ("the bad mother, hungry for diplomas, the abnormal woman, ambitious, consumed by penis envy") (Huston, *Bad Girl* 233). Kenneth's ultimatum to his "épouse féministe" ("feminist spouse") (233) in the spring of 1959, when he tells her that Dorrit is being neglected and needs a maternal presence, again equates being a good mother with being primary caregiver for the children. As he puts it, "[S]oit tu restes à la maison avec les enfants, soit je mets une vraie mère à ta place" ("[E]ither you stay at home with the children, or I will replace you with a real mother") (233). When Alison refuses to devote herself exclusively to mothering and give up her own needs, Kenneth divorces her and soon after finds a substitute in Alice, the good mother, who knows her place is in the home with the children.

In the domain of literary studies, much attention has been given in recent years to survivor discourse and to narratives of recovery, which suggest, as Kathryn Robson argues, that "it is only when the seemingly traumatic experience can be transformed into a narrative that the traumatic event can be put into the past" (11).[4] At the same time, many of these studies address the all-important question of the narratability of trauma, of how an experience that by its very nature "seems to resist narrativization" can be put into words

(13). Consequently, several critics have raised the question of what form this narrativization might take. Robson, for example, who has produced seminal work in the field of trauma studies, asks, "What kind of life-story can contain trauma within its frame?" (12), while Anne Whitehead posits, "If trauma is at all susceptible to narrative formulation, then it requires a literary form which departs from conventional linear narrative" (6).

Huston's creative form, with its nonlinear structure, lends itself well to her portrayal of Dorrit's experience of the effects of trauma over the course of her life as she struggles to cope with her rejection by the mother. In one of the textual fragments in *Bad Girl*, the narrator explicitly evokes many of the classic symptoms of trauma, particularly its "shock impact" (Luckhurst 79) and the way in which it is constantly relived: "Le trauma provoque une *sidération*. Ce n'est pas une mauvaise passe, c'est une *im*passe, une chose qui ne passe pas. En lui le temps se fige. Répétons: le trauma reste à jamais dans le présent. . . . Sa douleur demeure vive, à vif. . . . [L]e trauma est précisément une répétition" ("Trauma provokes a shock. It's not just a rough time, it's an *im*passe, something that doesn't go away. Time freezes at this moment. Repeat: trauma remains forever in the present. . . . The pain remains acute, an open wound. . . . [M]ore exactly, trauma is repetition") (Huston, *Bad Girl* 182).

In particular, the striking reference to "sa douleur [qui] demeure vive, à vif" suggests the presence of an indelible mark left by terrible events, thus recalling Cathy Caruth's definition of trauma as a "wound that cries out" (4). In Dorrit's case, references to the original wound, the pain caused by her mother's unthinkable "crime"—her abandonment of her daughter—are embedded throughout the text. The emphasis on the formidable difficulty of healing this wound again underscores the transgressive nature of the mother's "bad" behavior in a cultural context in which, as Rich reminds us, "[m]other-love is supposed to be continuous, unconditional. . . . Female anger threatens the institution of motherhood" (46). Indeed, the mother's departure leads to a significant rupture in the mother-daughter relationship: Dorrit does not see her mother for a year after she leaves the family, then not for another four years, after which she spends on average a week a year with her mother until Dorrit is an adult.

Likewise, Huston's creation of an intrauterine autobiography enables her to forcefully frame the repercussions of being unwanted from the daughter's perspective. By speaking to her fetal self, the narrator conjures up the undesired child in its most embryonic form within the originary space of the womb at a stage of development that is most often associated with the inception of the symbiotic relationship between a mother and her unborn child. The mother's attempts to provoke a miscarriage are thus portrayed as a kind of murderous impulse; as the narrator informs Dorrit after citing a letter she received from one of her friends, another woman who had been an undesired child, "Vous étiez toutes les deux promises à la mort, S. et toi, Dorrit" ("You were both destined for death, S. and you, Dorrit") (Huston, *Bad Girl* 103). In this fashion, the continuing psychological distress Dorrit will experience throughout her life is evoked by means of the corporeal image of the unwanted fetus being told of the suffering to come, and the theme of being undesired recurs frequently, as when Dorrit is told, "Ils n'ont pas de place pour toi, ils ne te désirent pas, ne t'ont pas fait exprès" ("They have no space for you, they don't want you, they didn't intend to conceive you") (18).

From the beginning of the narrative, the opposition between the mother's desire to miscarry and the unborn child's apparent determination to hang on is conveyed through the insistent repetition of the verb *s'accrocher*, thus suggesting, ironically, that both mother and daughter are, in different senses, fighting for their survival. At the same time, the idea of clinging on functions as a metaphor for Dorrit's continuing attempts to deal with the effects of childhood trauma, as illustrated in the following two citations: "Tu t'accroches. S'accrocher, Dorrit, ce sera l'histoire de ta vie" ("You hang on. Hanging on, Dorrit, will be the story of your life") (Huston, *Bad Girl* 12); "Tu *es*, toute, accrochage. S'accrocher est l'essence et la somme de ton être" ("You *are* nothing but your hanging on. Hanging on is the essence and the whole of your being") (17). In another telling textual fragment, the narrator refers more directly to Dorrit's reactions to her ordeal by using a reference to Virginia Woolf and Simone Weil, each of whom responded to trauma in very different ways, the former through writing and the joy she finds in "la musique des mots" ("the musicality of words") (191) and the latter through reading and reflecting on literary and philosophical works and by listening to music. Dorrit, we are told, will adopt both of these strategies in turn.

When Dorrit is a child, her psychological pain manifests itself primarily in her sense of guilt and the feeling of being unwanted. To her father's great consternation, she asks the women who gather for coffee after church if any of them would like to be her mother, and at times she fantasizes about having an archetypal Jewish matriarch—"cette *yiddishe mama* que tu n'as jamais eue. . . . [Q]ue n'eusses-tu donné pour avoir une mère juive envahissante, intrusive, autoritaire" ("this *Yiddish mother* that you never had. . . . [W]hat wouldn't you have given to have an engulfing, intrusive, authoritarian Jewish mother") (Huston, *Bad Girl* 51). At other moments, she expresses a kind of death wish, imagining that she could please her mother and somehow earn her love by expunging her existence, making it as if she had never been born: "Essayer de mourir, de disparaître, de n'être pas là. Pour faire plaisir à une personne que l'on aime—sa mère" ("Attempt to die, to disappear, to not be there. In order to please a person that one loves—one's mother") (103). Finally, as she grows a bit older, her need to be wanted also reveals itself in her "comportement séducteur" ("seductive behavior") (204), and the adult narrator sees a causal relationship between the desire to seduce and the fact that she was a rejected child: "*Parce que* tu étais une enfant non désirée, tu te pâmeras, dès l'âge de dix ans, en entendant les hommes susurrer qu'ils te désirent" ("*Because* you were an undesired child, once you reach the age of ten, you will swoon when you hear men whisper that they desire you") (200).

Most importantly, the title of the text points to the way in which Dorrit's sense of self is profoundly affected by the breakdown of her relationship with her mother, thus illustrating Judith Lewis Herman's contention that traumatic events "shatter the construction of the self that is formed and sustained in relation to others" (51). In *Bad Girl*, the faulty reasoning of the abandoned child leads to an all-enveloping sense of culpability. As the narrator argues, "Comment ne pas se sentir nulle quand votre mère vous quitte? Cela n'arrive jamais, qu'une mère quitte son enfant. C'est donc que l'enfant en question doit être nulle. Oui, tu mérites tout le malheur qui t'arrive, *bad girl*, même si tu ne sais pas pourquoi" ("How can you not feel worthless when your mother leaves you? That never happens, a mother leaving her child. It must be that the child in question is worthless. Yes, you deserve all the misfortune that happens to you, *bad girl*, even if you don't know why") (Huston, *Bad Girl* 251). Indeed, the fetal Dorrit is warned that self-condemnation will form a significant part of her identity: "Bientôt tu seras coupable, car née; et après, ça ne s'arrêtera jamais" ("Soon you will be guilty, since you will have been born; and afterward, it will never end") (195). References to guilt permeate the narrative, often in relation to specific aspects of the mother's behavior. When, after breaking a Christmas ornament, Dorrit is confronted with her mother's surprising outburst of anger, for example, she concludes, "[T]u es coupable vois-tu, Dorrit, tout le mal du monde est de ta faute" ("[Y]ou are guilty, you see, Dorrit, all the suffering in the world is your fault") (137).

The extent and intensity of the ramifications of being unwanted are reinforced by the interrelated images of limbo, murder, and punishment, all of which are associated with the theme of culpability. First, the notion of limbo, which the narrator links firmly to the leitmotif of abortion, is used to elicit a sense of placelessness and suggests the void at the center of Dorrit's identity created by her mother's infanticidal desires: "Ton vrai chez toi, c'est dans les limbes, avec les autres avortons" ("Your true home is in limbo with the other miscarried fetuses") (Huston, *Bad Girl* 99). Furthermore, being relegated to limbo—the realm inhabited by the souls of unbaptized children—is depicted as a life sentence that the guilty Dorrit will be condemned to serve: "Vu que la vie dans les limbes est une punition, tu te sentiras coupable, auras l'impression d'avoir commis un meurtre" ("Given that life in limbo is a punishment, you will feel culpable, will be under the impression that you have committed a murder") (104). As the narrator explains, the victim of this crime is the person Dorrit would have become had she stayed in Canada and remained English speaking rather than moving to France and adopting French as her primary language in an attempt to redefine her identity in the absence of the mother. In this way, the image of limbo is used to set up a correlation between the mother's abandonment of Dorrit and Dorrit's own renunciation of her native tongue. This correlation serves to bring out Dorrit's belief that she deserves to be severely punished, in part for pretending her stepmother was her biological mother and that the stepmother's language, for a brief period, was her maternal language: "Ayant renié la mère, il te sera facile de renier la mère patrie. . . . Menteuse et traîtresse, tu mériteras la peine de mort" ("Having disowned your mother, it will be easy for you to disown your mother country. . . . A liar and a traitor, you will deserve the death penalty") (104).[5] Ultimately, then, the trauma of being rejected is portrayed as leading to a loss of self that will prompt Dorrit to endeavor to reconstruct her shattered sense of identity in a country and a language that are not associated with her mother.

At the same time, however, the fact that Huston adopts an autobiographical format in order to give voice to her childhood trauma suggests that the conceptualization of *Bad Girl* itself can be seen as a positive aspect of the process of working through mental and physical suffering. When discussing the work of psychology professor James Pennebaker, Suzette Henke, for example, calls attention to his argument that "the very process of articulating painful experiences, especially in written form, can itself prove therapeutic" (xi). Huston herself acknowledges the crucial importance of literature in her reconstruction of self, evoking in particular the salutary influence of Romain Gary, another multilingual writer in exile whose works influenced her profoundly: "He was the first one to show me how literature could help you deal with the multiple identities you build when you're a foreigner. And how you could also, this way, get over the traumas you might have experienced when you were a kid" (Bisson). Numerous observations in *Bad Girl*, too, highlight the idea that the narrator's coming to writing was a way of coping with the problematic events of her childhood and ultimately provided her with a means of survival. As the narrator presciently discloses to the embryonic Dorrit, "L'art te sauvera, Dorrit" ("Art will save you, Dorrit") (Huston, *Bad Girl* 224). Likewise, Kenneth recognizes that the impetus behind his daughter's writing lies in her damaged childhood and the disfunctional relationship with her mother, referring in a letter he sends her to "*cette douleur dont l'élan a fait de toi une écrivaine stupéfiante*" ("this pain whose power has made an astounding writer out of you") (194). In this sense, the narrator suggests that the negative experience of having a "bad" mother is the primary source of her creativity and has played an important role in her becoming a prolific and successful author.

The subtitle of *Bad Girl*, *Classes de littérature*, points to the importance of the fact that the text traces out a kind of genealogy of the narrator's evolution as a writer. In an interview in *Le Devoir*, Huston brings forth the idea that *Bad Girl* is not an autobiography in the traditional sense but rather what she refers to as "une classe de littérature, c'est-à-dire une réflexion précise sur ce qui m'a fait écrire" ("a literature lesson, that is, a focused reflection on what made me a writer") (Massoutre). The "classes de littérature" elicited in the text include a wide variety of influences and situations that have shaped Huston as a person and especially as an author: her exposure to religion and music, the presence of other languages in her life, her discovery of the power of her own beauty, and her experience of conflict. In particular, being constantly uprooted and always having to assume the role of "la nouvelle" ("the new girl") at school and at church is described as "une classe de littérature puissance x" ("a literature lesson to the nth degree") (Huston, *Bad Girl* 158) and resulted in her setting her novels in very different time periods and geographical spaces. Similarly, Huston characterizes the personal letters her mother sent her as a key element of her survival, since they allowed her to "instaurer un dialogue littéraire qui est devenu vital. Une des belles classes de littérature de ma vie, la plus importante" ("set up a literary dialogue that became vital. One of the best literature lessons of my life, the most important") (Cloutier). In addition, references to those who helped the narrator come to terms with her abandonment and the knowledge that she was unwanted are embedded throughout *Bad Girl*. Indeed, Huston incorporates into the narrative extended allusions to the many writers, painters, artists, and filmmakers whose work has influenced her own thinking, ranging from authors Samuel Beckett, Romain Gary, Annie Ernaux, and Göran Tunström to creative artists Anne Truitt, Louise Bourgeois, Camille Claudel, and Clotilde Vautier.

Alongside these intertextual allusions, *Bad Girl* refers to specific moments of her genesis as a writer, particularly those that associate creativity with the absence of the mother. The narrator notes, for example, that she invented her first characters immediately after her parents' divorce, and she perceives a direct link between the fact that she was "privée de tout sentiment de sécurité à l'endroit de l'amour maternel" ("deprived of any sense of safety in regard to maternal love") (Huston, *Bad Girl* 145) and the development of an "*empathie désespérée*" ("desperate empathy") (146) that led her to become a novelist. In this sense, as she elucidates, writing provided her with a way of being in control, thus suggesting that creating fictional realms served as an antidote to the instability of the world of her childhood and the attendant feeling of vulnerability it brought her. In the narrator's words, "ayant été élevée sur des sables mouvants . . . écrire reflétera ton besoin de gouverner seule. De prendre seule toutes les décisions. De bâtir seule des univers sur cette fondation aérienne, immatérielle . . . et donc d'une solidité à toute épreuve: les mots" ("since you will have been raised on shifting sands . . . writing will reflect your need to command alone. To make all decisions by yourself. To build worlds by yourself on this aerial, ethereal, and therefore rock-solid foundation: words") (207). With its emphasis on the emergence of the narrator as an author, *Bad Girl* also constitutes an interesting twist on the conventional giving birth to baby / book plot. Whereas most books of this type portray a mother-writer who completes her book while she is expecting, Huston's narrative ends with her own birth, and frequent parallels are established between the conception of *Bad Girl* and Dorrit's gestation period: "Ne t'en fais pas, tu auras bientôt le droit de naître; encore quelques dizaines de pages et ce sera le moment" ("Don't worry, you will soon have the right to be born; a few dozen pages more and it will be time") (105). In a figurative sense, then, Huston conveys the impression of giving birth to herself, thus illustrating Marilyn Yalom's contention that "the act of writing can be seen as an effort to reclaim one's life, as a labor through which one may become mother to oneself as well as to literary progeny" (103).

In *Of Woman Born*, Rich makes the compelling argument that it is "[e]asier by far to hate and reject a mother outright than to see beyond her to the forces acting upon her" (235). While Huston's account of having had a bad mother—according to the standards of the time—focuses primarily on the daughter's long struggle to cope with the repercussions of childhood trauma, it also demonstrates that she has come to understand how her mother's decisions were shaped by historical and social factors. Indeed, Huston clearly articulates both the mother's position and the daughter's suffering as a consequence of her mother's struggle for autonomy when she affirms: "C'était [sa mère] une féministe avant l'heure qui avait de très belles aspirations pour son épanouissement personnel et qui est admirable. On peut souffrir d'un geste admirable" ("She was a feminist before her time who had great aspirations for her personal fulfilllment, and this is admirable. Yet one can suffer as the result of an admirable act") (Cloutier). In this sense, she reminds us that the notions of good and bad mothers are historically determined and that it is incumbent on us as readers to look beyond "our comforting representation of the good mother" (Sardin 309–10) in order to reflect on changing conceptualizations of motherhood.

NOTES

1. Married to Tzvetan Todorov for many years and mother to two children, Huston currently spends time in Switzerland, Germany, and France with her companion, Swiss painter Guy Oberson.
2. A future novel will explore the controversy surrounding the oilsands in the region of Fort McMurray, Alberta.
3. In an interview with Georgia Makhlouf, Huston observed that she chose the name Dorrit because of the way it sounded. It was only after *Bad Girl* had been published that she discovered that Dickens's Dorrit was an orphan.
4. The term "narrative recovery" refers to "both the recovery of past experience through narrative articulation and the psychological reintegration of a traumatically shattered subject" (Henke xii).
5. Soon after her father's remarriage, Huston was sent with her stepmother to Germany, where she lived and attended school for several months.

WORKS CITED

Bisson, Julien. "Prizewinning Parisienne." *France Today*, 18 Oct. 2011.

Caruth, Cathy. *Unclaimed Experience: Trauma, Narrative, and History*. Johns Hopkins University Press, 1996.

Cloutier, Mario. "Nancy Huston: Mettre au monde." *La Presse*, 1 Nov. 2014, https://www.lapresse.ca/arts/livres/entrevues/201410/31/01-4814591-nancy-huston-mettre-au-monde.php.

De Balsi, Sara. "Censure et écriture translingue." *Censura e auto-censura*, edited by A. Bibbò, S. Ercolino, and M. Lino, *Between*, vol. 5, no. 9, 2015, pp. 1–26.

Henke, Suzette. *Shattered Subjects: Trauma and Testimony in Women's Life-Writing*. Macmillan, 2000.

Herman, Judith Lewis. *Trauma and Recovery: The Aftermath of Violence—from Domestic Abuse to Political Terror*. Basic Books, 1992.

Huston, Nancy. *Bad Girl: Classes de littérature*. Leméac, 2014.

———. *Cantique des plaines*. Actes Sud, 1993.

———. *Danse noire*. Actes Sud, 2013.

———. *Désirs et réalités: Textes choisis 1978–1994*. Leméac, 1995.

———. *Journal de la création*. Seuil, 1990.

———. *La virevolte*. Actes Sud, 1994.

———. *Lignes de faille*. Actes Sud, 2006.

———. *Plainsong*. HarperCollins, 1993.

Luckhurst, Roger. *The Trauma Question*. Routledge, 2008.

Makhlouf, Georgia. "Nancy Huston: Mélomane en littérature." *L'Orient Littéraire*, Aug. 2018, http://lorientlitteraire.com/article_details.php?cid=6&nid=6502.

Massoutre, Guylaine. "De Nancy Huston à Siri Hustved et Linda Lê." *Le Devoir*, 25 Oct. 2014, https://www.ledevoir.com/lire/421941/nature-et-culture.

Rich, Adrienne. *Of Woman Born: Motherhood as Experience and Institution*. 10th anniversary ed. W. W. Norton, 1986.

Robson, Kathryn. *Writing Wounds: The Inscription of Trauma in Post-1968 French Women's Writing*. Rodopi, 2004.

Rye, Gill. *Narratives of Mothering: Women's Writing in Contemporary France*. University of Delaware Press, 2009.

Sardin, Pascale. "Towards an Ethics of Witness, or the Story and History of 'Une Minuscule Détresse' in Annie Ernaux's *L'Evénement* and Nancy Huston's *Instruments des Ténèbres*." *French Studies*, vol. 62, no. 3, 2008, pp. 301–12.

Trapenard, Augustin. "Nancy Huston, plus qu'une bad girl." *France Inter*, 30 Oct. 2014.

Whitehead, Anne. *Trauma Fiction*. Edinburgh University Press, 2004.

Yalom, Marilyn. *Maternity, Morality, and the Literature of Madness*. Pennsylvania State University Press, 1985.

8

Forgiving the Horrible Mother

Children's Needs and Women's Desires in Twenty-First-Century Québécois Film

AMY J. RANSOM

Pour en finir avec la petite Aurore

One of Québec's most written about films, *La petite Aurore, l'enfant martyre* (*Little Aurora's Tragedy*, Jean-Yves Bigras, 1952) is a nasty little melodrama based on a real-life case of child abuse from 1920 (Larochelle and Lessard).[1] It establishes early on the "horrible mother" as a stock trope of Québécois cinema, and, indeed, Heinz Weinmann positions it as a foundational work in his psychosocial analysis, *Cinéma de l'imaginaire au Québec* (1990). Aurore Gagnon, the child martyr, and her wicked stepmother, Marie-Anne Houde, are seen as emblematic of the French Canadian nation abandoned by the weak-willed father, her care left in the hands of an abusive *marâtre* (Weinmann, *Cinéma* 28–29). Elevated to the status of national myth, the story has proven perennially popular, from the original stage play, which ran from 1920 to 1952 (Weinmann, *Cinéma* 28); to Bigras's film; through the television docudrama, *L'affaire de la petite Aurore* (1994); to a big-budget, big-screen adaptation, *Aurore* (Luc Dionne, 2005). Indeed, as Éric Bédard demonstrates in an insightful analysis of Dionne's remake, along with two other popular film adaptations of literary classics involving maternal abandonment and the victimization of young women, *Séraphin, un homme et son péché* (*Séraphin: Heart of Stone*, Charles Binamé, 2003) and *Le survenant*

(*The Outlander*, Érik Canuel, 2005), this antifeminist myth remains surprisingly popular in contemporary Québec.

Fortunately, in contrast with the negative images of pre-1960s Québec society conveyed by those films, a number of twenty-first-century filmmakers have begun to offer a revised image of the horrible mother, one that constructs images of failed motherhood not to condemn but rather to understand and forgive. Beginning with two watershed films released on the cusp of the new millennium, Léa Pool's *Emporte-moi* (*Set Me Free*, 1999) and François Bouvier's *Histoires d'hiver* (*Winter Stories*, 1999), this chapter examines how a significant corpus of films focalized through the viewpoint of a child protagonist negotiates situations of maternal neglect and abandonment, working—admittedly to varying degrees—toward forgiving the horrible mother. These two films represent significant precursor texts to an entire wave of twenty-first-century films that revisit 1960s Québec by privileging the child's point of view as witness to social change and suggesting that the province may begin to leave behind its own martyr complex "pour en finir avec la petite Aurore" ("to finally be done with little Aurora").

As Jane Moss observes, films like Jean-Marc Vallée's record-breaking *C.R.A.Z.Y.* (2005) and Michel Poulette's telefilm *Histoire de famille* (2006) generally depict a new post-1960s Québécois family as "less patriarchal, less xenophobic, and less homophobic" (113).[2] With these progressive values, we also see a distancing from the traditional antifeminist binary images of the mother as either self-sacrificing or selfish and "horrible." Thus, three films released in 2008 (Philippe Falardeau's *C'est pas moi je le jure* [*It's Not Me, I Swear!*], Léa Pool's *Maman est chez le coiffeur* [*Mommy's at the Hairdresser's*], and Francis Leclerc's *Un été sans point ni coup sûr* [*A No-Hit, No-Run Summer*]) followed by a second miniwave (Michel Monty's *Une vie qui commence* [*Life Begins*, 2010] and Richard Roy's *Frisson des collines* [2011]) all focalize their narratives through the eyes of a more-or-less problem child faced with a life-changing event involving the loss of one or both parents.[3] All set in the 1960s, they use the family as a metonym for the changes occurring in Québec society as a whole, but although they depict mothers who abandon their children, they acknowledge that this "abandonment" is necessary not just for the child's development but also for that of the mother. By revealing the dysfunctions of the traditional French Canadian patriarchal family, these films offer a partial feminist re-vision, suggesting its replacement by a modern Québécois family that acknowledges women's and children's emotional needs. Following Judith Halberstam's notion (outlined by Loïc Bourdeau in the introduction to this volume) that "from the perspective of feminism, failure has often been a better bet than success" (4), these films acknowledge the impossibility of "success" for women under the image of the mother that was circumscribed for them in pre–Quiet Revolution ideology.[4]

Just Whom Are We Setting Free? Léa Pool's *Emporte-moi*

The imperative title of Léa Pool's *Emporte-moi* expresses the intimate flow of need and desire from one individual to another. The film's focalizing protagonist is the adolescent daughter, Hanna Riel (Karine Vanasse), so viewers and critics may presume that she utters the command, wishing for someone to *Set Me Free*, as rendered in the film's official English title. Not quite the *porte-moi* of a small child wanting to be carried, *emporte-moi* expresses ambivalence toward the maturation process, both a longing for autonomy and a desire to be held and loved. The film's coming-of-age elements as Hanna reaches menarche, has her first sexual experiences, and temporarily runs away from an untenable domestic situation support this reading. Furthermore, one of the figurative meanings of the French verb *emporter* is to be carried away by death, and the film's opening underwater sequence, in which Hanna appears floating almost lifelessly, immersed in the Saint Lawrence, invokes the release of suicide, as well as the safety of the mother's womb. Hanna's mixed desire is underscored as she later feigns drowning at a family beach outing and again sinks to the bottom of a swimming pool. In addition to the various forms of "acting out," through which Hanna asserts independence while at the same time crying out for attention, she nonetheless expresses very clearly that what she wants most of all is her mother's love.[5]

At one level, then, *Emporte-moi* offers yet another installment in Québec's oft-invoked family romance of absent mothers and fathers, lost sons and daughters.[6] Without denying the validity of Janis Pallister's reading that the film's central theme is the quest for the mother ("la quête de la mère est le thème central du film" [89]), I will argue that *Emporte-moi* nonethe-less marks a significant turning point in the tide of culturally constructed resentment, taking the first steps toward forgiving the so-called horrible mother. If we also read the film title's imperative from the point of view of Hanna's unnamed mother (Pascale Bussières),[7] we begin to see a repeated blurring of the boundaries between mother and daughter, the film title's insistence on the dysfunctional situations of both mothers and daughters in early 1960s Québec. Denied the opportunities that the film's hopeful conclusion suggests that her daughter will have thanks to the Quiet Rev-olution, Hanna's mother remains trapped in the role of the long-suffering, self-sacrificing mothers of the Grande Noirceur and before found in the films analyzed by Éric Bédard.[8] Unable to fulfill all the demands made upon her, she also cries out for release through the film's title and, indeed, suffers a nervous breakdown and attempts suicide. Thus, although the mother's absence—both emotional (she has nothing left to give after working all day in a garment factory and then typing her husband's writing all night) and physical (she is taken from the home in an ambulance for an institution-alized "rest cure")—triggers the child's crisis, the film refuses to condemn the mother for it. Rather, *Emporte-moi* underscores the fact that both of these women are victims of a social system on the eve of its destruction, a destruction partially brought about by its own denial of the needs and desires of women and children.

Emporte-moi thus opens up a space, allowing subsequent films to perform (sometimes only partial) feminist critiques of the patriarchal family to begin forgiving the so-called horrible mother. Through its repeated mirroring of mother and daughter (Gilbert and Santoro 146), Pool's 1999 film refuses to condemn the mother's desire to be released from the unbearable tensions of her own life. In spite of her unfulfilled desire for maternal love, Hanna repeatedly defends her mother, seeing the latter's potential to "be some-body" in different circumstances. In the early classroom sequence when Hanna reveals her confused identity (daughter of a French Canadian and a Holocaust survivor), she idealizes her mother as a great fashion designer rather than admit the reality that she is merely a seamstress in a garment factory. Hanna consistently rejects her father, blaming him for her mother's exhausted abjection. Indoctrinated by pre–Quiet Revolution ideology of the patriarchal family and the wife's supporting role in it (Baillargeon 151) and thus tragically unable to escape this *huis clos identitaire*, a dead end for a more fulfilling identity, Hanna's mother insists instead on her husband's genius. In contrast, because of the changes instituted in Québec society (such as the secular education from which Hanna benefits), her daughter will be allowed to pursue a career of her own.

From *Emporte-moi* to the Montreal Expos: *Histoires d'hiver* and *Un été sans point ni coup sûr*

Although it looked back with some nostalgia upon a signal era in Québec's history, *Emporte-moi* also looks forward with its conclusion's promise that Hanna will break the cycle in which her mother has been trapped. She may even have succeeded in partially freeing her mother, as the film's conclusion reunites them at the Riel family farm on the shores of the Saint Lawrence. Released only two weeks later in February 1999, François Bouvier's *Histoires d'hiver* also allows its mother figure to grow; furthermore, its focalizing boy protagonist, Martin Roy (Joël Dalpé-Drapeau), establishes a precedent for similar characters in a spate of films produced in the new millennium. Above all, although there remains something of a generation gap between child and parents, this film—as does Pool's, but in a different way—establishes complicity between Martin and his elders, a complicity that will increasingly facilitate intergenerational understanding in this corpus.

Building on Marc Robitaille's 1987 book, *Histoires d'hiver, avec des rues, des écoles et du hockey* (Winter stories, with cities, schools, and hockey), Bouvier's film—like the other films in this corpus—invokes the family as microcosm to comment on (but also to remythologize) the 1960s and Québec's narrative of its transition to modernity. Whereas Pool depicts a daughter's desire for complicity with her mother, Bouvier establishes complete complicity between the boy and his uncle (Proulx 104). Perhaps in order better to evoke Claude Jutra's classic *Mon oncle Antoine* (1971), *Histoires d'hiver* shifts its emphasis from parents to an uncle named Maurice, who is caricatured as a dyed-in-the-wool (*pure laine*) working-class French Canadian via his profession as a mechanic and his colorful use of the word *joual*, Montreal urban vernacular.[9] Maurice, who dies in the film, represents a dying generation forced to make room for the white-collar engineers of the Quiet Revolution, like Martin's father. The film uses the male-dominated realm of hockey to bind the relationship between Martin and his uncle Maurice (Denis Bouchard) but also temporarily to exclude his father (Luc Guérin). Not only does the loss of the uncle allow the boy to become a man (this is explicitly stated in the voice-over narration, performed by Luc Picard), it also facilitates a *rapprochement* with his father.

Along with its narrative of Québec's modernization and *bourgeoisification*, *Histoires d'hiver* touches briefly on the gradual liberation of the province's women as a significant aspect of the national narrative about the 1960s. This decade of global *prise de conscience*, the epiphanies experienced by minority and/or oppressed groups not just in Québec but around the world, also witnessed a "feminist revolution" (Baillargeon 11, 181ff.) in which women expressed their desire for a greater role in the public sphere and the need for fulfillment beyond the roles of wife and mother. This striving, however, is trivialized here, as the cartoonish Jacqueline (played by comic actress Diane Lavallée) seeks self-expression through arts and crafts. At the film's beginning, she fills the new-found free time opened up by the home appliances made available in the developing consumer culture by indulging in paint-by-numbers kits. Admittedly, by the film's end, she, like her son, has been seen to grow as she begins an original painting. Yet the painting's subject matter—her immediate circle of family and friends—and the fact that she relies on a photograph pinned to the top of her canvas as a model betray the limits that continue to define her. Nonetheless, this largely male-centered film's inclusion of such a character *and* the critical link it establishes between a mother's growth and that of her child point toward an evolving image of the mother in Québec.

A decade later, another adaptation of a Marc Robitaille narrative takes this process a clear step farther. Also featuring a twelve-year-old boy named Martin (Pierre-Luc Funk), exploring Québec's summer sport of baseball instead of winter's hockey, Francis Leclerc's *Un été sans point ni coup sûr* brings the mother more to the foreground, establishing a very clear complicity between mother and son and taking her search for fulfillment outside the home.

While Martin is clearly the center of the film's attention, his mother,

Mireille (Jacinthe Laguë), represents a second focalizing character, and her development parallels that of her son. Indeed, the film opens on a sequence in which their complicity is clearly established as the white-collar husband and father, Charles (Patrice Robitaille), returns from work to find his authority undermined. Mother and son have colluded to reject the father's summer tradition of sending Martin to scout camp, instead requesting that he stay home to play baseball. The film's voice-over narrative insists on Charles's resistance to change but ultimately concludes on his limited acceptance of a new status quo. Not only does he reluctantly agree to coach Martin's team, he eventually accepts Mireille's desire to work outside the home. Whereas *Histoires d'hiver* never depicts Jacqueline Roy outside the home, *Un été* allows Mireille to leave the kitchen (Valade); at first, she simply sprawls listlessly on the sofa, clearly bored and unfulfilled. By film's end, however, she appears almost fully liberated, working outside the home, albeit in the traditionally female realm of a flower shop. Furthermore, although the couple's stability is temporarily threatened by the approach of other men, in the end Mireille's desire for her husband returns when he stands up to an opposing coach (Roy Dupuis). The film thus acknowledges the mother's need for a fulfilling role in the public sphere and for a partner who arouses sexual desire.

Since both films are based on light-hearted, nostalgic representations of childhood experiences in 1960s Québec authored by Marc Robitaille, *Un été* necessarily resembles *Histoires d'hiver* in many ways. Indeed, Robert Proulx's incisive comparison of Bouvier's film and its literary model largely applies to Leclerc's adaptation as well; not only do both films develop their adult characters in greater detail, they also provide "une image plus complète de la société Québécoise de la fin des années 1960 ainsi que des enjeux individuels et collectifs qui s'y jouaient" ("a more complete image of late 1960s Québécois society, as well as the individual and collective issues being played out at the time") (Proulx 108). What differs, however, between the two films is the role they assign women's liberation in their visions of social change. Completely nonexistent in either of Robitaille's stories, the mother's quest for personal development is invented out of whole cloth; but Leclerc takes it much more seriously and definitely farther than does Bouvier, addressing the contemporary question of women's liberation. It is tempting to attribute this to generational differences between these filmmakers: Bouvier was born in 1948, whereas Leclerc was born in 1971. Indeed, Leclerc belongs to a "nouvelle génération" of filmmakers (Chartier 145; Lever 87), including Denis Villeneuve, Louis Bélanger, and Philippe Falardeau, the director of another film in the present corpus.

Negotiating the Mother's Loss: *Maman est chez le coiffeur* and *C'est pas moi, je le jure!*

Critics immediately perceived the significance of Léa Pool's *Maman est chez le coiffeur* and Philippe Falardeau's *C'est pas moi, je le jure!*, both released in 2008 and based respectively on the childhood experiences of siblings Isabelle and Bruno Hébert (Charles 12). With one of these films directed by an established icon of the province's film industry and the other by a rocketing star, academic analyses also quickly appeared (Charles; Clément).[10] Both films make essential contributions to the cultural process of forgiving the "horrible mother"; along with the films of Xavier Dolan (discussed in detail in Loïc Bourdeau's contribution to this collection), they represent some of the best explorations of the mother-child relationship in world cinema.

In contrast with Marc Robitaille's lighter touch, Bruno Hébert's semi-autobiographical novels *C'est pas moi, je le jure!* (1997) and *Alice court avec René* (2000), although they are extremely funny, narrate the struggles of a "problem child," Léon Doré, within a dysfunctional family in 1960s Québec. His mother's departure for a work assignment in Greece exacerbates his tendency for mythomania and acting out, ultimately leading to a stay in a psychiatric facility. Falardeau's film, adapted from Hébert's novels, maintains this focalization, while Pool's, based on an original screenplay by Isabelle Hébert, focuses more directly on an older sister. Both also stage the literal abandonment of her children by their mother; this abandonment is deeply felt and has a nearly tragic impact upon the family unit. Yet both filmmakers tell this story in such a way that the mother's departure represents not an insurmountable trauma but rather a temporary yet necessary step for the mental health and development of both the mother and her children.

Like *Emporte-moi*'s Hanna, *Maman est chez le coiffeur* presents Élise Gauvin (Marianne Fortier) on the cusp of adolescence, striving for autonomy.

At the same time, she wishes to hold on to her mother, Simone (Céline Bonnier), resenting her abandonment. She also feels responsible for the family crisis because she inadvertently brought their father's (Laurent Lucas) affair with another man to her mother's attention, triggering Simone's departure. Unlike the other films discussed here, the mother successfully juggles a fulfilling career with her other roles, as seen in the film's initial sequence, in which she dictates a report on the Vietnam War over the phone, but only after she has baked her children a cake to celebrate the end of the school year. She patiently helps her youngest son dress himself properly and later laughs as he tickles her feet while she works. She braids her daughter's hair and listens as her older son plays the piano. Indeed, this film reverses the paradigm of the frustrated housewife who desires autonomy; here, her husband's closeted homosexuality is the source of her frustration, as indicated in a bedtime scene in which Simone initiates sexual relations and he rejects her advances.

When Simone requests an assignment in London in order to deal with the pain of her husband's betrayal, the children at first perceive her departure as an abandonment. Élise, the eldest, is angry; the middle child, Coco (Élie Dupuis), sublimates his emotions by constructing a go-cart; and the youngest, Benoit (Hugo St-Onge-Paquin), already at risk because he is labeled "slow" in school because he cannot yet read, engages in (self-)destructive behaviors.[11] Not only does he mutilate his GI Joe doll and start a fire in the garage, but several foreboding scenes suggest that he may drown. Similarly abandoned, the unnamed husband is genuinely angry and hurt;[12] although he no longer feels sexual desire for his wife, his pain goes beyond the self-interested need for someone to take care of the children so he can pursue his career, as demonstrated in a scene involving his own emotional breakdown when he learns she plans to take the children to London. His inadequate preparation for taking care of his children nonetheless leads him to consider institutionalizing Benoit, thus further destabilizing the family.

To be sure, Simone's departure causes her children serious pain, particularly her youngest son, who retreats physically and emotionally into an inner world that he explores inside a broom closet. The elder children, though they clearly resent their mother's departure while at the same time missing her affection, display better coping mechanisms. Élise finds solace in the natural world and an unconventional friendship with the local pariah, a middle-aged man (Gabriel Arcand) with a distinctive strawberry birthmark and some apparent social or developmental delays. Coco has a circle of friends and his soapbox car project, which provides a creative outlet. Nonetheless, the film depicts the mother's departure as resulting in developmental progress for the other characters. Élise asserts her agency, learning to fish, experimenting with her budding sexuality, and defying her father; the latter develops the domestic skills necessary for raising his children (he goes from ordering pizza to learning to cook a full meal); even Benoit learns to read, motivated by a postcard from Simone. Above all, however, Simone's children support her decision by presenting a united front to the outside world. Their complicity with their mother appears in the film's title, a catch-phrase they use in response to neighborhood busybodies. By replying "Mommy is at the hairdresser's," the children ironically protect her from the judgmental gaze of outsiders. Via secondary characters like the inquiring Madame Corbeil (Kathleen Fortin) and Madame Paradis (Paule Ducharme), Pool lampoons the 1960s contradictory vision of the supposedly "modern" housewife still yoked to traditional norms for Catholic French Canadian femininity (Collectif Clio 419–22). The film concludes with Élise's rebellion against her father as she runs off with Benoit so that he cannot be taken to Bruno Bettelheim's boarding school in Sherbrooke, her last words indicating to Benoit that they will join their mother in London.[13]

Although Philippe Falardeau's adaptation of Bruno Hébert's *autofictions* is clearly more male centered than Pool's, and it denies the mother the professional career that justifies her departure, *C'est pas moi* nonetheless makes clear that mother and child remain connected in spite of the distance that separates them, and the child ultimately forgives her. Its focalizing character, Léon Doré (Antoine L'Écuyer), is a trickster; the title phrase ("It's not me, I swear!") protests his innocence for the repeated antics of an imaginative and inventive boy left unsupervised precisely because of his mother's absence. Once again, blame for the family's dysfunction is laid at the father's feet, however, because a good bit of this boy's "acting out" might have been avoided had the father not somewhat vengefully denied his children contact with their mother.

Early on, the film establishes complicity between mother and son, whose nonconformist creativity is consistently smothered by the family patriarch. Before she leaves, for example, Madeleine teaches Léon their motto, which reveals their shared rebel spirit, "C'est mal de mentir, mais c'est pire de mal mentir" ("It's bad to lie, but worse to lie badly"), and joins him in throwing an egg onto a busybody neighbor's roof. Philippe Doré (Daniel Brière), modeled on the real-life Liberal activist and Trudeau friend Jacques Hébert (Charles 7), is a straw man, a paternalistic, white-collar bourgeois. Through depicting his explicitly political activities, which also show him in league with the Catholic Church, this film offers the closest thing to a critique of the engineers of the Quiet Revolution as not really being so revolutionary after all. He is clearly mismatched with his wife, Madeleine (Suzanne Clément), a free spirit in tie-dyed caftans who finally has enough of his conformity and flees to Greece. In her absence, Léon certainly feels her loss deeply; in his solitude, he entertains himself by breaking into a neighbor's home, where he expresses his pain indirectly through destruction. Like Hanna in *Emporte-moi*, he also runs away from home to help a young female friend visit her estranged mother. That said, the film's blackly humorous opening sequence of Léon's attempted suicide (he experimentally hangs himself from a tree) precedes his mother's departure and actually establishes the depth of her maternal love for this unique son. In addition to their natural complicity, dream/fantasy sequences in which Léon vividly imagines his absent mother coupled with the completely negative portrayal of the father (who can blame her for leaving him) and her ultimate return in the film's conclusion make clear that she is forgiven.

In their depictions of the 1960s as an era of absent mothers and weak fathers, these films offer a certain cultural reflection on various academic analyses of the period in question. In the wake of works like Heinz Weinmann's psychosocial analysis of Québec film expressing various aspects of Freud's "family romance" in *Cinéma de l'imaginaire au Québec* (1990) and Guy Corneau's *Absent Fathers, Lost Sons* (1989), it has become a commonplace in the scholarly discourse to see the Quiet Revolution as an allegorical rejection of paternal authority and the self-assertion of the newly enfranchised sons. In Québec's complex situation of a dual colonization, paternal authority may be located both in the political and the economic authority of Anglophone elites and the Canadian federal government, itself still not completely liberated from its colonial ties to Great Britain, as well as in that of the nonetheless francophone Catholic Church, with its patriarchal models. As Baillargeon, Lamoureux, and others assert, women's enfranchisement through the feminist movement, which seconded the nationalist one, was also an important element in Québec's social evolution at this time. Finally, it is not insignificant that the mothers in these particular films leave Québec for careers abroad; not only do they thus figure women's rejection of the traditional roles of wife and mother as sole avenues for feminine fulfillment, they also reflect Québec's newfound desire to stop looking inward, the belly-button gazing frequently decried by intellectuals in the 1960s, and end a long period of perceived isolation in order to look outward and join the rest of the Western world in its march toward (post)modernity.

Losing the Father: *Frisson des collines* and *Une vie qui commence*

Both of Pool's films and Falardeau's film critique traditional French Canadian family structures as suffocating women's and children's desires, thus hampering their full flowering as individuals. As Jane Moss observes, a film like *Maman* (in which the heteronormative society forces a gay man to closet his sexuality) also reveals the coercive pressures it places on grown men (113). This theme is central to Michel Monty's *Une vie qui commence*, in which unhealthy French Canadian patriarchal family relationships are blamed for the loss of the young protagonist's father. Étienne (Charles-Antoine Perreault) loses his idolized father, the physician Jacques Langevin (François Papineau), to the slow suicide of drug addiction, linked directly to the actions of his social pillar grandfather. In this film and in *Frisson des collines*, blame is thus shifted away from the immediate father figure, a man who is adored and emulated, onto the grandfather's generation. In both of these films, the father's death also entails a temporary loss of the mother to her grieving process. In their androcentricity and their fantasy-like depiction of these mothers, however, their feminist revision remains only partial.

Indeed, *Une vie* depicts Julie Le Breton's character, Louise, as an unbelievable stereotype of the 1960s fantasy wife depicted in women's magazines

(Collectif Clio 419–22). Frequently cast as a sensuous redhead, Le Breton's Louise by day feeds her children in a spotless modern kitchen and vacuums with her hair and makeup perfect; by night she is a playful sex kitten in her husband's bed. Furthermore, still a product of an ideology in which "real" men bear the burden of being the family's breadwinner and "real" women stay home (Collectif Clio 446), she is completely ignorant of the family's economic situation after her husband's death. When he collapses under the social burden, she struggles to pick up the pieces, including packing up and selling their suburban house to pay the debts he has left them with, moving to a flat in Montréal, and finding employment for herself.

While she certainly is forced to mature, Louise does not appear to *grow*; instead of achieving greater fulfillment, she actually becomes increasingly rigid, falling back on traditional values to cope with her economic burden and her adolescent son's increasingly idiosyncratic behavior. Out of misplaced loyalty to her late husband, she impractically rejects financial assistance from her in-laws while at the same time enrolling her son in a strict Catholic *collège classique*—precisely the type of institution that produced her father-in-law's generation.[14] She becomes shrill and shrewish, even hysterical when Étienne, unable to cope with his own grief, acts out a form of denial of his father's death by doing everything in his power to emulate him: he wears a suit, refusing to change clothes, "diagnoses" his friends' and brother's illnesses, and even begins to take the drugs found in his father's pocket. Although mother and son eventually reconcile, the viewer's image of Louise is ultimately too confused to elicit sympathy.

Richard Roy's *Frisson des collines* stages a very similar tale of a boy's permanent loss of his father (Patrice Robitaille) and temporary loss of his mother (Anick Lemay) during her grieving process. Cowritten by Roy and Michel Michaud, the film's scenario draws on a number of elements found in earlier films in this corpus: an adolescent in crisis, his or her youthful antics and awakening sexuality, the excitement of late 1960s social change, and so on. Even the casting of tow-headed actor Antoine-Olivier Pilon in the lead role of Frisson (his nickname is linked anecdotally to his parents' first kiss) invokes that of Antoine L'Écuyer in *C'est pas moi*. As in *Histoires d'hiver*, the adolescent shares complicity with an avuncular figure, his late father's band mate, Tom Faucher (Guillaume Lemay-Thivierge); instead of sports, this boy's engagement with popular music of the period helps him through his period of difficulty. Finally, the culminating adventure of *Histoires d'hiver*—a trip to see the Canadiens in the Montréal Forum—is paralleled by Tom agreeing to bring Frisson to Woodstock so he can see his idol, Jimi Hendrix, play.

As in *Une vie*, the father-son relationship is strong and healthy; the traumatic loss of the father (he is electrocuted while working as a lineman—perhaps a reference to the 1960s creation of Hydro-Québec) is compounded by the mother's temporary abandonment of her son to her obsessive mourning. Anick Lemay's character, Lucille, is rather pale and lifeless even before her husband's death; they are shown as a happy couple, with the door demurely shut on their nonetheless clearly active sex life. However, the depiction of her as being at loose ends without the family breadwinner and the concluding hints that she will pair with Frisson's second father substitute, local veterinarian (Paul Doucet), leave her no role other than that of housewife and mother, apparently unable to function independently in the decade's supposed new society. The film provides a more liberated image of women from a younger generation through Frisson's older sister, Camille (Viviane Audet), who is having a secret affair with the local priest (he plans to leave the church so they can marry), and his resplendent new teacher, Hélène Paradis (Évelyne Brochu).

Both may be described as "nice little films," successfully negotiating state-subsidizing bodies' demands for a Québec-specific, territorialized "national" cinema while at the same time meeting popular audiences' desires to see familiar stars in a by-now-familiar subgenre (the 1960s family film). Ideologically speaking, however, these last two films take a step backward from the 2008 films. With their idealized (albeit absent) fathers and their nostalgia for the preliberation mother portrayed by LeBreton and Lemay, they lack the critical punch we find in the work of Pool and Falardeau or, for that matter, even Leclerc. Eventually, these mothers complete the grieving process and return to care for their sons, but neither character advances personally: Le Breton's character seeks refuge in the conservative values of her ultra-Catholic in-laws, and Lemay's remains a housewife, simply transferring her wifely duties to another man.

A Range of Forgiveness

Director Francis Leclerc attributes the recent popularity of the 1960s in Québécois cinema to the fact that the "deciders" at funding agencies like SODEC and Téléfilm Canada are baby boomers (Protat 4–5), and he acknowledges that for *Un été sans point ni coup sûr*, he had to rely on coscenarist Michel Robitaille for a true-to-memory image of that decade, since Leclerc hadn't been born yet. Leclerc also speculates about a spate of 1980s films as his generation comes to the fore (Protat 6); in fact, such a boom has already begun, as seen in Ricardo Trogi's comedies, undisguised *autofictions* focalized by a budding adolescent male based on the filmmaker/scenarist's own memories of that decade, *1981* (2009) and *1987* (2014).

Whereas we cannot deny that popular cinema in Québec continues to vehicle black-and-white images of the "horrible mother" and the victimized child, it does so in order to condemn the pre–Quiet Revolution values of the Grande Noirceur, as Bédard argues. We can nonetheless conclude, based on the corpus of films examined here and their more nuanced treatments of the mother, that complex female characters have become increasingly present on the province's big screens and that women's roles in Québec society, both public and private, must be acknowledged. In particular, these films indirectly address the role of the women's liberation movement as part of the various movements for national autonomy during the 1960s. This alone demonstrates the success of efforts by feminist scholars like those of the pioneering Collectif Clio and, more recently, Denyse Baillargeon, among others, to ensure that women's roles in the development of Québécois national identity and self-representation are acknowledged. Furthermore, while we expect that a woman filmmaker such as Pool, frequently labeled as "feminist," even though she rejects the label herself (Green 60–61), would pave the way for films that revise a deep-rooted image of the mother, it is significant that male filmmakers of a younger generation also offer such visions, as seen in Leclerc's *Un été* and Falardeau's *C'est pas moi*. Significantly, these acknowledged *auteurs* allow their mothers greater latitude in terms of progressive lifestyles that can combine motherhood with a career. Finally, even the more ambivalent imagery found in the works of filmmakers more closely linked with popular media, like Monty and Roy and the older Bouvier

(Castiel 14), reveals that Québec has come a long way toward forgiving the horrible mother.

NOTES

1. For classic interpretations of this film, see Loiselle (39–54); Tremblay-Daviault (38–41); Weinmann (*Cinéma* 27–50). For a more recent discussion, see Beaulieu (49–51). Although the film is considered an unquestionable "classic" of Québec film, opinions vary widely on the film's aesthetic merits, ranging from Weinmann's qualification as one of the province's "premiers grands films" (*Cinéma* 13) to Bédard's admission of its "évidentes faiblesses" ("obvious weaknesses") (88). I find its sadomasochistic spectacularization of child abuse somewhat exploitative.

2. For a complete account of *C.R.A.Z.Y.*, this now-iconic film that also records the 1960s experiences of a young protagonist, see Schwartzwald.

3. *Frisson des collines* doesn't appear to have an official English title; it refers to the main character's nickname, Frisson (shiver), and might be rendered "Frisson of/ from the Hills."

4. The years 1960–66, known as Québec's "Quiet Revolution," marked a period of profrancophone political reforms and the secularization of Québec's social services, such as education and health care. Before this period of modernization, the dominant clerical-national ideology dictated traditional gender roles for French Canadian men and women.

5. For a more extended reading of this film, see Gilbert and Santoro.

6. Heinz Weinmann's applications of Freud's family romance to Québec's history in *Du Canada au Québec: Généalogie d'une histoire* (1987) and to its cinema in *Cinéma de l'imaginaire au Québec, de la petite Aurore à Jésus de Montréal* (1990) remain the best known works in the commentary provoked by Guy Corneau's psychological study *Absent Fathers, Lost Sons* (1989).

7. The film's credits indicate only "Mère" and "Père." Although the film gives Hanna's father's full name, David Cohn, we never learn the Christian name of her mother, whose surname, Riel, Hanna nonetheless bears.

8. Associated with Maurice Duplessis's terms as prime minister of Québec (1936–39 and 1940–59), this period has been considered as Québec's Dark Ages. A time of clerical influence and political conservatism, it is frequently contrasted with the Quiet Revolution, which followed it.

9. *Joual*, a transcription of urban working-class Montrealers' pronunciation of the word for "horse" in French (*cheval*), has moved from a term referring to a distinct dialect to being used as shorthand for all vernacular forms of French spoken throughout the province.

10. Julia Morgan Charles and Frédéric Clément develop separately the problem of nostalgia in these films' representations of Québec society in the 1960s through the microcosm of the family, thus supporting and supplementing the arguments made here.

11. In this imaginative iteration of the real-life Hébert family, Benoit parallels the Léon character in Bruno Hébert's novels and Philippe Falardeau's film.

12. Like *Emporte-moi*, this film only credits the parents as "La Mère" and "Le Père," but conversely, we never learn the father's first name in *Maman*.

13. Pool's mention of the once-respected psychologist who (erroneously) made an entire generation of mothers feel guilty for having "caused" their child's autism appears to be yet another jab at the father and his glib faith in science.

14. First founded by the Jesuits, the private system of the *collège classique* prepared French Canadian elites for university with a classical curriculum. The schools were replaced after the Quiet Revolution with the new, secularized system of the *cégep* (*collège d'enseignement général et professionnel*).

FILMOGRAPHY

1981. Dir. Ricardo Trogi. Perf. Jean-Carl Boucher. Go Films, 2009. DVD.

1987. Dir. Ricardo Trogi. Perf. Jean-Carl Boucher. Go Films, 2014. DVD.

Aurore. Dir. Luc Dionne. Perf. Marianne Fortier, Serge Postigo, Hélène Bourgeois-Leclerc. Cinémaginaire, 2005. DVD.

C'est pas moi je le jure! (*It's Not Me, I Swear!*). Dir. Philippe Falardeau. Perf. Antoine L'Écuyer, Suzanne Clément, Daniel Brière. Christal Films, 2008. DVD.

C.R.A.Z.Y. Dir. Jean-Marc Vallée. Perf. Marc-André Grondin, Michel Côté, Danielle Proulx. TVA Films, 2005. DVD.

Emporte-moi (*Set Me Free*). Dir. Léa Pool. Perf. Karine Vanasse, Pascale Bussières. Cité Amérique, 1999. VHS.

Frisson des collines. Dir. Richard Roy. Perf. Antoine-Olivier Pilon, Anick Lemay, Guillaume Lemay-Thivierge. Les Films Séville, 2011. DVD.

Histoire de famille. Dir. Michel Poulette. Perf. Juliette Gosselin, Danielle Proulx, Luc Proulx. Christal Films, 2006. DVD.

Histoires d'hiver (*Winter Stories*). Dir. François Bouvier. Perf. Joël Dalpé-Drapeau, Luc Guérin, Diane Lavallée. Aska Films, 1999. DVD.

L'affaire de la petite Aurore. "Les grands procès" (season 2, episode 5). Dir. Mark Blandford. Perf. Yvan Ponton, Léa-Marie Cantin. TVA, 1994. VHS.

La petite Aurore, l'enfant martyre (*Little Aurora's Tragedy*). Dir. Jean-Yves Bigras. Perf. Yvonne Laflamme, Lucie Mitchell. L'Alliance Cinématographique Canadienne, 1952. VHS.

Le survenant (*The Outlander*). Dir. Erik Canuel. Perf. Jean-Nicolas Verreault, Anick Lemay, Gilles Renaud. Les Films Vision 4, 2005. DVD.

Maman est chez le coiffeur (*Mommy's at the Hairdresser's*). Dir. Léa Pool. Perf. Marianne Fortier, Céline Bonnier, Laurent Lucas. Arte/Equinoxe, 2008. DVD.

Mon oncle Antoine. Dir. Claude Jutra. Perf. Jacques Gagnon, Jean Deuceppe. ONF, 1971. VHS.

Séraphin: Un homme et son péché (*Séraphin: Heart of Stone*). Dir. Charles Binamé. Perf. Pierre Lebeau, Karine Vanasse, Roy Dupuis. Alliance Vivafilm, 2002. DVD.

Un été sans point ni coup sûr (*A No-Hit, No-Run Summer*). Dir. Francis Leclerc. Perf. Pierre-Luc Funk, Patrice Robitaille, Jacinthe Laguë. Alliance Vivafilm, 2008. DVD.

Une vie qui commence (*Life Begins*). Dir. Michel Monty. Perf. Charles Antoine Perreault, Julie Le Breton, François Papineau. Alliance Vivafilm, 2010. DVD.

WORKS CITED

Baillargeon, Denyse. *Brève histoire des femmes au Québec*. Boréal, 2012.

Beaulieu, Étienne. "Le murmure du hors-champ: La voix et l'image dans trois films québécois." *Revue des Sciences Humaines*, vol. 288, Oct.–Dec. 2007, pp. 45–55.

Bédard, Éric. "Ce passé qui ne passe pas: La Grande Noirceur catholique dans les films *Séraphin: Un homme et son péché, Le survenant* et *Aurore*." *Globe: Revue Internationale d'Études Québécoises*, vol. 11, no. 1, 2008, pp. 75–94.

Castiel, Élie. "Entrevue: François Bouvier; La mémoire indélébile." *Séquences*, vol. 201, Mar.–Apr. 1999, pp. 14–16.

Charles, Julia Morgan. "La Maison où j'ai grandi: The Changing Landscape of Nostalgia in Quebec's Contemporary Coming of Age Films." MA thesis, McGill University, 2009.

Chartier, Daniel. "Le cinéma du pays de la neige devient pluriculturel." *Études Romanes*, vol. 59, 2009, pp. 141–53.

Clément, Frédéric. "Voix de femmes, voies de femmes: La fin des années 60 dans le cinéma récent." *Perspectives étudiantes féministes: Actes électroniques du colloque étudiant le 12–13 mars, 2010*, edited by Valérie Soly, pp. 158–76.

Collectif Clio. *L'histoire des femmes au Québec depuis quatre siècles*. Les Quinze / Club des Loisirs, 1983.

Corneau, Guy. *Absent Fathers, Lost Sons*. 1989. Trans. Larry Shouldice. Shambhala, 1991.

Fradet, Pierre-Alexandre. Rev. of *Frisson des collines*. *Séquences*, vol. 273, July–Aug. 2011, p. 62.

Gilbert, Paula Ruth, and Miléna Santoro. "Transforming Visions: Pedagogical Approaches to Léa Pool's *Emporte-moi* (*Set Me Free*)." Special issue of *Women in French Studies*, 2006, pp. 139–55.

Green, Mary Jean. "Léa Pool's *La Femme de l'hôtel* and Women's Film in Québec." *Québec Studies*, vol. 9, 1989–90, pp. 49–62.

Halberstam, Judith. *The Queer Art of Failure*. Duke University Press, 2011.

Hébert, Bruno. *Alice court avec René*. Boréal, 2000.

———. *C'est pas moi, je le jure!* Boréal, 1997.

Lamoureux, Diane. "The Paradoxes of Quebec Feminism." *Quebec Questions: Quebec Studies for the Twenty-First Century*, edited by Christopher Kirkey, Stéphane Gervais, and Jarett Rudy, 2nd ed., Oxford University Press Canada, 2016, pp. 352–71.

Larochelle, Diane, and Rénald Lessard. "Un cas tragique: Aurore l'enfant martyre." *Cap-aux-Diamants: La Revue d'Histoire du Québec*, vol. 32, 1993, p. 59.

Lever, Yves. "Cinéma québécois et mémoire." *Le cinéma au Québec: Tradition et modernité*, edited by Stéphane Albert Boulais, Fides, 2006, pp. 77–87.

Loiselle, André. *Stage-Bound: Feature Film Adaptations of Canadian and Québécois Drama*. McGill-Queen's University Press, 2003.

Moss, Jane. "Family Films: Québec Style." *American Review of Canadian Studies*, vol. 41, no. 2, 2011, pp. 109–16.

Pallister, Janis. "L'*angst* de l'adolescente: *Emporte-moi* de Léa Pool." *Nouvelles Études Francophones*, vol. 22, no. 1, 2007, pp. 89–108.

Protat, Zoë. "Entretien avec Francis Leclerc." *CinéBulles*, vol. 26, no. 3, 2008, pp. 2–8.

Proulx, Robert. "À la croisée des chemins entre le récit et le film." *Sélection des Actes du Colloque international d'études françaises de l'APFFUE, Université de La Rioja*, Logroño, Spain, 2004, pp. 99–109.

Robitaille, Marc. *Histoires d'hiver, avec des rues, des écoles et du hockey*. VLB, 1987.

———. *Un été sans point ni coup sûr*. Les 400 coups, 2004.

Schwartzwald, Robert. *C.R.A.Z.Y.: A Queer Film Classic*. Arsenal Pulp Press, 2016.

Tremblay-Daviault, Christiane. "Avant la Révolution tranquille: Une Terre-Mère en perdition." *Femmes et cinéma québécois*, edited by Louise Carrière, Boréal Express, 1983, pp. 21–52.

Valade, Claire. "Vivre sa vie: *Un été sans point ni coup sûr*." *Séquences*, vol. 255, July–Aug. 2008, p. 45.

Weinmann, Heinz. *Cinéma de l'imaginaire au Québec, de la petite Aurore à Jésus de Montréal*. l'Héxagone, 1990.

———. *Du Canada au Québec: Généalogie d'une histoire*. l'Héxagone, 1987.

9

Politics and Motherhood in Xavier Dolan's *J'ai tué ma mère* and *Mommy*

LOÏC BOURDEAU

In her 1994 contribution to *Recherches Féministes* titled "Le corps et la fiction à réinventer: Métamorphose de la maternité dans l'écriture des femmes au Québec," Lori Saint-Martin provides an analysis of novels in which the mother figure has finally become a subject.[1] Indeed, while the mother has been omnipresent in Québécois literature and theater, her "expérience quotidienne . . . , ses désirs, sa voix, n'ont droit de citer dans le roman que depuis peu" ("daily experience . . . , desires, voice, have only recently been included in novels") (Saint-Martin 116). In the texts that Saint-Martin analyzes, as well as in more contemporary works, "tout un pan de l'expérience des femmes . . . accède finalement à la fiction" ("a whole array of women's experiences . . . finally has a place in fiction") (116). Interestingly, however, representations of mothers in Quebec cinema have proven quite scarce. As film scholar Bill Marshall points out, "It is certainly the case that the father-son relationship is often privileged in Quebec cinema (or conspicuous by its absence, which usually amounts to the same thing)" and often serves to bring forth Quebec's "failure to attain phallo-national maturity" (106). Critic Martin Bilodeau writes about Xavier Dolan's first feature film, *J'ai tué ma mère* (2009): "J'ai beaucoup exercé ma mémoire cette semaine afin de trouver dans le cinéma québecois un personnage de mère aussi fort et présent au centre de l'image que celui interprété par Anne Dorval" ("I have thought long and hard this past week to find in Quebec cinema such a strong mother as the one portrayed by Anne Dorval"). What seems to be original in Dolan's maternal portrayal lies in the same representational shift that has taken place in literature; that is, finally a mother can express her own subjectivity. As Saint-Martin reminds us, quoting Marianne Hirsch, new stories cannot emerge so long as mothers remain objects rather than "des sujets sociaux, psychologiques et linguistiques" ("social, psychological, and linguistic subjects") (132). Contemporary productions successfully offer new forms of maternal empowerment. As far as cinema is concerned, Dolan certainly plays a part in this endeavor.[2]

Although Quebec cinema does not frequently engage with the mother figure, the topic is discussed quite extensively in contemporary media. Indeed, this coverage inundates our newsfeeds, channels, papers, and daily discussions with issues pertaining to women's rights and motherhood. Such a proliferation provides the basis of this chapter as I investigate Dolan's maternal representations in *J'ai tué ma mère* (2009) and *Mommy* (2014) and propose a reading of these figures as archetypes of the contemporary Québécoise and her social, economic, and political struggles. *J'ai tué ma mère* tells the story of sixteen-year-old Hubert, who lives with his divorced mother, Chantal. Both struggle to communicate and to have common interests, which weighs on the relationship. Chantal, a secretary, enjoys watching her TV shows, decorating her home with kitschy decorations, tanning at the salon, and wearing faux fur, and she has a tendency to change her mind from one day to the next. Hubert, on the other hand, hates kitsch, creates his own abstract art, has a passion for literature, and dislikes "sa classe de morons" ("his class of morons"). Given the aggravated nature of their interactions, Chantal decides to send him to boarding school, which he utterly despises. He eventually escapes to a place by the sea where he had spent a happy childhood. Chantal finds him, and the film points to a form of reconciliation.

Similar struggles take place in *Mommy* between Diane (Die, which she signs with a heart in place of a dot), a widowed single mother, and her violent, ADHD-suffering son, Steve, who is expelled from yet another institution.

In spite of a new law allowing her to give up her legal rights to her son, Diane decides to take care of him. Their neighbor Kyla, an emotionally depressed teacher on sabbatical, quickly comes into the picture to help Diane and homeschool Steve. The son's mental problems give rise to violent outbursts that make it increasingly harder for Diane to take care of him. Unlike the first film, mother and son are extremely close and affectionate, but tensions arise nonetheless.

This chapter focuses exclusively on these two works to shed light on the cinematic progression at play and rather called for by the features' titles and thematic similarities. I argue that *J'ai tué ma mère* addresses motherhood at conceptual and historical levels, whereas *Mommy* offers insights into more current and identifiable specimens of womanhood/motherhood. It came to my attention that *Mommy* is at times perceived as Dolan's way to redeem "his" mother in *J'ai tué ma mère*. Such a perplexing remark reveals two issues. First, it is oblivious to the final scene, in which Chantal tells off the school principal, rejects his patriarchal accusations of her incompetence, and happily reunites with her son. Second, it suggests that Chantal was indeed a bad mother in need of redemption, thus failing to notice how the entire film tries to deconstruct social expectations vis-à-vis mothers, subsequently reinforcing that motherhood as performed by Diane in *Mommy* (caring and fully dedicated to her son's well-being) is the right model. I would agree with journalist Mark Olsen, who notes: "His latest film builds upon themes of identity and redemption explored in his 2009 debut." If the rapprochement is relevant, then redemption as its justification proves a problematic oversight.

While both films rely on a mother-son dynamic, the first work demonstrates the crippling effects of historically inherited normative discourses, whereas the second reflects on the impact of present sociopolitical difficulties. Although these issues arise from specific political decisions in the Québécois context, they should easily resonate with decisions made presently in other Western countries. To borrow from Bill Marshall and Gill Rye in their introduction to a special issue of *Quebec Studies, Women's Writing and Filmmaking in Québec*, this chapter seeks to demonstrate how Dolan's work is not only "firmly anchored in the Québécois context" but also representative of more universal concerns (7).

In a volume titled *Horrible Mothers*, a discussion of Dolan's cinematographic representation of mother-son conflict in *J'ai tué ma mère* is quite fitting. The title of the film suffices to shed light on the difficult relationship between two entities: "je" (Hubert) and "ma mère" (Chantal). While the intent behind this affirmation, "j'ai tué ma mère," lies in separation—the survival of one individual, of "je"—the film refuses to treat Hubert as the sole center of narrative gravity. Just as the title demands, at the level of syntax, a relationship between a subject and an object, so too does the plot demand that we not overlook one character (the mother) by privileging the other's perspective (Hubert's). In fact, the opening scene reverses the subject-object hierarchy as the mother appears first in a close-up of her mouth, then her face, and then her upper body. Slowly moving back, the camera makes room for the son, who is sitting next to her at the dining table. By trapping them in the frame, the mother on the left and the son on the right, Dolan establishes the inseparable and inescapable nature of their rapport. In a similar manner, the next scene takes place in the mother's car while they are on their way to school and work. Soon they are arguing about the radio station and other minor subjects. Here also the frame locks them in the same space. By focusing specifically on the mother during arguments, Dolan places Chantal in a broader context, portraying her authority as fragile and unable to criticize historically charged stereotypes of motherhood.

In times of crisis, Chantal will seek to, if not victimize herself, perform maternal selflessness and genuine care.[3] Two scenes depict Dolan's strategy while shedding light on the burden of social norms:

> *Chantal*: J'serais curieuse que tu fasses un sondage auprès de tes chums.... Demande-leur donc si leurs parents les conduisent à l'école le matin.
>
> *Hubert*: Arrête de me demander de faire des sondages à chaque fois. Tu dis n'importe quoi! 50 pour cent de mes chums se font conduire par leurs parents! 50 pour cent!
>
> ...
>
> *Chantal*: Tu me demandes pas comment était la mienne de journée?
>
> *Hubert*: Non.... [S]i y avait quelque chose de spécial qui s'était passé tu me l'aurais déjà dit, c'est sûr ! Puis, même chose pour moi.[4]

The first exchange is from the argument in the car, which the mother hopes to win by resorting to a scientific (and purportedly unbiased) experiment. Statistics become an example of the dominance of the normal in their relationship. The mother relies on the survey method to show her son that she is somewhat "exceptional." Taking him to school is presented as a favor; she is not like any other parent. Yet the son quickly retorts that they are nothing but an average family. Chantal proceeds to drop him off in the middle of the street, concerned that she might be late to work. Historian Andrée Lévesque explains in *Making and Breaking the Rules: Women in Quebec, 1919–1939* (1994) that "[w]hether she was being described by priest, doctor, or politician, the mother was primarily a figure of love and self-sacrifice" (23). In his portrayal of Chantal, Dolan thus posits the historical legacy of the *mère québécoise*, whose "kindness, forbearance, compassion, gentleness, and suffering" (24) represent alleged innate qualities praised by society in opposition to Chantal's own priorities and desires.[5] The construction of the scene itself, from her trying to be an extraordinary mother to dropping off her son in the street, epitomizes the difficulties of living up to societal expectations and, at the same time, living one's life.

In a similar manner, the second dialogue demonstrates Chantal's forced attempt at making small talk, even though she has nothing "spécial" to tell.[6] What emerges from these scenes and from other instances in the film is the prevalence of Chantal's attempt to uphold conservative values of motherhood—and her subsequent failures to do so—as a response to historical discourses on the matter. *J'ai tué ma mère* offers alternative models of motherhood (especially in the person of Hubert's boyfriend's mother), the inclusion of which actually reinforces the traditional nature of Chantal's performance and her overall inscription into the aforementioned past discourses.

It is true that Lévesque's case study predates the advances and benefits of the Quiet Revolution and the women's liberation movement, which "includ[ed] ending physical and sexual violence against women and systemic discrimination against women in the workplace, establishing daycare and parental leave, the recognition of women's work in the family, and the equality of spouses in marriage" (Baillargeon 243). Nevertheless, examples such as Michel Tremblay's iconic play *Les belles-soeurs* (1968) and Fanny

Britt's essay mentioned below show that similar considerations operate on a cyclical basis. Of course, demographic studies show significant changes in Québec's birth rate, thus highlighting the impact of these advances. From the "revanche des berceaux" ("revenge of the cradle") to headlines about Quebec's low birth rate (e.g., the *Montreal Gazette*: "Fewer Babies Born in Quebec as Fertility Rate Continues Downward Spiral"), it becomes evident that women of the post-1970s era enjoy greater freedom to decide whether they want to have children.[7] Yet the perception of child-free women remains quite negative. In May 2018 journalist Alexandra Schwartz wrote: "Women rarely get the chance to exercise their free will over their own fertility without encumbrance or coercion" and that, although having children yields the "promise of social validation," it comes at a cost. As time unfolds, stigmatization persists.

My discussion of *Mommy* later in this chapter, as well as the current debates over abortion and women's rights and the recurring social judgments as to what is a good or bad mother, further underlines the persisting rhetoric of control and surveillance from which Chantal suffers.[8] Above all, this rhetoric reinforces the expectation that women exist to be mothers. In Britt's *Les tranchées: Maternité, ambigüité et féminisme, en fragments*, two women recount:

> On va trinquer à notre liberté, pis à notre rébellion par rapport aux modèles féminins traditionnels.
> Rébellion, schmébellion.
>
> . . .
>
> Non mais c'est vrai. Nos amis qui ont des enfants pensent qu'on "défie le patriarcat" tous les soirs de la semaine, mais la vérité, c'est que la plupart du temps, je me couche avec une hostie de chape de plomb sur le cœur, pis que je passe mes nuits à me débattre avec questions de marde, à me demander où-quand-comment je vais trouver la porte qui mène à la vie signifiante que je suis supposée mener pis que je mène visiblement pas, vu que partout où je regarde, on me montre qu'une vie signifiante, ça inclut des enfants.
> Pis le pire c'est qu'on angoisse même pas sur des problèmes qu'on a. On angoisse sur des problèmes qu'on pourrait avoir. (19–20)[9]

Decades separate Lévesque's mothers from those of Dolan and Britt, but the daily concerns and fights have changed little. As feminist and psychoanalyst Luce Irigaray puts it, "[W]e [women] are brought up (whether consciously or not) to be trained in repetition, to adapt to a society's systems, and educated to do *like*, to be *like*, without any decisive innovations or discoveries of our own" (*Je* 31). Although discourses in support of women's freedoms have gained more ground and attention, and "innovations or discoveries" are more widely available to women and mothers, they continue to be torn between their desire to define themselves alone and to fit in a schizophrenic world that supposedly advocates diversity and liberty while at the same time giving greater value to (good) mothers. Chantal is one such example of this psychological split.

Because of the tense nature of their interactions, Hubert one evening suggests that he rent a studio apartment close to school using his grandmother's inheritance. Chantal initially agrees.

> *Hubert*: *Je te parle.* J'ai trouvé une solution de pour nous deux. Pour notre relation. *Tu écoutes.* Je pense qu'il faut que je déménage dans un appartement. Je serais proche du métro, je serais proche de l'école, je serais proche de mes amis. . . . C'est parce que tu es toujours sur mon dos. Je sais que ça va fonctionner.
> *Chantal*: Tu vas faire ça avec l'argent de mamie?
> *Hubert*: Oui! voilà exactement ce que je pensais. On est vraiment sur la même longueur d'onde.
> *Chantal*: Oui, c'est une bonne idée. . . .
> *Hubert*: Je suis content, je t'aime, je t'aime. Je t'aime ma petite maman d'amour.[10]

The following evening, however, things have changed:

> *Hubert*: *Maman faut que je te parle.* J'ai visité l'appartement.
> *Chantal*: Quel appartement?
> *Hubert*: Et bien l'appartement dont je t'ai parlé. Il est tellement parfait pour moi, j'en reviens pas.
> *Chantal*: J'ai repensé à ça aujourd'hui, ça a pas de bon sens. . . .

Hubert: Excuse-moi? Je t'en ai parlé hier et tu m'as dit que c'était une bonne idée. Je t'en ai parlé hier! (my emphasis)[11]

While these instances somewhat reestablish Chantal's authority, she becomes in the eyes of the viewer mostly responsible for the various arguments. In addition, Dolan also undermines her power because it is presented as so fickle. In both scenes, Hubert repeatedly calls for his mother's attention (she is absorbed in her television program), and she fails to place the welfare of their relationship over her personal interests. It even seems that her initial agreement with her son's idea might have merely been a ploy to secure a peaceful evening for herself in front of the television. Perhaps too she was lulled and blinded by the repeated use of "proche" and "je t'aime" as the promise of a closer bond with her son, thus echoing the way "culture . . . has blindly venerated the mother-son relationship to the point of religious fetishism" (Irigaray, *Je* 39).

Nevertheless, the viewer should not be tempted to "haïr" Chantal the way Hubert hates her ("j't'haïs"). Again, this requires that we understand and accept the Québécoise's historical baggage and tease out the various contributing elements of her sociological oppression.[12] To further engage with the status and power of motherhood, Lévesque writes:

> Woman is defined by maternity; given its essential qualities, it would be against nature for her to deviate from its course. Paradoxically, however, the entire apparatus was devoted to incubating and orienting her nature. Her first dolls were there to be cuddled, dressed, fed, and, of course, loved. With the advent of puberty, the lesson became more pointed. According to Dr. L. P. Mercier, "It is at this point that the girl must begin to realize that, by reason of her physical and moral qualities, her entire life is headed for the one great aim, of motherhood." (27)

To let her teenage son move out implies an actual physical split in the relationship, which would damage her image and tarnish her "moral qualities." Further, in comparison to her son's boyfriend and mother, a relationship that resembles that of friends, she would doubtlessly be perceived as a horrible mother, one who drove her son out of the house. Who would wish to be "against nature," "to deviate," to reject life's "one great aim"? In a black-and-white confessional vignette, Hubert explains with great awareness the power of lasting expectations: "Elle voulait pas m'avoir. Elle a agi comme si j'étais un fardeau. Elle était pas faite pour être mère. Elle s'est mariée puis elle a eu un enfant parce que c'est ce que tout le monde attendait d'elle. C'est ce que tout le monde attend encore des femmes d'ailleurs. Presque tout le monde" ("She didn't want me. She behaved as though I was a burden. She wasn't made to be a mother. She got married and had a child because that's what everybody expected of her. In fact, that's what everyone expects of women. Almost everyone").

Hubert's commentary strikes home not only because of its accuracy but also because of the absence of the father in the picture. While there is a reference to marriage, it is *she* who had a child. In that sense, Dolan's work is of a kind with Québec's literary tradition, in which fathers are predominantly absent. As scholar Rachel Killick notes in her introduction to Tremblay's *Les belles-soeurs*: "Men as well as women were losers in the arrangement [imposed by the Catholic Church], since the exaggerated promotion of the image of 'mère de famille,' passing over the men, gave considerable power to the domestic partnership of women and parish priest" (xvi). Because the church had so much power and determination to control women in order to guarantee Québec's "physical survival" (xv), men lost power in the very system that should have promoted them.

Chantal's authority, when it is not unstable, functions by proxy; that is, it is mediated through a third party. Because of their disagreements, the mother appeals to the father in hopes that Hubert will respect the decision to send him to boarding school in the country. In this particular scene, it is through a parental "we" that authority can be upheld, yet it is a "we" that is mostly paternal/patriarchal and posits the father as superior to Chantal. The screen places the father at the center of the scene, while mother and son surround him on each side. He cites Latin sayings—in a rather pompous manner—which further establishes his supposed superiority. In fact, he quickly turns to the mother to give her the translation. What follows is an outburst of violent anger from Hubert, which Dolan chooses to express through a metaphorical explosion. More powerful than the son's "fuck you," the image of an exploding window, of shattered glass, communicates the intensity of his feelings.

The mother's decision to resort to the father's intervention initially seems to lessen her own authority and might testify to her own failures as a mother. Chantal, who does not manage to conform to normative standards of motherhood and whose personal preferences and priorities unfold throughout the film, participates at first in further empowering and legitimizing patriarchal discourses. "L'ordre social fonctionne comme une immense machine symbolique tendant à ratifier la domination masculine sur laquelle il est fondé" ("The social order functions like a big symbolic machine aimed at ratifying the masculine domination upon which it is founded") (Bourdieu, *La domination* 22–23). Chantal, as one part in this "machine," helps to "ratifier" the very order that oppresses her. Hubert's father, who is "un lâche qui . . . a dumpé . . . [Chantal] sous prétexte qu'il n'était pas à la hauteur de son rôle de père" ("a coward who . . . dumped . . . [Chantal] because allegedly he wasn't up to the task of being a father"), comes back to try to exert his paternal power, as though from some "divinely preordained design" (Killick xvi). He cannot, however, be taken seriously, and he damages the very image of patriarchy. If the viewer might be tempted to blame Hubert's attitude on the lack of a father figure, the latter's intervention quickly discredits him. What right does he have over a child he has not raised? Dolan provides a poignant critique of patriarchy, an ultimately crippled system. The filmmaker excludes the possibility of giving power to the father and refuses the idea that "une différence biologique entre les sexes . . . peut apparaître comme la justification naturelle de la différence entre les genres" ("a biological difference between the sexes . . . can appear as the natural justification to gender differences") (Bourdieu, *La domination* 24–25). This biological difference eventually becomes the natural justification of men's superiority over women.

The movie's penultimate scene, in which, during a phone conversation, Chantal rejects the school principal's criticisms of her childrearing method, puts another dent in the patriarchal order. In light of these two instances, it is quite clear that Dolan's interventions seek to deconstruct patriarchal authority, which, in turn, echoes Québec's status as a progressive and feminist province. In "Le Québec, paradis du féminisme" (2017), philosopher Loyola Leroux lays out the various measures in favor of women and parity: "La lutte au patriarcat et ses symboles est très en avance au Québec avec la possibilité pour les femmes de garder leur nom de famille" ("The fight against patriarchy and its symbols is ahead of its time in Quebec with the possibility for women to keep their last name"), or Québec "est la province qui possède le plus grand pourcentage de mères monoparentales" ("is the province with the highest percentage of single mothers"). In that sense, Quebec offers a diversity of possibilities for women and mothers and thus a diversity of maternal experiences. As the film gives us a glimpse of one mother-son relationship, it does not claim to represent all mothers, and it rejects judgment or moralization.

Following the success of *J'ai tué ma mère* in 2009 at the Quinzaine du Festival de Cannes, where it received three prizes, Xavier Dolan declared: "Jamais je n'ai été aussi fier d'être Québécois. . . . Quand on est confronté à un environnement étranger, on réalise alors la profondeur de ses racines. Ici et maintenant, je sais d'où je viens et j'ai hâte de partager mes prix et mon film avec ma famille: les Québécois" ("I've never been so proud of being Québécois. . . . When one is confronted with a foreign environment, one realizes then the depth of one's roots. Here and now, I know where I'm from, and I look forward to sharing my awards and my film with my family: all Québécois") (O. Tremblay). Proud of his Québec roots, the filmmaker acknowledges the undeniable influence of his motherland on his work. *J'ai tué ma mère* is indeed the product of such attachment and influence, where past and present interact. Not only did he not kill the maternal character, he reinstated her to a central position and shed new light on Québec's burdensome legacy of motherhood and its impact on the contemporary Québécoise.

As *J'ai tué ma mère* plays with and relies on the past, on Québec's identity and national struggles, *Mommy* should demonstrate in the following discussion the inscription of motherhood into contemporary reality, the now of Quebec.

Mommy: Womanhood and Motherhood in Contemporary Québec

After three feature-length films in which mothers were not central—*Les amours imaginaires* (2010), *Laurence Anyways* (2012), and *Tom à la ferme* (2013)—Dolan created another conflicting duo.[13] *Mommy* opens in a manner quite similar to *J'ai tué ma mère*, presenting the mother-son relationship as the crux of the story. Unlike the film, however, the question of inseparability is very much in the background. Although it is "filmed almost claustrophobically in the perfect-square shape 1:1 aspect ratio" (Schou), which establishes closeness and inescapable exposure, mother and son are in two distinct spaces. While Chantal and Hubert were trapped in the shot unconditionally, Diane and Steve's reunion is conditional. In terms of the progression of Dolan's maternal representations, it makes sense that the mother-son relationship is not a given. His films demonstrate patterns and strategies to *unmother* women, to let them express their own desires and subjectivities outside the realm of motherhood. Diane is perhaps the most developed archetype of the unmother, "personnage de veuve un peu dégrossie, presque vulgaire que ses proches surnomment D.I.E." ("a somewhat rough widow, almost vulgar and whose relatives call D.I.E.") (Houdassine). Her nickname, which she signs with a heart in place of the dot, even strengthens her image as an independent woman, one who has actually killed the mother—the one normative model offered to women—to become two distinguishable and self-chosen identities: a woman *and* a mother.

According to Dolan, *Mommy* "parle de gens qui s'aiment profondément mais dont l'amour est mis à l'épreuve par la vie elle-même, par la maladie et par le système qui les ostracise" ("speaks of people who deeply love each other but whose love is being put to the test by life itself, by the disease, and by the system that ostracizes them") ("*Mommy*"). The following analysis investigates, for the most part, such problems as motherhood, ostracism, and systemic marginalization in conjunction with concrete political developments in Québec. (It will seem as though so much more could be said about this film, and I would agree. The focus in this analysis is first to make connections between the fiction and Québec women's and mothers' lived conditions today. *Mommy* becomes a lens through which to understand a variety of factors that still hinder women's emancipation.) Diane has been asked to attend a meeting at her son's psychiatric institution following new instances of violence, and the camera tracks her determined steps through the building. The strong-willed mother must decide what will happen to her expelled son in a new political context. Indeed, the opening shot—white text on a black screen—reads:

In a fictional Canada, a new government comes into power during the federal elections of 2015. Two months later, its cabinet passes the s-18 Bill, amending the Canadian health services policy. Specifically, the bill includes the highly controversial s-14 law, which stipulates that the parent of a child with behavior problems has, in a situation of financial distress, physical and or psychological danger, the moral and legal right to commit his child to a state psychiatric hospital, without further legal review.

From the beginning of the film, *Mommy* focuses on the choice to be or not to be a caregiver. Whereas Chantal "a eu un enfant parce que c'est ce que tout le monde attendait d'elle" ("has had a child because that's what everyone expected of her") (*J'ai tué ma mère*), Diane has the option to give up her rights over her child. The viewer might wonder, if Diane were to do that, would she be any less of a mother? She refuses to do so, in spite of medical recommendations. The mother's refusal is also a refusal to let normative institutions determine one's identity, just as "the woman was [once and only] qualified for those physical and social functions for which her biology and education had destined her" (Lévesque 27).

Out of the hospital and into the world, Diane and Steve prepare to start a new life, with all that it entails: finding a home, going to work, going to school, and so forth. To this extent, Dolan's latest production concerns itself with the mundane and somewhat banal realities of life. More subtly, he questions processes of (political) domination and its effects on people. As such, the opening of the film presents those forces that come in contact with and regulate everyone's life. Further, it attests to the inevitably hierarchical nature of power, from federal to legal and medical and, finally, to parental.

In the edited volume *Pierre Bourdieu: L'insoumission en héritage* (2013), French writer and intellectual Édouard Louis writes about politics: "Comment la politique—et en l'occurrence, une politique de gauche—peut-elle produire la vie bonne si ceux qui font la politique sont si peu concernés par les effets de la politique? Si elle ne les frappe pas comme elle frappait les personnes de mon enfance?" ("How can politics—and in particular, left-wing politics—produce the good life if those who are making politics are so little concerned with the effects of politics? If it doesn't hit them like it would hit the people of my childhood?") (12).

Although *Mommy* does not engage with current political affairs in Québec in an attempt to transcend the limitations of location and time, its characters do not escape either the effects of politics or a social reality that dictates where they live or what they can or cannot do or afford. Politics sets the film in motion just as it invades, exists in, and affects every subsequent scene. As Diane struggles to provide her son with "la vie bonne" ("the good life"), what support does she receive? What politics are being enforced to help her succeed?

Released in 2014 but set in a fictional 2015, the viewer can nonetheless make connections with the actual politics of 2014, a time when Canada was preparing for new federal elections and saw the Liberal Party come to power. While Justin Trudeau's progressive platform was appealing, his victory was also "the product of an anti-Conservative voting bloc that seemed to have forged a subconscious pact to embrace whoever the front-runner was heading into the last week of the campaign" (Keehn). It would be expected of the Liberal Party—seen from a European perspective as center or left-wing and leading "une politique de gauche" ("a politics of the Left") socially—to care about the effects of politics on people, to support diversity, and to fight for gender equality.[14] While this study relies on an understanding of Liberal politics in Québec, no political party is exempt from understanding the repercussions of its work on women. However, an interesting question is whether the Liberals' proclaimed progressive policies really do produce social progress.

In her provocatively titled book *Les libéraux n'aiment pas les femmes*, Québec essayist Aurélie Lanctôt argues that the Liberals "se définissent souvent par opposition à ceux qui se cramponnent à une vision réactionnaire des structures sociales et de la vie politique, où les femmes n'ont qu'un rôle auxiliaire et des possibilités limitées . . . chérissent la liberté des individus, de tous les individus. . . . [I]ls font sans relâche la promotion de l'ambition chez les femmes, ils défendent farouchement l'accès à la contraception et à l'avortement, et encouragent le décloisonnement des représentations traditionnelles de la famille" ("often define themselves in opposition to those who hold on tight to a reactionary conception of social structures and political life, where women only have an auxiliary role and limited possibilities . . .

cherish individual freedom, of all individuals. . . . [T]hey tirelessly promote ambition among women, they fiercely defend access to contraception and abortion, and encourage the breaking down of traditional representations of family"). Yet the current context of economic austerity and "les politiques de relance économique bénéficient d'abord aux hommes, tandis que les vagues de compression frappent surtout les femmes" ("politics of economic stimulus benefit men first, whereas waves of economic cuts hurt women above all"). As an example, Prime Minister Philippe Couillard's plan to reform Quebec's single-fee daycare system and cut budgets to save the province money led to significant backlash.[15] In response, "[l]e Conseil du statut de la femme (CSF) reproche au gouvernement . . . de ne pas avoir pris la peine d'évaluer l'impact sur les femmes. . . . Or, une hausse de tarif pourrait inciter certaines mères à renoncer à leur emploi, pour demeurer au foyer" ("[t]he Council on Women's Status blames the government . . . for not having taken the time to assess the impact on women. . . . In fact, a rate increase could incite women to renounce their jobs, to stay at home") (Richer).

The question of care is pivotal to *Mommy*. The title itself denotes the dependence of a child on a mother, echoing the infantile call for attention and care. Because the medical institution can no longer care for Steve, Diane has to reorganize her life and find ways to earn a living, as well as make time for homeschooling. Though not ideal, she proves to be a very loving and pragmatic, or realistic, mother.[16] At a time when prices and the overall cost of living are increasing, Lanctôt notes, "[P]our celles [les femmes] qui vivent seules, les perspectives économiques n'ont rien de très enviable" ("[F]or those [the women] who are single, the future is economically bleak"). Having lost her permanent job because she had to start anew with Steve, Diane becomes in turn a housekeeper and a translator, all the while dealing with her son's ADHD and violent outbursts. Yet Anne Dorval accurately describes her character as a "femme forte qui ne s'apitoie jamais sur son sort, qui ne fait jamais pitié, malgré toutes les tuiles que le destin lui envoie" ("strong woman who does not feel sorry for herself, who never incites pity, despite all the blows life throws at her") (Houdassine).[17] While politics can sometimes seem to consider issues of economic benefit and loss in a vacuum, *Mommy*—just as the CSF did—demands that the full equation be considered, that every single element be taken into account. Only then, no longer in a vacuum, can there be politics that do not contribute to a vicious cycle of violence, oppression, and marginalization.[18]

Experiencing financial precariousness and worried about living in a heavily populated area of town, Diane and Steve are marginalized/marginalize themselves spatially on the outskirts of the city:

Steve: Où c'est qu'on vit à c't'heure?
Diane: Saint-Hubert, proche d'la 116.
Steve: C'est glam? J'ai-tu une chambre?
Diane: Ben là, y me reste encore assez de cash qu't'aies une chambre. . . . [V]as-tu dormir en cuiller à 40 ans toi?

. . .

Diane: Tu r'gardes pas à déco. J'ai loué ça; une vieille madame qu'est morte y a même pas deux mois.[19]

Living on the wrong side of the tracks, their visibility is undermined, as is their stability. Steve's question about where they live "à c't'heure" also attests to habitual geographical displacement and the question of support, a crucial matter when mental illness is part of the picture. In a 2014 *Le Devoir* piece titled "Santé mentale: Une priorité oubliée," Amélie Daoust-Boisvert reports: "Pressions budgétaires sur services psychologiques publics, report du plan d'action en santé mentale, annulation d'une campagne de prévention, financement réduit aux organismes communautaires: l'inquiétude est vive dans le milieu de la santé mentale, où on se demande si cette problématique n'est pas reléguée au dernier rang des préoccupations du gouvernement" ("Budgetary constraints in mental health public services, report of an action plan on mental health, cancelling of a prevention campaign, limited funding for community organizations: many worry in the mental health care system, where one wonders whether this issue might be relegated to the bottom of the government's agenda").

If a psychiatric institution is unable to provide proper care for Steve, how will he get better outside when psychological support is scarce? What the outside world actually offers is the potential for human relations. Dolan depicts "chaos," "florid dysfunction," "twin volcanoes of love and frustration"

(Scott) in order to counter the political view that a country must be led like a company, that people are mere human resources. They struggle, they laugh, they dance, they are human. The use of pastel colors and upbeat music alleviates the heaviness of other violent scenes and helps to create an emotional connection with the viewer.

I would further argue that Dolan manages to criticize social issues not by depicting individuals who complain about their lives but by depicting individuals who simply try to make do with the struggle. In "On the Myth of Sexual Orientation," scholar Margot Francis draws a comparison between sexual orientation and race: "As James Baldwin suggests, when talking about racism: 'as long as I complain about being oppressed, the oppressor is in consolation of knowing that I know my place, so to speak'" (4). Trapped in the square frame with the characters and their exacerbated emotions, Dolan subtly exposes the viewer to the variety of factors that contribute to social domination without inspiring pity. As he explains, he makes "des films sur des gens différents . . . les laissés-pour-compte. . . . [C]ela [lui] permet de les accompagner dans leur combat" ("films about people who are different . . . those left behind. . . . [I]t allows [him] to accompany them in their fight") (Lorit). As a consequence, the viewer too feels compelled to accompany those people and rally to their cause.

The other classic image that emerges in *Mommy* is that of the struggling teacher. Diane enlists Kyla, her neighbor and a teacher on sabbatical, to homeschool Steve. Stuttering and shy, Kyla hides the loss of a child and the impossibility of returning to work. Lanctôt shows that "[d]éjà en 2010, une étude . . . sur la santé des enseignants révélait que 60% d'entre eux présentent des symptômes d'épuisement professionnel . . . d'anxiété en lien avec leur travail" ("as early as 2010, a study . . . on teachers' health reported that 60 percent of them showed signs of burnout . . . anxiety in relation to their job"). As education budgets decrease—"le salaire des enseignants du Québec est de 22% inférieur à la moyenne canadienne" ("teachers' salaries in Quebec are 22 percent lower than the Canadian average")—mental problems increase. Having recently moved from Toronto with her husband and daughter to this marginal space, Kyla too starts anew and finds in her neighbors an outlet for her teaching, away from paralyzing professional and maternal duties. As film critic Mary Corliss writes, "She and Diane get along like loving sisters, especially when they open the box wine and dissolve helplessly into giggles." In these moments, they are no longer mothers with responsibilities.

Kyla's teaching approach proves successful with Steve, to whom she is entirely dedicated. The one-on-one relationship, however, comes with great exposure to violence.

> *Kyla*: La musique, Steve, baisse ça là.
> *Steve*: Pourquoi y a pas d'fucking jus d'orange dans c't'e fucking d'maison-là?
> *Kyla*: Il reste dix minutes à nos tr . . . tr . . .
> *Steve*: Trente. Trente minutes. . . . [D]is-le t'es capable.
> . . .
> *Kyla*: J'accepte pas ça.
> *Steve*: . . . Tape-moi sur la gueule, tape-moi sur la gueule.
> *Kyla*: J'fais ça pour te rendre service, Steve.[20]

Finally, "he rips off Kyla's necklace, she wrestles him to the floor and, her nose to his, fiercely lays down the law" (Corliss). Here lies the pedagogical struggle, the lack of resources for teachers. In fact, "on ne saurait trop souligner l'importance de l'école et la valeur inestimable du travail des enseignants—qui dans les faits sont surtout des enseignantes" ("one cannot stress enough the importance of school and the inestimable value of teachers—who in reality are mostly women") (Lanctôt). But that which is valued demands support. To some extent, Kyla does help Steve, but his mental problems eventually outdistance her meager resources. At least Diane and Kyla have found female solidarity in a system that crushes them.

In this story of "dysfunctional love and family" (Scott), Dolan continues to give a voice to the marginalized. In fact, I would draw on Irigaray and her reminder about motherhood: "Une autre chose à laquelle nous avons à veiller, c'est surtout de ne pas retuer cette mère. . . . Il s'agit de lui redonner la vie. . . . Lui donner droit aux paroles, et pourquoi pas parfois aux cris, à la colère" ("Another thing we have to watch for is to ensure that we are not killing the mother once more. . . . It's about giving her life again. . . . Giving her access to speech and, if necessary, sometimes to screams, to anger") (*Le corps-à-corps* 28). Using "verbal battles waged at maximum volume in raw Quebecois patois" (Corliss), Dolan gives voice and draws attention to multilayered systemic issues.

In *Surveiller et punir* (1975), Michel Foucault writes: "La visibilité est un piège" ("Visibility is a trap") (202). To be on-screen is to be made visible, to be unable to escape the viewer's gaze, but also to trap the viewer in a given reality. Since *J'ai tué ma mère*, Xavier Dolan has shown his understanding of the power of cinema to expose a variety of struggles and denounce oppressive norms. In his first production, the ghost of the pre–Quiet Revolution Québécoise haunts Chantal, who fails to reach social expectations. Even at a time of liberation, conflicting conventions maintain her in a state of uncertainty. Likewise, her visibility is a trap; she worries about the external gaze and judgment. Yet *Mommy*'s Diane proves a strong-willed character determined to get and do what she wants. But visibility, as far as she is concerned, can also be problematic because of her son's unique behavior. Yet she demonstrates an acute knowledge of the powers that be and refuses, on the one hand, to show any signs of failure and, on the other, to conform.

Beyond the maternal character, Dolan forces a broader reassessment of social dysfunctions, thus showing the intimate and intricate connection between the power of cinema and the power of politics. As Lanctôt notes about school, "Dans cette relation humaine, de personne à personne, ces enseignants éduquent la jeunesse" ("In this relationship between humans, between people, these teachers educate our youth"). In a similar way, Dolan's cinema sheds light on human relations in an attempt to educate, to allow the viewer to consider the big picture rather than one isolated element of it. His productions have a purpose, a political design. And in the argument that one political party might be more progressive than the other, Dolan shows that people's struggles exist beyond the political spectrum and demands that we see beyond single-issue politics. Staging "les laissés-pour-compte" ("those left behind"), the marginal, and using colors such as "orange and pink and yellow, as if it had been shot in California" (Osenlund), *Mommy* reminds me of Justin Trudeau's victory speech: "Sunny ways, my friends. Sunny ways. This is what positive politics can do" ("Justin Trudeau's"). Xavier Dolan finds beauty in hardship and delivers films about hope. Now can politics deliver more than hope?

Throughout the text and the endnotes, all translations of film dialogue are taken from the DVD subtitles. I have translated quotes from other sources unless noted otherwise.

1. The novels are Monique La Rue's *La cohorte fictive* (1979), Madeleine Ouellette-Michalska's *La maison Trestler* (1984), and Élise Turcotte's *Le bruit des choses vivantes* (1991).

2. I would not presume to be aware of every single film that comes out in Québec each year. However, a quick look at some of the blockbusters confirms the initial tendency to make fathers the central characters of the stories. Ken Scott's *Starbuck* (2011), Jean-Philippe Pearson's *Le bonheur des autres* (2011), Denis Villeneuve's *Incendies* (2013), and François Bouvier's *Paul à Québec* (2015) all tell more or less complicated family stories in which fatherhood clearly makes for the greater part of the plot. Whether they are, respectively, about a sperm donor meeting his biological children, an older man starting a new life with a younger woman, children looking for their brother-father, or a dying grandfather, these films do not engage equally with maternal characters in spite of the equally complex struggles they face. Mothers end up being in underdeveloped supporting roles; the audience sympathizes with them, yet not as much as with their male counterparts. Contemporary representations of men and fathers can be lauded for proposing alternative masculinities, but men and fathers should not be lauded simply for assuming their parental roles. Discussing the 2017 Women's March—a worldwide grassroots movement to oppose President Donald Trump and "send a bold message to [the] new government on their first day in office, and to the world that women's rights are human rights" (Tatum)—some pieces featured the stories of fathers "who were forced to parent their children alone for a day," thus adding to the preconceived image of "mothers as de facto caregivers and fathers as bumbling helpers who balk at the housework that mounts when their wives leave town for a day" (Cauterucci). While the aforementioned films offer much more nuanced and layered portrayals of women, motherhood remains an inherent and automatic predisposition, while men must learn to be fathers.

3. Chantal's over-the-top tendencies at times resemble those of Germaine Lauzon in Michel Tremblay's *Les belles-soeurs* (1968): "Désâmez-vous pour élever ça, pis que c'est que ça vous rapporte? Rien! Rien pantoute! C'est même pas capable de vous rendre un p'tit sarvice! J't'avertis, Linda, j'commence à en avoir plein le casque de vous servir, toé pis les autres! Chus pas une sarvante, moé, icitte!... J'demande pas la lune! Aide-moé donc, pour une fois, au lieu d'aller niaser avec c'te naiseux-là!" ("Work hard to raise them, then what do you get out of it? Nothing! Nothing at all! They can't even do you a little favor! I warn you, Linda, I have had it up to

here serving you, you and the others! I'm not your servant here! . . . I'm not asking for the moon! Come on, help me, for once, instead of going out to fool with this fool!"). She who serves everyone selflessly presents herself as a saint and martyr. For both Tremblay and Dolan, it is about denouncing "the central social myth of female fulfillment in devotion to the family" (Killick xix).

4. Chantal: "I'd be curious if you did a survey among your classmates. . . . Ask them if their parents give them a ride to school in the morning."

   Hubert: "Stop asking me to do surveys every time. You don't know what you're saying. Fifty percent of my mates get a ride from their parents! Fifty percent!"

   . . .

   Chantal: "You don't ask me how my day was?"

   Hubert: "No. . . . [I]f anything special had happened you would have told me already, for sure! Same for me."

5. Another instance of Quebec's past shadowing Dolan's work rests in his portrayal of Chantal as *mater dolorosa*. Though brief, one scene depicts the mother as a nun crying tears of blood and hugging a golden cross. In this powerful shot lie evident references to historical clerical authority. Not only does Dolan play with the image of Chantal, the saint who is being abused by her child, he also brings back the memory of a time when, to quote Baillargeon, "[t]he role played by nuns in Quebec was considerable" (238). She explains further: "The impressive magnitude of the nun's activities was a direct consequence of the Quebec government's reluctance to intervene in education and social welfare. . . . In the Church's view, dispensing charity within a religious framework was the best way to help the destitute while preserving the Christian family social order."

6. Later on in the film, trying to patch things up with his mother, Hubert cleans the house, does laundry, and cooks for her. At dinner, he asks her about her day at work. Surprised at first, she replies: "Bien, on est un petit peu dans le jus, mais ça va" ("Well, we're pretty busy, but it's okay"). Even when things go seemingly well and Hubert cares, her brief and vague response testifies to her inability to sustain a full conversation. She does not ask questions in return, and silence dominates once more.

7. A discussion on Radio-Canada's *Plus on est de fous, plus on lit* shows how low birth rates are also linked to women deciding to postpone motherhood until after they have made a career for themselves. Many then suffer from infertility. A variety of factors must be considered, but the stigma remains ("Mon corps").

8. See "Des milliers" as an example of the continued politicization of abortion rights during term elections. See also "Le mouvement pro-vie" on the expansion of the pro-life movements and centers in Canada and Quebec.

9. "'Let's toast to our freedom, and to our rebellion against traditional feminine models.'"

'Rebellion, schmebellion.'

. . .

'For real it's true. Our friends who have children think we're "defying patriarchy" every night of the week, but the truth is most of the time, I go to bed feeling a damned burden in my heart, and I spend my nights fighting stupid questions, asking myself where-when-how I am going to find the door that opens onto the meaningful life I'm supposed to lead and that I'm clearly not leading, given that everywhere I look, I'm shown that a meaningful life includes children.'

'And the worst part is we're stressing over problems we don't even have. We're stressing over problems we could be having."'

10. Hubert: "*I'm talking to you*. I found a solution for the both of us. For our relationship. *You hear me*. I think I should move into my own apartment. I'd be close to the subway, I'd be close to school, I'd be close to my friends. . . . It's because you're always on my case. I know it's going to work."

    Chantal: "You're going to do this with Grandma's money?"

    Hubert: "Yes! Exactly what I was thinking about. We're so on the same page."

    Chantal: "Yes, it's a good idea. . . ."

    Hubert: "I am happy, I love you, I love you. I love you my lovely little mom."

11. Hubert: "Mom, I need to talk to you. I visited the apartment."

    Chantal: "What apartment?"

    Hubert: "Well, the apartment we talked about. It's so perfect for me, I can't believe it."

    Chantal: "I thought it over today, it doesn't make sense . . ."

    Hubert: "Excuse me? I talked to you about it yesterday, and you said it's a good idea. I told you about it yesterday!"

12. As Bourdieu would explain, a form of "symbolic violence," which "to put it as tersely and simply as possible, is the *violence which is exercised upon a social agent with his or her complicity* . . . social agents are knowing agents who, even when they are subjected to determinism, contribute to producing the efficacy of that which determines them insofar as they structure what determines them" (*An Invitation* 167).

13. One could quite correctly argue that mothers are never really in the background, perhaps even less so in *Tom à la ferme*, but the plot revolves more around other, more predominant issues such as a love triangle, an identity crisis, and power struggles.

14. At the time when the film was made and released, a Liberal Party government was already leading the Québec province. In this article, I look specifically at what policies Prime Minister Philippe Couillard and his cabinet members have produced and implemented and their impact on women. *Mommy* provides archetypes of struggling women who in turn echo the situation of the Québécoise today. This is certainly not to say that the Liberal Party is responsible for all of society's ills.

15. Couillard's former campaign opponent from the Parti Québécois, Pauline Marois, asked him to reconsider his position. See "Pauline Marois."

16. She works hard to provide for her son, she hires a lawyer to defend his case, and she even makes the decision to reinstitutionalize him when he becomes too dangerous. Indeed, without his knowledge, after a pleasant trip Die drops Steve off at the hospital. This heartbreaking scene highlights not only Die's understanding of her son's mental condition, her limited means to help, but also her unwavering support and love. As strong as she presents herself, she is in fact devastated.

17. I would draw a parallel with Édouard Louis's autobiographical novel, in which he describes his childhood with his poor working-class family. About the publication of his book, he writes of his mother's reaction: "[C]e qui a le plus choqué ma mère, c'est que j'ai écrit que ma famille était pauvre. Pour elle, c'était la pire chose, parce que le monde social et les dominants font croire aux gens pauvres qu'ils sont responsables de leur situation, et qu'ils finissent par l'intérioriser" ("[W]hat shocked my mother the most was that I wrote that my family was poor. For her, it was the worst, because the social world and the dominants make poor people believe that they are responsible for their situation and that they finish to internalize it") (Vincent). Likewise, Dolan's Diane belongs to a similar struggling milieu and worries about the way she is perceived. For instance, she pours boxed wine into a nicer glass bottle to hide her economic circumstances, she smokes and then quickly sprays the smoke with deodorizer as if to hide the truth, and she pours whiskey in her coffee cup in the morning. Dolan plays with visibility and meaning. The truth seems to be hidden, covered up. However, I would not go so far as to say that it translates how Diane has internalized the dominants' discourse of responsibility. In fact, I would argue that she strategically plays with appearances to maintain control. Later on in the film she uses her charms to seduce a friend and lawyer, hoping he might help with Steve's legal troubles for free. The way she controls her emotions adds to the refusal to appear vulnerable and her refusal to let the system win.

18. Adding to Lanctôt's arguments, studies carried out in 2014–15 confirm that "[e]n additionnant les coupes générales, les hausses de taxes et de tarifs et les réductions ou gels de salaires, ... les femmes ont assumé 3,1 milliards de compressions de plus que les hommes" ("[a]dding general cuts, tax and price raises, and salary decreases or freezes, ... women have suffered $3.1 billion in compressions more than men") (Rettino-Parazelli).

19. Steve: "Where do we live now?"
    Diane: "Saint-Hubert, by the 116."
    Steve: "Glamorous! Do I have my own room?"
    Diane: "Come on, I have enough cash for you to have your own room. . . . [Y]ou gonna spoon with me at age forty?"

. . .

Diane: "Don't look at the decorations. I rented this; an old lady died less than two months ago."

20. Kyla: "Turn down the music, Steve."

Steve: "Why is there no fucking orange juice in this fucking house?"

Kyla: "We got ten minutes left out of our th . . . th . . ."

Steve: "Thirty. Thirty minutes. . . . [S]ay it, you can do it."

. . .

Kyla: "I don't accept this."

Steve: ". . . Punch me in the face, punch me in the face."

Kyla: "I'm doing you a favor, Steve."

FILMOGRAPHY

J'ai tué ma mère. Dir. Xavier Dolan. Perf. Xavier Dolan, Anne Dorval. K-Films, 2009. DVD.

Mommy. Dir. Xavier Dolan. Perf. Suzanne Clément, Anne Dorval, Antoine Olivier Pilon. Metafilms, 2014. DVD.

WORKS CITED

Baillargeon, Denyse. "Quebec Women of the Twentieth Century: Milestones in an Unfinished Journey." *Quebec Questions: Quebec Studies for the Twenty-First Century*, edited by Stéphan Gervais, Chistopher Kirley, and Jarrett Rudy, Oxford University Press, 2011, pp. 231–48.

Bilodeau, Martin. "Une voix de bruit et de fureur." *Le Devoir*, 6 June 2009, https://www.ledevoir.com/culture/cinema/253629/une-voix-de-bruit-et-de-fureur.

Bourdieu, Pierre. *An Invitation to Reflexive Sociology.* Trans. Loic J. D. Wacquant. University of Chicago Press, 1992.

———. *La domination masculine.* Seuil, 1998.

Britt, Fanny. *Les tranchées: Maternité, ambiguité et féminisme, en fragments.* Atelier 10, 2013.

Cauterucci, Christina. "Dads, Who Are Parents, Do Not Deserve Praise for Parenting While Moms Marched." *Slate*, 23 Jan. 2017, http://www.slate.com/blogs/xx_factor/2017/01/23/dads_don_t_deserve_praise_for_parenting_while_mom_marches_against_trump.html.

Corliss, Mary. "Xavier Dolan's *Mommy*: The Fireworks of Family Love and Pain." *Time*, 23 Jan. 2015, http://time.com/3679470/mommy-movie-review-xavier-dolan/.

Daoust-Boivert, Amélie. "Santé mentale: Une priorité oubliée." *Le Devoir*, 20 Aug. 2014, https://www.ledevoir.com/societe/sante/416331/sante-mentale-une-priorite-oubliee.

"Des milliers de manifestants pro-vie interpellant les partis politiques à Ottawa." Radio-Canada, 14 May 2015, https://ici.radio-canada.ca/nouvelle/720784/marche-pro-vie-ottawa.

"Fewer Babies Born in Quebec as Fertility Rate Continues Downward Spiral." *Montreal Gazette*, 19 Apr. 2017, http://montrealgazette.com/news/quebec/fewer-babies -born-in-quebec-as-fertility-rate-continues-downward-spiral.

Foucault, Michel. *Surveiller et punir*. Gallimard, 1975.

Francis, Margot. "On the Myth of Sexual Orientation: Field Notes from the Personal, Pedagogical, and Historical Discourses of Identity." *Queerly Canadian*, edited by Maureen Fitzgerald and Scott Rayter, Canadian Scholars' Press, 2012, pp. 1–22.

Houdassine, Ismaël. "Mommy—Anne Dorval: 'Xavier Dolan m'a donné mon plus beau rôle.'" *Huffington Post (Quebec)*, 20 Sept. 2014, https://quebec.huffingtonpost.ca /2014/09/20/mommy-anne-dorval—xavier-dolan-ma-donne-mon-plus-beau-ro le_n_5854500.html.

Irigaray, Luce. *Je, tu, nous: Toward a Culture of Difference*. Routledge, 1992.

———. *Le corps-à-corps avec la mère*. Pleine lune, 1981.

"Justin Trudeau's 'Sunny Ways' a Nod to Sir Wilfrid Laurier." CBC, 20 Oct. 2015, http:// www.cbc.ca/news/canada/nova-scotia/ns-prof-trudeau-sunny-ways-1.3280693.

Keehn, Jeremy. "What Justin Trudeau's Victory Means for Canada." *New Yorker*, 20 Oct. 2015, https://www.newyorker.com/news/news-desk/what-justin-trudeaus -victory-means-for-canada.

Lanctôt, Aurélie. *Les libéraux n'aiment pas les femmes*. Lux, 2015.

"Le mouvement pro-vie gagne du terrain." *La Presse*, 20 Mar. 2010, http://www.lapresse .ca/le-soleil/actualites/societe/201005/28/01-4284935-le-mouvement-pro-vie -gagne-du-terrain.php.

Leroux, Loyola. "Le Québec, paradis du féminisme." *Huffington Post (Quebec)*, 8 Mar. 2017, https://quebec.huffingtonpost.ca/loyola-leroux/quebec-paradis-feminisme -8-mars_b_15209856.html.

Lévesque, Andrée. *Making and Breaking the Rules: Women in Quebec, 1919–1939*. Trans. Yvonne M. Klein. 1994. University of Toronto Press, 2010.

Lorit, Mathilde. "Xavier Dolan: 'Sans cinéma, je meurs.'" *Madame Figaro*, 10 Mar. 2014, http://madame.lefigaro.fr/celebrites/xavier-dolan-sans-cinema-meurs -031014-964951.

Louis, Édouard, ed. *Pierre Bourdieu: L'insoumission en heritage*. Presses Universitaires de France, 2013.

Marshall, Bill. *Quebec National Cinema*. McGill-Queen's University Press, 2000.

Marshall, Bill, and Gill Rye. Introduction. *Women's Writing and Filmmaking in Québec*, special issue of *Quebec Studies*, vol. 59, 2015, pp. 3–8.

"*Mommy*: Xavier Dolan fait la paix avec la figure maternelle, Cannes Chavire." *L'Obs*, 22 May 2014, https://www.nouvelobs.com/culture/20140522.AFP7834/mommy -xavier-dolan-fait-la-paix-avec-la-figure-maternelle-cannes-chavire.html.

"Mon corps ne vous appartient pas." *Plus on est de fous, plus on lit*, 22 May 2018, https://ici.radio-canada.ca/premiere/emissions/plus-on-est-de-fous-plus-on-lit/episodes/407707/audio-fil-du-mardi-22-mai-2018.

Olsen, Mark. "In *Mommy*, Xavier Dolan Looks Things in the Eye." *Los Angeles Times*, 18 Jan. 2015, http://www.latimes.com/entertainment/movies/la-et-mn-ca-xavier-dolan-20150118-story.html.

Osenlund, R. Kurt. "Xavier Dolan on Mommy Issues & Celine Dion." *Out*, 20 Jan. 2015, https://www.out.com/movies/2015/1/20/xavier-dolan-mommy-issues-and-celine-dion.

"Pauline Marois Calls Out Philippe Couillard over Daycare Cuts." CBC, 14 Mar. 2016, http://www.cbc.ca/news/canada/montreal/quebec-daycare-cuts-pauline-marois-1.3490032.

Rettino-Parazelli, Karl. "Crise d'équité." *Le Devoir*, 3 Mar. 2015, https://www.ledevoir.com/economie/433298/relance-economique-les-femmes-ont-ete-plus-penalisees-que-les-hommes-conclut-l-iris.

Richer, Jocelyne. "Le CSF dit craindre un retour au foyer." *Le Devoir*, 29 Jan. 2015, https://www.ledevoir.com/societe/430323/hausse-du-tarif-de-garderie-le-csf-dit-craindre-un-retour-au-foyer.

Saint-Martin, Lori. "Le corps et la fiction à réinventer: Métamorphoses de la maternité dans l'écriture des femmes au Québec." *Recherches Féministes*, vol. 7, no. 2, 1994, pp. 115–34.

Schou, Solvej. "Cries for Help, Embraced by Praise." *New York Times*, 18 Jan. 2015, https://www.nytimes.com/2015/01/18/movies/cries-for-help-embraced-by-praise.html.

Schwartz, Alexandra. "Sheila Heti Wrestles with a Big Decision in 'Motherhood.'" *New Yorker*, 7 May 2018, https://www.newyorker.com/magazine/2018/05/07/sheila-heti-wrestles-with-a-big-decision-in-motherhood.

Scott, Anthony Oliver. "Parent and Child as Two Volcanoes under One Roof." *New York Times*, 23 Jan. 2015, https://www.nytimes.com/2015/01/23/movies/xavier-dolans-mommy-depicts-a-clashing-mother-and-son.html.

Tatum, Sophie. "Women's March on Washington: What You Need to Know." CNN, 17 Jan. 2017, https://www.cnn.com/2017/01/16/politics/womens-march-on-washington-need-to-know/index.html.

Tremblay, Michel. *Les belles-soeurs*. Ed. Rachel Killick. Bristol Classical Press, 2000.

Tremblay, Odile. "Trois prix pour *J'ai tué ma mère*." *Le Devoir*, https://www.ledevoir.com/culture/cinema/251835/trois-prix-pour-j-ai-tue-ma-mere.

Vincent, Catherine. "Edouard Louis: 'Trump et le FN sont le produit de l'exclusion.'" *Le Monde*, 11 Dec. 2016, https://www.lemonde.fr/livres/article/2016/12/11/edouard-louis-trump-et-le-fn-sont-le-produit-de-l-exclusion_5047058_3260.html.

Loïc Bourdeau holds a PhD from the University of California, Davis. He is currently assistant professor of French and francophone studies at the University of Louisiana at Lafayette. His research focuses on twentieth- and twenty-first-century French and Québec literature and cinema with particular theoretical interest in queer and feminist studies. He has published on, among others, Michel Tremblay, Anne Hébert, Xavier Dolan, Simon Boulerice, and Edouard Louis.

Ariane Brun del Re holds an MA in French from McGill University. She is currently pursuing her PhD at the University of Ottawa under the supervision of Dr. Lucie Hotte. Her research focuses on francophone literatures from Canada.

Natalie Edwards is associate professor of French studies at the University of Adelaide. Her research focuses on late twentieth- and twenty-first-century literature in French. She is interested in literary representation of and by minority writers such as women, immigrants, and refugees. Her PhD work at Northwestern University provided her with extensive training in postcolonial and feminist theory, and she brings this to bear on literary texts from the French and francophone literary traditions. She has published two books on French and francophone women's autobiography and has coedited ten volumes on minority literature from across the francophone world. Her work has appeared in journals such as the *French Review*, *French Cultural Studies*, *A/b: Autobiography Studies*, *Contemporary French and Francophone Studies (SITES)*, *Women in French Studies*, the *Australian Journal of French Studies*, *Studies in Twentieth- and Twenty-First-Century Literatures*, *Life Writing*, and the *Irish Journal for French Studies*. In 2018–19 she was appointed visiting international fellow for the Society of French Studies (UK).

Prior to her appointment as lecturer in French translation at Newcastle University in September 2016, **Pauline Henry-Tierney** worked as a lecturer in French studies at Nottingham Trent University and as a graduate teaching assistant at the University of Manchester, where she also completed her doctorate in French studies, funded by a French Graduate Scholarship. She was awarded her PhD in French studies in December 2015 for her dissertation "Transgressive Textualities: Translating Gender, Sexuality and Corporeality in Contemporary French and Francophone Women's Writing."

Lucie Hotte is professor of French studies at the University of Ottawa. She holds the research chair in "production et réception des littératures minoritaires." Hotte teaches courses on Franco-Ontarian, Acadian, West Canadian, and Québec literatures. She has published numerous articles and a monograph, and she has coedited several volumes on literature by minorities. Hotte has secured several grants and received prestigious awards for her academic contributions (Prix Champlain, Member of the Royal Society of Canada).

Susan Ireland is Orville and Mary Patterson Routt Professor of Literature at Grinnell College. She grew up in England and taught in France for eight years before coming to the United States in 1982. She holds a PhD in French literature from the University of Colorado. Her research interests include contemporary French fiction, Québec women writers, the Algerian novel, and the literature of immigration in France and Québec. She has published articles in these areas and has edited *Immigrant Narratives in Contemporary France* and *Textualizing the Immigrant Experience in Contemporary Québec* with Patrice Proulx. She is also an editor of *The Feminist Encyclopedia of French Literature*.

Susan Pinette is associate professor of modern languages and literatures and director of Franco American Programs at the University of Maine. She received her doctorate in French at the University of California, Irvine. Her research examines contemporary Franco-American literature, where she shows its significance to the broader arenas of North American francophone communities and American studies. She has published on Lahontan, Diderot, and Kerouac and is currently working on a book-length manuscript on Franco-American fiction. As director, she has developed various curricula for Franco-American studies, received state and federal funding grants, and served as a liaison between the academic community, business leaders, governments, and the public.

Patrice J. Proulx is professor of French at the University of Nebraska at Omaha. She holds a PhD in French from Cornell University. Her research and teaching interests include twentieth- and twenty-first-century French and francophone literature, cultural studies, and francophone film. She is especially interested in exploring literary themes related to history, memory, and the transmission of stories. In addition, she served as editor of *The Feminist Encyclopedia of French Literature* and coedited *Immigrant Narratives in Contemporary France* and *Textualizing the Immigrant Experience in Contemporary Québec.*

Amy J. Ransom is professor of French at Central Michigan University. She has published over two dozen articles on Québécois science fiction, fantasy, and horror film and literature, including *Science Fiction from Québec: A Postcolonial Study* (2009). In addition to her book *Hockey PQ: Canada's Game in Québec's Popular Culture* (2014), she is currently working on a book-length study of Québec film since the year 2000. She is also a book reviews editor for the *Journal for the Fantastic in the Arts* and editor-in-chief of *Québec Studies.*

Chelsea Ray is associate professor of French language and literature at the University of Maine at Augusta. She received her doctorate in comparative literature at UCLA, where she focused on nineteenth- and twentieth-century French and Russian literature. Her research interests include French and Russian women writers, translation studies, and gender studies. Her scholarship is currently focused on women writers in Paris at the turn of the century. She has published in *South Central Review* (MLA).

Alison Rice is associate professor of French and francophone literature and film at the University of Notre Dame. Her first book, *Time Signatures: Contextualizing Contemporary Francophone Autobiographical Writing from the Maghreb* (Lexington Books, 2006), closely examines the writing of Hélène Cixous, Assia Djebar, and Abdelkébir Khatibi. *Polygraphies: Francophone Women Writing Algeria*, published by the University of Virginia Press (2012), focuses on Maïssa Bey, Marie Cardinal, Hélène Cixous, Assia Djebar, Malika Mokeddem, Zahia Rahmani, and Leïla Sebbar. Alison Rice's current project, "Francophone Metronomes: Worldwide Women Writers in Paris," is an in-depth study of women writers of French from around the world, complemented by a series of filmed interviews.

anger, female, 139

animalistic language, 37n6, 63–64, 65, 67, 73n16

antifeminism, 149–50

Aranese dialect, 59–60, 72n5, 73n9, 74n19

Arcan, Nelly, 11, 23–39; *Paradis, clef en main*, 37n8; *Putain*, 11, 23–39

Arcand, Gabriel, 158

archetypes of motherhood, 4, 170, 180, 190n14

assimilation and coming-out stories, 47–48

attachment parenting, 87

Audet, Viviane, 162

Aurore (Dionne), 149

austerity, 183

autobiography, 12, 124, 124n3; vs. fiction, 125n7; intrauterine, 135–36, 140; trauma and, 135, 140, 143, 146n4

autofiction, 23, 34, 37n1, 108–10, 158

"bad faith," 33

Bad Girl (Huston), 12–13, 83–84, 133–47; divorce in, 138, 144–45; French language in, 142–43; as a literature lesson, 144; style of, 135, 139

Badinter, Elisabeth, 87, 94

The Bad Mother (Andersen). See *La mauvaise mère* (Andersen)

Baillargeon, Denyse, 42, 154, 163, 173, 189n5

Baumrind, Diana, 88

Beaupré, Norman, 41–42

beauty, prostitution funding, 33

the "beauty myth," 30, 33

Beauvoir, Simone de, 16n4, 24, 30, 31, 32, 33; *La vieillesse*, 30; *Le deuxième sexe*, 30

Becoming a Man (Monette), 43–47

Bédard, Éric, 149–50, 152, 163, 164n1

Bérubé, Allan, 11, 49, 50–51

Bettelheim, Bruno, 26, 158, 165n13

Bigras, Jean-Yves, 149, 164n1

bilingualism, 72n4

Bilodeau, Martin, 169–70

birth rates, 42, 61, 73n11, 174, 189n7

Blais, Marie Claire, 73n16

Blanco, María del Pilar, 49

Bleu sur blanc (Andersen), 111, 114, 117–18, 120

bodies: aging, 29–30, 36; degenerative illnesses of, 30–31; desexualized, 31–32; fragmented images of, 25–26; motherhood changing, 31–32; territorialization of, 31; women controlling their own, 66–67

Bologna, Caroline, 18n11

Bonnier, Céline, 157

Bosch, Hieronymus, 26

Bouchard, Denis, 154

Bouliane, Gretchen Richter, 58

Bourdieu, Pierre, 178, 190n12

Bouvier, François, 150, 153–54, 155–56, 163, 188n2; *Histoires d'hiver*, 150, 153–54, 155, 161, 162; *Paul à Québec*, 188n2

Brière, Daniel, 159

Britt, Fanny, 1, 7, 173–74

Brochu, Évelyne, 162

Brossard, Nicole, 5

Brun del Re, Ariane, 12

Bussières, Pascale, 152

Camille (character in *Frisson des collines*), 162

Cantiques des plaines (Huston), 134

Canucks, 44, 47, 48, 50

McClintock, Anne, 42

Melançon, Johanne, 110

Mello, Tam'ara, 58, 71

mémère figure, 42, 51–53, 67

men: and masculinity, 88, 138, 188n2; patriarchy hurting, 160, 161, 177; relationships between, 153–54. *See also* fathers

mental health: abandonment and, 143, 156; language for, lacking, 64; large families' toll on, 66; politics affecting, 184, 185; social media and, 6–7

metamorphosis, 28–29

Michaud, Michel, 161

migration: Catholic alarm at, 61; narratives, 50–51; to New England, 11–12, 61

Miller, Nancy K., 100

mill towns, 43–44

Mireille (character in *Un été sans point ni coup sûr*), 154–55

the Mirror Stage, 26

Mommy (Dolan), 13, 170–71, 174, 179–87, 190n14

Monette, Paul, 11, 43–47, 54n3

Mon oncle Antoine (Jutra), 153

Monty, Michel, 150, 160–61, 163

morality, 17n7, 87

Morrell, Carolyn, 97–98

Moss, Jane, 150, 160

The Mother-Daughter Plot (Hirsch), 37n5

mother-daughter relationship, 24–25, 29, 112–16, 136–37; blurring of boundaries in, 152; dread in, 30–31; guilt in, 114–16

motherhood: alternative models of, 8–9, 71, 173; ambivalence about, 58, 107–8; American practices of, 12, 81, 87; bodies changed by, 31–32; expectation of, 174; failing, 4, 10,

12, 14, 108; fear of, 24, 30–31, 117, 136; and female anger, 139; for Franco-Americans, 11, 57–58, 61, 67; fulfillment and, 136–37, 155, 189n3; history of, 15n2, 94–95, 146, 171; institutionalized, 134–35; mechanization of, 69–70; as patriarchal, 2–3, 25, 29, 137–38, 151; as a profession, 34; and professional work, balancing, 86, 157, 189n7; rebellion against ideals of, 71–73, 134–35, 174; self-sacrifice and, 10, 65, 90n1, 135, 136, 172–73; surrogate, 66

mothers: absent, 82, 83–84, 89, 137–38, 156–58; animalistic language for, 37n6, 63–64, 65, 67; authority of, 172, 175–78; caregiver role assumed of, 188n2; children relinquished by, 180–81; criticism of, from others, 18n11, 69, 178; death of, 27, 34–35, 36, 70, 114–15; empathy for, 145–46; forgiving, 134, 150, 152, 158, 159, 163–64; images for, 23–24, 25–29, 34–35, 63–64, 67; judgment of, by others, 6, 69, 158, 174, 179, 187; leaving Québec, 160; as martyrs, 25, 188n3; motherland linked with, 41, 42; myth of, 41, 57–58, 61, 71, 116, 133; needs of, 63, 107–8, 121, 152–53; non-Franco-American, 44, 46–47, 49; overbearing, 4; "perfect," 1, 2–3, 137; as powerless, 29, 172; power of, 81; "redeeming," 171; silencing, 37n5; single, 170, 179, 183; "stay-at-home," 80, 82–83, 87, 161

Mothers of Invention (Santoro), 5

mother-son relationship, 154–55, 159, 171–92; inseparability in, 175–78, 180; permissiveness in, 79–82, 84–86, 87–89

sex work. *See* prostitution

shame, 15n3, 45, 108, 109, 117, 118–19, 121–22

shaming, 11, 18n11

silencing, 27, 37n5, 72n3

Sleeping Beauty, 26–27, 30, 36

social location, 182

social media, 1, 4, 6–7, 10–11, 16n6

social norms, 136–37, 172–73, 178, 187, 190n12

social reproduction, 11

Sol (character in *Lignes de faille*), 77, 78–81, 82, 84–86, 87, 88; and food, 79–80, 87, 90n2; religious convictions of, 80–81; and violence, 79, 88–89; visiting Germany, 86, 90n5

Sollors, Werner, 48, 49

sons, fathers and, 82, 88, 169

Spaces of Creation (Connolly), 3

spanking, 85

Starbuck (Scott), 188n2

stepmothers, 149

Steve (character in *Mommy*), 170–71, 180–81, 183–84, 186, 191n16

St-Onge-Paquin, Hugo, 157

subjectivity, 5, 16n5, 27, 29, 36, 169–94

subject-object hierarchy, 172

suicide, 34, 37n8, 63, 64, 69, 160; children attempting, 159; imagery, 151; mothers attempting, 152

Sukenick, Lynn, 24–25

surveillance, 6, 7, 17n8, 174

survival, 140, 143

survivance, 61–62, 65–66, 70, 71–72, 101

Takai, Yukari, 42

Tatum, Sophie, 188n2

teaching, 100–101, 185–86, 187

technology, 4, 6–7, 17n8

Tess (character in *Lignes de faille*), 79–83, 84–86, 87

Tilmant, Isabelle, 95

Todorov, Tzvetan, 86, 146n1

tolerance, rejection of, 14–15

Tom à la ferme (Dolan), 179, 190n13

translation: by Chabot, 72n2, 73n15, 74n21; of *Putain*, 28, 37n4, 37n7

Trapenard, Augustin, 135

trauma: of abandonment, 12–13, 120–21, 138–39, 141–42, 143, 156; autobiography and, 135, 140, 143, 146n4; in literature, 138–39, 143, 146n4; as repetition, 139; the self shattered by, 141–42, 143, 146n4; surviving, 140–41

Tremblay, Michel, 2, 173, 177, 188; *Encore une fois, si vous permettez*, 2; *Les belles-soeurs*, 2, 173, 177, 188n3

Trogi, Ricardo, 163

The Trouble with Normal (Warner), 17n8

Trudeau, Justin, 182, 187

Trump, Donald, 188n2

ugliness, 30, 32, 33

uncle figures, 153–54, 161–62

Un été sans point ni coup sûr (Leclerc), 150, 154–55, 163

Une vie qui commence (Monty), 150, 160–61

United States: exodus to, 61; Iraq War and, 78, 79; permissive parenting in, 81, 87; traveling beyond, 90n5. *See also* Franco-American identity

unmothers, 180

upward mobility, 46–47

utilitarianism, 15n1

Val d'Aran, 59, 73n7

Vallée, Edith, 95

values. *See* Catholicism; Quiet Revolution

CPSIA information can be obtained
at www.ICGtesting.com
Printed in the USA
BVHW032327121119
563680BV00004B/13/P

9 780803 293984